SUE WRIGHT

Peacemaker's Dream

D1500913

Contents

Preface

The story of Pocahontas is a story that has been told many times. Usually the books are either academic text books or cartoons aimed at children. In my previous book 'Tempest - Bermuda 1609' I introduced the character of Pocahontas/Little Mischief at the end. The true story of Pocahontas, also known as Matoaka, then took flight in my imagination and this sequel took a very different direction.

The story of the invasion of The Powhatan people was so outrageous I felt it had to be told. But I soon realised the minefield of conflicting reports of the truth, few of which came from the Powhatan themselves.

My research took me to places I had never been before, and to the confirmation that history is often reported by the victors, with little or no voice given to the oppressed.

I have done my very best to write a book that you will enjoy, but also one that gives a hint of the experiences of the indigenous people of America. I can only give my interpretation based on my studies, but in doing so, I hope to have incorporated many voices rather than just a few, embellishing with my imagination to provide something that people might relate to.

I apologise in advance, if I have written anything that does not accurately reflect the position of the Powhatan in 1600s, I mean no disrespect. In fact, it is my attempt to acknowledge the wrong-doings of Colonial settlers.

This book is fiction, but based on the facts as far as I could ascertain them. It may be your starting point for further investigation if the story stirs you as it did me.

Sue Wright

Acknowledgement

Many thanks go to Lee Bogle who gave his permission for his beautiful painting 'The Prayer' to be used for the cover of this book.

You can find more of Lee's work at www.leebogle.com

Thanks to Nigel Wright, my Editor who spent many hours helping me with my manuscript.

Glossary

ALONGQUIAN
Powhatan Language

APOOK
Tobacco

HOBBOMAK
Arrangement of rock located
in an area with powerful energy

Huskanasquaw
Female coming of
age ceremony

Huskanaw
Male coming of age
ceremony

Kitchi
Brave

Mamanantoweck
Spiritual

person/Prophet

Manito aki
Spirit World

Matchacomoco
Great Council of
Alliance

Midewewin
Medicine Dance

Nantaquoud
Son

Nikomis
Grandmother

Powa
Energy

Powagan
Guardian Spirit

Puccoon
Red pigment

Qiakros
Priests

Quioccosan
Large building
used for

ceremonies

Sunsquaa and Sunks
Wise women and men

Tassantassas/Longcoats
English Colonists

Tsenacommacah
Land ruled by Powhata

Tuckahoe
Poisonous underwater root
that can be processed into flour

Weroance
Chief

Werowocomoco
Pocahontas's village

Yehakin
House

Characters

Henry Spelman
Young English lad,
interpreter for Powhatan

John Smith
Explorer, Colonial Governor,
Admiral of New England,
author

Japasaw/Ioppasus
Kocoum's brother
Pocahontas's brother in law

Kekataugh
Chief of Kekoughtan territory

Kocoum
Pocahontas's first husband,
brother of Japazaw of the
Potowamac

Ko-kee

Pocahontas's son

Matachanna
Pocahontas's sister

Nikomis
The Beloved Woman,
The woman that fell from the Sky

Opechancanough
Pocahontas's uncle
Powhatan's brother

Parahunt
Pocahontas's brother

Pocahontas/Matoaka/Amonute
Daughter of Powhatan
Beloved Woman

Pochins
Pocahontas's brother

Powhatan/Wahunsenacwh
Pocahontas's father
Chief of Powhatans

Samuel Argall
Admiral, Adventurer and Naval Officer

Thomas Dale
Deputy Governor of Virginia 1611 - 1616

Thomas Rolfe

Pocahontas's son

Thomas Savage

English lad that lived with Powhatans

Uttamatamakin/Tomakin/Tomocomo

Pocahontas's brother in law

EPIGRAPH

THE LEGEND OF THE WOMAN WHO FELL TO EARTH
(An ancient Native American Tale)

Full Bloom was promised to a Weroance from down the river.

Before the Weroance would marry her, he made her do a series of tests. She did so well at these tests that the Weroance knew she was more powerful than him.

After they married, she moved in with his family and soon after, the Weroance became very ill. His friends and family told him that it was because of his new wife, and he must get rid of her.

To get rid of her was extremely difficult, because her medicine was more powerful than his.

However, a plan was hatched. The Weroance had a beautiful tree that hung with many lights, brighter than the light of the milky way at night or the sun during the day. The flesh of his previous wife hung there and her aura gave the tree light. He received what powers he had from this wonderful tree.

His friends told him to uproot the tree and show his wife what he had done so that she would bend over and fall into the pit made by the uprooted tree.

As she fell into the nothingness below the tree she tried to hold onto whatever she could - she grabbed corn, tobacco and roots encrusted with soil. As she fell through the darkness some waterbirds were floating by and they moved together to catch her and stop her falling. They did not know what to do with her though. Then turtle saw what had happened and offered for his back as a sanctuary for her. Then other creatures saw what had happened and they dove to retrieve mud that had fallen from her hands to create a world that she could live in. Otter and toad went, and then muskrat. Muskrat tried so hard stuffing his mouth with soil that he sadly died, but all the creatures packed his mud onto turtle's back to make a home for Sky Woman.

Full bloom was pregnant when she fell, and she gave birth to her daughter, Winona or Blossom. In time Winona also fell pregnant and gave birth to twins. Ahone came into the world the usual way, but Okee tore his way out of his mother's body, killing her. Good and evil were born.

Nikomis took her daughter's body and hung it from a tree. Her daughter's head became the moon and her body became the sun and stars. This new tree of light in a new place marked the end of a cycle of creation. The soil on the turtle's back became the earth that they lived on. There was good and there was evil, and Nikomis had provided corn and tobacco as she fell... All the creatures had helped to build the earth on Turtle's back.

CHANGE IS COMING (1604)

For weeks people had been talking in hushed voices, stopping whenever she came near and looking furtively at one another. Her name floated on the wind like the smell of venison cooking over hot coals. Maybe they were going to send her away to another tribe as they were tired of her mischief and her constant questions... maybe they going to sacrifice her to the Gods in return for spiritual protection for the tribe? Was this the end for her?

Even although Matachanna, her older sister, had made it very clear that only adults were invited to the 'special meeting', she had to find out what was going on - this was a matter of life or death. She was Pocahontas, the daughter of The Great Powhatan, and if they were not going to tell her what this was all about, she would have to take matters into her own hands. She was eight years old, and she had a right to know if she was going to be sacrificed.

She watched them filing in to the quiccosan[1] and waited outside until everyone had entered. Then, lifting the doorflap, screwing up her face and counting to ten, she crept in like a small mouse, hardly daring to breathe.

She crouched down by the entrance, looking around her while her eyes adjusted to the darkness.

The quiccosan was the largest building that she had ever seen. It was so long she could hardly see from one end to the other, especially in the dark smoky atmosphere. The rounded roof seemed as high as the sky, and the large fire that burned Apook[2] in the middle, made it fragrant and warm, if a little stifling. She had to hold her breath to stop herself coughing as the tobacco fumes clogged up her throat and made her eyes water. There was a door flap at each end of the large building, and strong mountainous pillars down the middle, the tops of which bore the faces of members of the Manito[3] Aki. The pillars held up the roof, affirming the presence of the spirits presiding over everything that happened in the Great House.

She looked up to the faces of the Gods majestically staring down at her, stern and judgmental, and bowed her head. Her respects paid, she glanced back at the door flap from where she had come, and then forwards to a potential hiding place, pausing, considering - was this really a good idea? She prayed once more to Oke[4] to keep her invisible and then summoning all the energy she had, she ran, crouching down as small as she could until she reached a bench to hide behind. She looked up at the wooden faces of the Gods once more and put her hands together at her heart and mouthed a silent apology for her rude intrusion.

She looked around to see if anyone earthly was watching, breathing a sigh of relief when she saw that all eyes were on her father. They sat side by side on long benches around the Quiccosan, dressed in colourful ceremonial dress, intricate headdresses signifying their varying ranks. Their bodies, painted with flowers or animals, glistened in the heat of the fire. Their faces were drawn, concentrating. Despair hung in the air like a heavy blanket. Maybe they were sad that they had to get rid of her? They were all people that had known her since she was born and they all loved her, and she loved them, but sometimes you had to do things you do not want to do when there is a good reason – she had been told this many times, and she almost forgave them.

The Great Powhatan, her father, put his hands together in front of his heart as he bowed his head. Pocahontas saw the sparkle had gone from his crinkly eyes as he looked at the assembled group. He, especially, would be devastated if he lost her. She was his favourite daughter, his 'Little Mischief'. He would miss her if she was sacrificed.

He raised his arm for silence. She held her breath.

"We have talked often my brothers and sisters, but you *must* understand that the Spirits are sending us warnings. The Quiakros[5] have seen what is to come... it has been foretold for many moons that great change is coming." He paused and looked around, struggling to draw himself up to full height but giving in to powerlessness as he shook his head.

" This will be a new kind of foe, one that does not talk to the winds as we do. We must prepare ourselves. My dream vision commands that we embrace change. We know that change can be difficult, but it is not always bad. We will learn better ways from our new friends, forging an alliance that will be strong and safe against further enemies."

Nothing about her yet... hopefully he would get on with it as she was starting to get pins and needles, and so far this was very boring. Just about change, and someone coming. Nothing to do with her.

Her Uncle Opechancanough, The Great Powhatan's younger brother, cleared his throat. Everyone turned to look at him, including Pocahontas. Opechancanough always spoke his mind, he was sure to get to the point and put her out of her misery.

"Great Powhatan, how can this be right? We must defend our lands, our food, and our people - if not, we will be overrun and wiped out. You are surrendering control before we have even seen these new invaders or *tried* to defend ourselves. They will not come over the seas at great peril to themselves to help us - they will come to take our lands and kill our people."

Powhatan looked at Opechancanough, and Pocahontas had rarely seen such determination in his eyes. It was not to do with her, but nevertheless it was getting very interesting...

Her father spoke. "The great festival of Nikomis, the winter feast celebrating the grandmother, The Woman That Fell From The Sky, will bring us answers, my brother. My beautiful daughter Pocahontas will receive her dream vision as prophesied by the Manito Aki. This will be the greatest dream vision that we have received for many generations. The Quiakros will interpret Pocahontas's dreams and they will tell us what to do. It is not up to you or me, it is up to the visions of Pocahontas."

Pocahontas froze like a cornered hare... '*up to the visions of Pocahontas? Invaders?*' What did it all mean? She watched, trembling, to see what would happen next. Her Uncle's face was puce. Everyone else was sitting on the edge of their seats waiting for the drama between the two brothers to unfold.

"But Powhatan... we *must* prepare for war... we cannot rely on the visions of a child!" Opechancanough had disbelief written all over his face.

Powhatan raised his arm, looked at Opechancanough and shook his head. "The Gods have spoken, my brother. It is true, she *is* just a child, but she is also the most important Beloved Woman we have had for generations. I cannot ignore the Prophesies."

Opechancanough stared at his brother. Powhatan stared back, his face unflinching.

"There is nothing more to say then" Opechancanough muttered through gritted teeth, getting up and marching out of the Quiccosan, the door flap swinging violently behind him.

Pocahontas pulled back into the shadows as he passed. She looked after him, and then towards her father, her face drained of colour, bile rising up to her throat ...*the most important dream vision for generations... it is up to the Dream Visions of Pocahontas...*

Powhatan paused, regaining his composure, and then turned back to the assembled group who were murmuring amongst themselves, clearly shocked by what they had just witnessed.

He stood up raising both arms in the air for silence. "There will be some among you that doubt. Just remember, one thing is certain - change *is* coming. We will learn how to manage change by being alert and by listening to the Gods and the Visions that are sent – even if they *are* sent to children. We must trust in the messages sent to us by the Gods." He bowed his head, sat down and closed his eyes to signify the ending of the meeting.

She was the child on whom they all depended. She should have listened to Matachanna, and never come to the meeting. The words played in her ears.... '*It is up to the Dream Visions of Pocahontas*'....

As Powhatan sat with his eyes closed, everyone withdrew and left the Quioccosan,[7] sombre and deep in thought. Pocahontas crouched in her hiding place, waiting for the moment to strategically leave without being seen.

She was getting pins and needles in her legs from crouching. The Quiccosan had emptied out now, and she was left on her own with Powhatan. She tried to stretch out her leg to get the circulation going, and panic overwhelmed her as she saw, as if in slow motion, the huge bench that she was hiding behind started to topple over. She reached over to steady it, but it was too late.

"Crash!"

There she was, thoroughly exposed, scrabbling around on the floor like a beetle, with no hiding place, her eyes wide and focussed on her father, waiting for the sky to fall in when he realised her crime. Powhatan opened his eyes and looked in her direction, alert for danger.

"It is only me father, it is only Pocahontas. I came to see you, but I see it is not the right time, so I will just go." She looked at him with wide eyes, rising from her crouched position, hobbling as her circulation started to flow. She started to move towards the door, gaining speed.

"Oh Pocahontas, what are we going to do with you child?" He shook his head, but a faint smile touched his lips. "You know you should not be here, but right now your presence has lifted my heart at a time when my heart is very heavy. Stay awhile."

He patted the ground next to him, and as her anticipation of his wrath diminished, she breathed a sigh of relief and tiptoed towards him, sitting down cross legged. She looked up at him, wondering what he was going to say next, needing to know what it all meant, but his eyes were vacant, his smile faded as he looked into the flames. She wriggled, but his silence was telling her to wait. She crossed and re-crossed her legs and looked up at him again. His eyes were still focused on the yellow and blue flames as he breathed in the fragrant apook in silence. His breathing was hoarse and loud, almost as if he was asleep. She did not want to disturb him and he had said he wanted her to stay, so she held in her impatience.

She sat for a while picking her fingernails and wriggling her toes, but she really needed to go and think things through, if Powhatan was not going to answer her questions. She glanced up at him to see if his face had changed at all. He was still the same. She was not sure if he still knew she was there. Maybe he was asleep? She had to do something. She moved her small hand towards his arm and touched him, smiling up at him. He looked down at her as if seeing her for the first time. It was now or never.

"Father, I heard what you were saying to Uncle Opechancanough, and I think this needs further consideration." She was trying to sound grown-up, talking 'father to daughter'.

He laughed. "If only it were that simple, my Little Mischief"

He wasn't supposed to laugh, this was serious. Her face crumpled "I didn't realise that my Visions would be so important. I am scared. I am just a child, I cannot do these things" she said.

He smiled as she looked up at him with big black eyes that were glistening with fear and anticipation. Her tiny naked flat chest was rising and falling as she waited, hoping that he could take from her the weight that had suddenly crashed down on her tiny shoulders - hoping he would say it was alright and that she had misunderstood.

He sighed as he stooped down and lifted her up onto his knee and put his arm around her, drawing her into him. She felt his strong firm body and his still and calm presence, and sighed. This was her father; this was the strong warrior that she knew. He would make it better. She relaxed into him.

He looked down at her. "It is alright Pocahontas. The Spirits will always protect you and give you what you need. You are only a Messenger. It is not *your* message that we are waiting for - it is the message that will be given to you by the Manito Aki. All you must do is open your heart."

Pocahontas screwed up her face. "I do not really know what it all means, father. I don't know how to open my heart. Say I am given a Vision and

I tell you the wrong thing?" Her mouth turned down and she sat up and stared into the fire, drawing her eyebrows together.

Powhatan pulled her back and gave her another hug. "Before you were born, it was prophesied that you would be a Beloved Woman whose Dream Visions would foretell the biggest changes in the world for hundreds of years. When the Spring Equinox is with us, you will go to a Hobbomak and you will stay there, not eating for many days. It is then that the Spirits will send you The Vision."

Their eyes met. Her face was long, and her eyes were watery, remembering what her Uncle had said.

"But father, I am only a child, I cannot do these things. I don't know enough."

"I know you will worry. It would be strange if you did not. All I can tell you Pocahontas, is that this is a process that has been going on for thousands of years. The spirits have said that you will be very special, and your name will be remembered for generations to come. There is nothing that you can do to stop this - the Spirits have spoken."

"But I don't *feel* special, I just want to play and have fun. Can't you choose someone else?"

Powhatan enveloped her in a bear like hug, smiling, but her body remained stiff, her eyes staring into the fire. She had known she had special powers for a long time. She saw things that others could not see. But she had ignored it, hoping it would go away. She wanted to please him so much, but she feared telling him about the Visions she had *already* seen, … She shivered, but not from the cold. She was beginning to realize that the nightmares that came to her day and night, were not just dreams, they were prophesies – and silent tears slid down her face as it became clear that Powhatan could not take it all away. It *was* up to her.

[1] Large building used for ceremonies

[2] Tobacco

[3] Spirit World

[4] Powhatan God

[5] Priests

A NEW FRIEND

Pocahontas tossed and turned in her small cot bed. It should have been warm, but her body was shivering, and thoughts were swirling around and around her head. These were not childish worries, these were worries that concerned the fate of every single person that she knew, and some that she didn't. And she was on her own with it. Why was she chosen? She saw things that other people didn't see, but so what? It was not at all helpful. It was just very annoying. She put up with it and tried to blank it out as much as she could, so she could get on with her day to day life. It was like a stab to the heart when she realised that her ability to communicate with animals, see what was written on the wind, and foretell the future in her dreams, *did* actually mean something. But it was useless… her dreams had never been useful to *her*…

She could hear movement and hushed voices outside of the Yehakin indicating that the day would soon be starting even though it must be dark outside. Her father's warriors were preparing for hunting and they had to be ready before the sun rose.

The fire still burned in the centre of the Yehakin. It had to be kept alight to keep away evil spirits, but despite its glowing heat, it had not managed to keep her frozen toes and fingers warm. The atmosphere was smoky, soot covering all the surfaces in the room, and she longed for clean crisp air to clear the cloying cobwebs of her mind.

She could hear Uttamatamakin, her brother in law, snoring loudly as he breathed in and out. He was snuggled up with Matachanna, her sister, and her father slept on the other side of the Yehakin. He was snoring too. Why did men always snore, she thought to herself, it was very annoying when one was trying to sleep. Powhatan's latest wife was sleeping next to him behind a screen, and his other eleven wives and their children were dotted around the large Yehakin according to their rank. So many people, snuffling, groaning and moving around. As she lay trying to sleep, the noise filled her head to bursting. She banged her head against the pillow, and put her hands over her ears to try and blank them out, but it was no use. She squeezed her eyes shut thinking 'everyone just go away and leave me alone!'.

She tossed and turned and tossed and turned, squeezing her eyes shut. Her feet were like blocks of ice. It was no good, she had to get up or her nose would drop off and her feet would fuse to the covers. Maybe if she went outside for a walk, she could clear her head and warm herself up.

She got out of her bed, quickly put on her leggings and deerskin mantle, and tiptoed across the Yehakin towards the entrance. As she raised the flap, the cold damp air hit her. The twilight made everything take on an eery misty appearance, the moist air almost translucent as it hung in pockets over the nearby water. She stopped for a moment, listening to the breeze swishing through the leaves. Maybe this had been a bad idea. Although she had been cold when lying still, it was much warmer inside the Yehakin, and it wouldn't be long before everyone else was up and Matachanna was serving up steaming bowls of corn meal and large wedges of Tuckahoe[1] bread slathered with animal fat. Her mouth watered at the thought. Should she stay?

No. She could have some food later. She would go and visit her favourite dog Kitchi to clear her head. He would know what to do. She set off towards the kennels.

Kitchi was a large dog with a very dense black and grey coat, large teeth and a ferocious growl, if provoked. She opened the kennel door that creaked with age, and peeked inside. The first thing that hit her was the familiar sweet smell of the dry bedding grass and the sounds of the dogs moving about whimpering, barking, and playing with one another. Kitchi came towards her wagging his tail. His eyes were smiling at her as he brushed against her. She read his greeting in his eyes.

"Well then, I suppose you are pleased to see me?" she said as she raised her hand to meet his fluffy head. She sat down on the dried grass that lined the enclosure, with Kitchi by her side rubbing his soft ears.

Pocahontas sighed and threw herself back on a mound of grass taking in the smells and the sounds, trying to transport herself away from all her troubles. "It's not happening Kitchi, is it? I am not being asked to save the tribe, really - am I?"

Kitchi looked at her with sad brown eyes. With her wisdom, Pocahontas knew he was telling her that it *was* true, and she sighed. Kitchi would not lie to her. She threw her arms around her huge furry friend, burying her face in his neck.

"Save the tribe? Don't be ridiculous. You are only a twig of a girl."

Pocahontas jumped and looked around to see where the voice was coming from. At first, she thought it was Kitchi answering her....

She then realised that the booming voice had come from outside.

"Who is there?" Pocahontas's voice trembled. Who had heard her outspoken words? What would they think of her? She would never have voiced her worries to anyone but Kitchi.

"It is me - Kocoum" the voice said.

"Kocoum?" she answered, her eyebrows raising. "Who is Kocoum? I don't know any 'Kocoum'. You should not be here" she said, trying to make her voice sound authoritative, and getting up to get a better view of the rude intruder.

As she stood, her arm on Kitchi's back, she saw a boy of about twelve years old as he bounded out from behind the door. He waited, his hands on his waist and fixed a strong gaze at her, drawing himself up to full height. "So - who are *you*, and what are *you* doing here? I am a trainee warrior in the tribe of the Great Powhatan. I should throw you out of here as you are trespassing… " he said.

Was he serious? "I am *not* trespassing" Pocahontas shouted, pulling away from Kitchi, and standing straight and tall, eyes flashing. "I am the *daughter* of the Great Powhatan. I am a Beloved Woman in training, and I don't need *you* to tell me what to do…. " she flicked her hair back and stared, her eyes unwavering. "Stand aside and apologise for your rudeness" she shouted, nostrils flaring, colour flooding her cheeks.

Kocoum looked at her for several seconds, his face quizzical. He then put his hand over his mouth as he burst out laughing. "Really? You are just a little girl, and you look so funny with your little angry red face and twigs for arms." His eyes were dancing. "Maybe I should get down on one knee and worship you, oh Great Daughter of The Great Powhatan." He made a large mock bow, and then started prancing around. He was giggling, glancing at her every now and then to see if she was watching him.

Pocahontas looked at him, her face still stormy. How dare he? It was far from funny. But even Kitchi started bounding around with him. She stood watching the two of them, hands on hips, face straight. She was entitled to feel angry, he had insulted her. But, the picture of him prancing around with the 'dancing' dog contrasted so drastically with her rigid stance that her mouth started to turn up at the edges.

She could not fight the rising bubbles of fun that came from deep in her stomach and she started to laugh. Then laughter took over and she laughed like she had never laughed before, unsure why she was laughing, which made it worse. It was not *that* funny. Who *was* this boy that he could do this to her?

When they had both exhausted themselves with laughter, there was an awkward pause. He looked at her, his eyes focussed on her face. "Friends?" He asked, eyebrows raised.

"Friends" she replied, smiling.

"Do you like climbing trees by any chance?" he asked.

"That's a silly question. Of course I do." Pocahontas's face lit up. Maybe she had at last found someone that liked adventure as much as she did.

They put a rope around Kitchi's neck, and she followed Kocoum as he headed for the trees. The sun was rising, and the grass was wet with the morning dew. The smell of the pine trees filled the air as the weak sun started to warm up the atmosphere, and noises from the settlement mingled with the sounds of the early morning bird call.

There was silence between them as they walked. Pocahontas had so much to think about, and now all she was thinking about was this boy. Her life was getting extremely complicated. She stole a glance at him. She had never met a boy like this alone. She had seen many training for her father, and there were many wandering around the village, but never had any of them spoken to her.

He was about twelve years old. His brown body was strong and a bit gangly. He was taller than most of the trainee warriors, and certainly a lot taller than she was. He had the dark shiny hair and black eyes of the Powhatan people, much like her own. What was he really like though? He could be arrogant but he could also be a clown. Now his face was soft as he smiled at Kitchi, murmuring as he fondled the dog's ears. Out of the corner of her eye, she saw him glance at her, and she quickly looked away, hiding under her hair, the blood rushing to her cheeks.

He smiled, looking at the ground.

"So, I know a great tree to climb" he said glancing back at her. "Let's go this way." They wandered through the trees for a while, trees that had tall trunks with branches sprouting out too high to reach - not good to climb, unless you had a rope to pull yourself up with. At last, Kocoum pointed ahead.

There, before her stood the most magnificent tree she had ever seen. It had a large canopy of leaves, a huge brown silver trunk, and low climbable branches fanning out from the middle. If trees could be friendly, this tree was a friend. She could feel the tree smiling and welcoming them.

"How amazing. It was made for climbing." She looked at him with wide eyes.

He puffed his chest out with pride. "You just have to know where to look. I come here all the time" he said nonchalantly. In command. "It is my special tree. You can climb almost to the top, and when you get up there, you can see for miles and miles."

"Does the tree have a name?" She asked.

"No of course not, it is just a tree!" He laughed.

"No tree is *just* a tree Kocoum. Especially a tree like this. I am going to call her Hurit, a name for beautiful things." She looked up, smiling at the branches waving in the wind.

"If you must" he said.

"Now, I will give you a 'leg up' to get to the first branch as you are so dinky..." he smiled, knowing how niggled she would be at not being able to get to the first branch herself.

She couldn't argue with him, as she could never scale the tall lower trunk without help, and she knew that if she tried, she would spoil her image.

He cupped his hands together and she held onto his shoulders, using his hands as a step. They were face to face looking into each other's eyes for a few seconds, before he hoisted her up above his head, towards the first extending branch of the tree. She landed on the first branch, her heart beating faster than it should have when climbing a tree.

"You ok?" he shouted.

"Of course I'm ok. This is nothing to me. I am used to much more difficult trees than this."

He smiled to himself. "You go to the next level then, and I will follow you up".

Pocahontas looked up towards the sky and saw the most beautiful green canopy over her head. Speckles of sunlight danced on her face as she gazed. She saw branches reaching out from the main trunk above her, just waiting for her to climb. She took the first tentative steps upwards and grabbed on to a branch just above her chin. She clasped on to the rough bark and eased herself up, arms straining, looking down at Kocoum. She climbed up and up, seeing the ground getting further and further away, until she was almost at the top of the tree. She had lied. This was the highest she had ever been.

"Don't climb any further Pocahontas - the branches will be too small and could give way when you get up there". He climbed to join her on a branch close by, and they both looked out at the scene in front and below them.

"Wow" exclaimed Pocahontas.

"Are you scared?" Kocoum asked. She could tell from the way he pursed his lips that he hoped she was.

"Of course not!" she said. "It is the most wonderful thing I have ever seen. Look over there, you can see the water - you can *even* see the birds landing on it. I can imagine flying through the trees and having Hurit as my home. I can feel the wind through my hair and on my face. She picked a leaf and threw it into the air. It circled round and round as it fluttered to the ground. Imagine what it would feel like to be that leaf." They both watched it, mesmerized by its swirling freedom.

His eyes turned skywards. "Sometimes I imagine I can fly. It must be so freeing to be able to fly over the trees and the water, or float like a leaf on the breeze."

"I definitely want to stay here forever" she said.

"Well, I think the favourite daughter of the Great Powhatan might be missed, don't you?" He laughed. "In fact, I think we had better head down for breakfast before everyone gets worried about you. We can always come here again. I don't want to be blamed for leading you astray."

She nodded her head slowly, her mouth turned down at the corners. "You are right, I know, but I feel so light up here. It is as if all my troubles are on the ground, and I am in the sky and they cannot reach me. Thank you for sharing your special place with me" she looked at him and held his gaze.

As he looked at her beautiful face, something stirred within him that he had never felt before. He turned away, but he was compelled to turn back for a sneaky moment.

They climbed down the tree to a very patient Kitchi who jumped up to lick Pocahontas's face with a wet sloppy welcome, his tail wagging furiously. She scurried around below the tree until she found the leaf that she had allowed to fall. "Now I can keep a part of Hurit to remind me how it feels to fly. Here, you have half of the leaf Kocoum,"she said, tearing the leaf in two, "and we can *both* remember what freedom feels like."

She crouched down with her hand on Kitchi's head and looked deeply into his brown eyes "We have to go back now, my friend" she said to him.

Suddenly her hand went to her mouth with shock. "Oh no" she whispered to herself as she saw it in Kitchi's eyes. "What does it mean Kitchi?" she whispered. The dog licked her hand. He knew. She tried to blink her eyes to get rid of the Vision, but there it was, as clear as could be.

We are together hand in hand - the world around us is covered with blood...

[1] Poisonous plant processed to make flour for bread

SPRING EQUINOX: 1604

Today was the day. Today was the Spring Equinox, the day she was to go to the Hobbomak[1] to receive her blessing from the Gods and to receive her Dream Vision.

The image in Kitchi's eyes after her wonderful day with Kocoum had scared her and she had told nobody. The world covered with blood - how unfair that she was sent such a Prophesy but was not given any guidance on what to do with it, or how to stop it. What did it mean?

She often saw Visions in her head, a bit like other people had dreams - but hers were not when she was asleep. She had tried to bring them on when *she* wanted them - but they had stubbornly refused. She had even tried to bring on the Vision she had seen in Kitchi's eyes so that she might get a fuller story, but it was impossible.

Her world was a very different place to that of most people, with the Spirits of animals and trees befriending her - the badgers, rabbits, dogs and deer told her things through their big brown eyes, and the trees whispered to her as if they were friends.

At first, she thought she was just imagining things and became annoyed at herself, trying to ignore the messages. She had been doing this for years, until Powhatan had told her that this is what happens to people such as her;

people that have been chosen by the Manito Aki. It was a special gift.

She did not understand why she was given only part of a Prophesy. That seemed unfair. It was as if she was supposed to find the answers – but how could she? She was only a child. She did not have the answers within her - or did she? Maybe she just had to try a little harder.

She and Kocoum had become the best of friends and she had tried to describe her mystical world, but he had just looked at her with wide eyes, asking her impossible questions that she had no answers for. It was something she could not put into words, something that only those connected to the spirits could really understand. So, she had stopped telling him when she saw a squirrel telling her the way to go, or when a deer beckoned them in the woods when they were playing. He was her closest friend and if *he* couldn't understand, no one could. She had to learn to use her gift well and hide it from those that did not understand. It was a lonely place to be.

Now it was Spring Equinox and it was her chance to formally connect with the Spirits with the blessing of Powhatan and all the wise men and women of the tribe. Maybe the answers that she had been searching for would be given to her. Maybe she would at last know what she had to do.

Sunsquaa had told her what was going to happen, and she was ready. Her Badger Spirit guide had also come to her one night in a dream to reassure her that all would be well. He kept coming to her in dreams, and had become her best friend in the other world.

"Why have you come to me Badger?" she asked him one night in a dream.

"Manito Aki sent me to you. Manito Aki loves your mischievous nature, and Manito Aki knows I am mischievous as well. He knew that we are of like Nature and Spirit and that I could look after you well" he had said.

She had been a little nervous about going to the Hobbomak, but Badger said he was going to stay with her when she entered the Hobbomak and Sunsquaa[2] was going to check on her every twelve hours to make sure that she was safe. The Spirits had decided the time was right for her. She would do her duty, even if fear overwhelmed her.

Despite her fear, part of her felt very special, as she had the blessing of the whole tribe. All day the women had been preparing her for her epic journey. Her hair had been braided and white feathers adorned her head. Her body was decorated with paintings of birds and flowers, and she had not eaten for two days (that part didn't feel too special as Pocahontas loved her food).

Then the evening came. It was a dark night, and Sunsquaa took her hand and led her past lines of people waiting to cheer her on. She walked down the line of well wishers, looking for Kocoum's face. When she saw him, her heart gave a flutter. Their eyes locked. It was brief, but as significant as if they had looked at each other for hours. The meaning was clear.

All eyes were on her, so she forced herself to look forwards. Ahead she saw the dark forest with tall trees like a dense cavern waiting to devour her small self. Her stomach lurched. The crowd of people and the cheering, petered out as she moved further and further away into the night clutching the hand of Sunsquaa. She looked back once wanting to see if Kocoum was still there, but Sunsquaa yanked her forwards into the silent darkness.

As they walked on, several times she caught sight of Badger weaving in and out of the undergrowth and she felt a warm feeling knowing that he was there to protect her.

The wind continued to swirl through the trees which were silhouetted against the light of the moon. They walked and walked and walked. She was starting to get tired. She had had only a few hours' sleep, and nothing to eat.

Her stomach started to grumble and gripe shouting for some warm corn gruel. She imagined a steaming turtle shell filled to the brim with hot food and she started to feel a longing to be back in her small bed in the Yehakin. She forced each step, her legs feeling like they were trailing through the thickest of mud. It would be disgrace to stop now, no matter how difficult it was. She had to receive her Dream Vision. The tribe depended on it. Her stomach somersaulted again.

Suddenly she saw the turn in the river. This must be it; this must be where if she looked up, she would be able to see the stones. There they were, the stones of the Hobbomak standing tall hard and grey in the moonlight, their long sinister shadows enveloping the earth around them. Pocahontas needed to get into the vortex of the stones, where the magic would be revealed to her. She hesitated for a moment. Her task weighed heavily on her shoulders as they walked towards the stones that had stood for centuries, tall and forbidding.

"You are here with the Gods" said Sunsquaa. "I must leave, but I will come back soon, to check that you are safe." Sunsquaa kissed her on her cheek, put her hands together and bowed. "Do not be afraid, little one. You are protected by the greatest powers on the earth. You have to do nothing, but be yourself." At that, Sunsquaa turned and walked away, looking back once over her shoulder. Pocahontas was alone.

She tiptoed into the centre and sat down cross legged on the ground, waiting. "Manito Aki, I am here" she whispered. She couldn't understand why it felt so ordinary. There didn't seem to be the magical feeling that she had envisioned when she set out. It was just hard and cold. Despite Sunsquaa's words, she was frightened. She looked towards the trees who whispered encouragement and she saw the figure of Badger doing somersaults to try and make her laugh. It did not work. She looked around her and she felt so small, as if she was an ant about to be crushed.

A rumble of thunder crashed through the trees, and the illumination from a sheet of lightening made the night turn into day for a second, throwing eery shadows dancing before her eyes. Then the cold blackness returned like a blanket hiding all in its path.

"Manito Aki, please speak to me." She had to scream at the top of her voice as the angry thunder roared, drowning her out. Pocahontas felt the cold icy drops of hail-like needles on her small body as she looked up at the stones that stood towering above her; not the friendly Manito that she had envisaged, but an angry torrent that offered her no shelter. Surely the spirits wanted her to come? Surely, they would protect her from the harshness of this other world. Her body was getting colder and colder as the icy pellets battered her body, causing her to roll her body up into a ball to protect herself from the stinging attack.

Gradually without her noticing, everything became hazy as consciousness started to leave her...

I never knew that I could fly - maybe sometimes in my dreams I floated in the air, but now I am truly flying. I have big wings and I am covered in white feathers I am a Beloved Woman. I have never felt so free. I look around and all I see are friends. They are large and small - from the big brown bear to the tiny little ant, I know that they are all like me. We are all creatures together, we are all as one, all creatures of the spirits. My heart is bursting with joy at the beauty of Mother Earth. Harmony. Synchrony. Life.

But wait, they are all looking at something from the top of a hill that looks down on the river.

Crowds coming across the sea like termites, skeletons, weak, sad and disease ridden. Skin and bone. Hands scrape frantically in the dust. Tears mingle with the dirty salt water that illusively quenches their thirst but kills them brutally. I drop food for the strangers, who clap and cheer as I fly away. One of their number smiles at me, I know his name is Smith. Manito Aki wants me to save them, embrace them to make them part of our tribe.

Now they are too weak even to take my food. I feed them one by one. They have tools to work the land, shiny things I have never seen before, fire sticks to kill. I bow, I smile, but they hold their hands to their chests and look at the parched earth with suspicion in their eyes - they do not share, they raise the stick... noise and fire burst out, making my heart heavy. I can do nothing... my people are hiding...

He glances up and catches my eye, pleading... his head goes down...the block is cold, the axe is sharp... on I go through time.

Kocoum and I walk hand in hand... but the world is covered with blood... as my heart is pulled from my body. Kocoum ... he is going further and further 'til I am all alone my tears splashing on the shiny copper kettle as my darkness begins.

A swirling misty wind wrenches me like an innocent from the arms of my protector. It is dark, and I am in a dark room...Crouched on the floor... humiliation... searing pain...

I cannot get out. Why am I here? It is cold and grey. Evil abounds. Friends have gone, no Badger, no Kitchi... I see myself crying until.... A fluttering, a warm glow... a friend...

the fragrance comes - warm, happy - acres and acres of apook... but the snake bites still...

I toss on the sea... A King and Queen - a castle, gold and silver balls on top of glittering pyramids, painted faces, music - it is getting louder so it is all I can hear. The painted faces are ghouls with angry eyes getting bigger, they are laughing at me in my beautiful dress... I cannot breathe, I see my people getting smaller... they are now the ants... They are being crushed by laughing crowds stamping on the flowers, on crops, and I cannot reach them. My heart is breaking... on and on they trudge... a trail of tears...

It is so cold, but he is holding my hand, he smiles with love and the seed is planted...

The ship, the pain. I am transforming, and my wings return. Badger shows me the way, and I fly with the leaf that falls. Kocoum holds out his hand to lead me...I find joy with him, my eternal love, but my heart is broken too. I ache for my love and the two little flowers as I leave the other world...

I swoop down one last time, just to see, before I soar with my childhood heart. We soar and soar over the land and the dark sea. I am home at last.

But what is this home? Many moons have passed... As I look down, I am flying over a parched land that is getting darker and darker as the earth dies bit by bit. Smoke is rising, tall grey structures with tiny windows, and I see the beautiful trees as they choke, the dolphins in the sea as they are poisoned, and my kin as they lie on the parched earth. They are crying. I am crying. Is it the creatures that came from the sea who destroy my earth, that makes it dark and covered with blood?

Manito Aki tells me it is the Gods and Nature that will save the day, but my name will go on. Manito Aki does not want the death of the world, so he will rescue us, transforming us, like the dolphins and the bears, taking us to another, better world...

The voice of Manito Aki floats on the wind... those who nurture the world

22

survive, those who take from her perish through their own greed...

She woke up to find Badger licking her hand. The dream had come and gone. All she had left was remnants of images in her head, but no understanding of what it meant.

The Gods had told her what the future held. Nothing would ever be the same again, she could read it in Badger's eyes and hear it in the wind. It was up to her now.

[1] Standing Stones with powerful energy field
  [2] Wise woman

THE STRANGERS ARRIVE: MAY 14, 1607

❦

(Pocahontas aged 11)

"Hurry up Kocoum" Pocahontas shouted, her chest rising and falling with the effort of running. "They are definitely coming. I heard the messenger talking to Powhatan. It must be the strangers that I saw in my Dream Vision. It *must* be." She was still not sure what the dream had meant, it was all very strange.

Kocoum rolled his eyes. He sauntered over towards her, completely unmoved by her urgency, stopping to kick a stone into the bushes. After all, she was not his boss, she didn't tell him what to do…

She watched him impatiently. He obviously did not realise the importance of what was about to happen.

Suddenly she felt faint. Everything before her became hazy and Kocoum faded from view… she shivered… the coldness of the Hobbomack overtook her and she was back in her dream vision…

"...I look around and all I see are friends...
   They are coming across
   the land in great numbers like ants."

She shook her head and the image disappeared. She looked around her to see if Kocoum had noticed, but time must have stood still as nothing had changed. He was still looking at the stone that he had kicked into the bushes. It was unsettling, but she had to pull herself together if she was going to find out what was going on. It had been three years since her Dream Vision, and the Quikros had not told her the meaning of it. Powhatan knew, but he was biding his time until the strangers arrived, to formulate a plan. So she had to take matters into her own hands again. Surely they would thank her in the end?

She beckoned Kocoum frantically with her hands. "Come on, we must go *now* as it is quite a long way away, and we want to be back before dark." She was jumping up and down with excitement. She knew this was a very daring thing that she wanted to do. Maybe the spirits had made her overhear the messenger and that was their way of giving her permission to get involved. What harm could there be in going? She would only look, she wouldn't talk to the strangers - that would be too scary, even with Kocoum at her side.

"Slow down, slow down Pocahontas" said Kocoum. "I think you are getting ahead of yourself. If Powhatan has had a messenger telling him of the arrival of strangers, I am sure he will be dealing with it. I am *also* sure he will not be wanting his eleven year old daughter and her friend poking their noses in. We know nothing about these people. They could kill us - we just don't know."

She looked at him and held out her hand. "Come ON Kocoum. I saw them in my vision, and I must do something. Please come with me, or I will go on my own." She knew that this would annoy him.

He stood and looked at her, raising one eyebrow, hands on hips, his black hair shining in the gentle May sunshine. "Pocahontas, this is not a good idea. It is definitely not a good idea for you to go on your own. We know absolutely nothing about these people."

He had walked right into her trap. "I *know* that Kocoum. Why do you *think* I want to go…" Her voice had a mocking tone to it. Then she turned more serious."I need to find out about them. That is my job. I must have answers for my father, so that he can make plans. They might just be like the others that have come and gone and will be off before we meet them - or they might be coming like the Prophecy foretells, to stay and make a life alongside of us. We do need to know though."

Kocoum groaned. "Yes, I know all that Pocahontas. But it is not the job of an eleven-year-old girl to find these answers. Your father will send warriors. It is only you interpreting a dream… and that is not your job either."

Pocahontas looked at him with her eyes flashing. He just didn't understand. She was about to explode at him, but stopped and thought for a moment. Instead, she ran up to him and threw her arms around him. "Please Kocoum. I really want to do this and I can't do it without you." She looked up at him with large brown pleading eyes, smiling at him, knowing he could never resist her. "But I *will* go on my own if you don't come." The pleading turning to determination.

He looked down at her, and she knew she had won. "I really don't think this is a good idea Pocahontas. I will go with you as long as we just look at them from afar, but not today - tomorrow when we are sufficiently prepared AND I don't want to approach them or talk to them, it is just too dangerous." He sighed.

"Of course Kocoum, we will do exactly as you say, and we will come back as soon as we have seen what they are doing. Of *course* I will not go down and talk to them. I am not stupid." She smiled. One step at a time.

The two children set off the following morning, prepared with water and some tuckahoe bread, in case they got hungry along the way. Pocahontas knew that it was quite a long way from her village, and they needed to be prepared for the journey.

They started climbing up the hill. They had crossed the river after leaving Pocahontas's village of Werowocomoco and traveled for several miles to get to the next river. Tribes up and down the river had reported to Powhatan

26

that men dressed in long coats were coming, and some had met them. Some tribes were pleased to see the strangers, and others were not. Pocahontas knew, from her Dream Vision, that she had to make friends with these strangers, at least she *thought* that was what the dream meant. Surely this was what the Manito Aki wanted her to do? Surely she was only carrying out the wishes of the Manito Aki? One day Kocoum would understand.

They got to the top of the hill and looked down. So far there was nothing. Kocoum laughed. "See, they are not coming after all."

"They will be here Kocoum - we just have to wait." Pocahontas's face held a set determination. She knew. She was not going to be put off by him. He just didn't understand these things.

They kept looking and eventually, after several hours, they saw three ships coming round the corner from the direction of the Chesapeake area, starting to head for land.

"Here they come Kocoum" Pocahontas shouted, jumping up and down. "I *knew* they would come. I told you so." She prodded him and pushed him. He came towards her and grabbed her from behind, picking her up in the air and swinging her around.

"So they have come, you little twiglet, so now what are we going to do." He faced her with raised eyebrows. "You know what you promised? You know we are not going to go near them?"

"Well, we must watch them to see what they are doing, and how many of them there are. Then maybe go over and say hello if they land" she said.

"Whoa… whoa…whoa… You PROMISED. We really don't know if they are friendly or not. They might eat us for dinner… "

Pocahontas could see that he was fidgeting and his eyes were wide with anxiety. *He* had not seen the vision. *He* did not know that they were the same as all creatures. She smiled. "OK Kocoum, let's just watch them for a while. We might be able to gauge how friendly they are… let's get a little closer, so we can hear what is going on."

"I don't suppose they will stay here anyway" said Kocoum. "It is not really a good place to have a camp, is it? Sure they can dock their large ships in that deep water, but they will soon find out that when it gets a little hotter, the mosquitoes will drive them absolutely mad and they are sure to get ill. When the fresh water dries up, they will find themselves drinking salt - and you know what happens when you drink salt water? I don't think they will be here that long if they have any sense. No good warrior would set up camp there, I think they are just scouting, and they will move upriver once they have inspected the land."

Tears mingle with the dirty
salt water that
illusively quenches their thirst,
but kills them brutally

She shook her head to get rid of the Vision. "Well, we will soon find out, won't we." She took his hand and started to walk towards where the strangers were about to land.

"Keep out of sight Pocahontas, we don't know what they are like yet" he whispered. "I think that they eat little girls for supper." He laughed, but he was not amused. He didn't know what she had brought them to, but he didn't want to lose face, so went along with it as usual. He should have known, however, that she would eventually take matters into her own hands.

She looked over at him. "Don't worry Kocoum, I promise we will be fine." He shook his head, knowing how impulsive she was, bracing himself for the unknown.

As they watched, the three ships pulled into the bank of the river. The ships looked very big compared to the dugouts that Pocahontas was used to. They looked even bigger than most of their Yehakins. Many men dressed in long coats jumped onto the bank and they shouted with glee, happy to have landed. Pocahontas watched with wide eyes as they started to unload the ships and erect what looked like teepees, for shelter.

"Look Pocahontas, they have teepees, they are not building anything permanent. Maybe they are not staying, as I thought" said Kocoum. "They have no women with them either - so they can't be here for good, or there surely would be women and children. They must just be exploring." Pocahontas could see him visibly relaxing.

"Let's go now" he said.

"No. Let's get a bit closer" she said grabbing his hand and pulling him roughly forward. "They look very strange. Look at the way that they are dressed in those funny long coats and hats and look at the colour of their skin. They are shouting at one another too… looks like they are angry. I need to get closer."

"Pocahontas, please… you can't get much closer, they will see us, and then we will be in real trouble." His eyes were wide, his face stern.

"Don't back out now Kocoum" she said, her eyes pleading with him. "Look, there is a pile of wood left over from a storm. We can run quickly behind that, and then we will be close enough to see what is going on." Before Kocoum could respond, Pocahontas shot out towards the pile of wood. He looked after her in despair.

"Come ON Kocoum" she beckoned him with her arm. "Don't leave me here by myself." She knew that he would be insulted by the inference that he would leave her, and she was right. She saw the anger in his eyes as he resolved himself to follow her. He looked in the direction of the Longcoats to make sure no one was looking his way, and ran. As he landed next to Pocahontas, one of the logs was nudged and it fell off the pile and started rolling down the hill towards the strangers clanking and bouncing as it went.

The strangers looked up from what they were doing, eyebrows raised and alert.

"There is someone over there" shouted one of the men, pointing.

"Quick, get the gun, we don't want a repeat of what happened before. It could be a hostile native."

Pocahontas stayed as quiet and still as an arrow being aimed. Her heart lurched. Maybe she had misjudged, maybe Kocoum was right. What had she done?

One of the men had a long thick stick that he pointed towards the pile of wood that the children were hiding behind.

29

"Come out of there with your hands up." The man shouted something that the children did not understand, so they just stayed stock still and hoped for the best.

"You will have to shoot" one of the men said. "We can't take the risk."

All of a sudden Pocahontas heard a loud bang and remembers...

they raise the stick and noise and fire burst out, making my heart heavy.

They huddled behind the logs, clinging to one another, scared to look or move. Kocoum's arm had been hit by something coming from the fire-stick and was bleeding. Pocahontas's face was white with fear, her lips trembling. "We are going to die Kocoum. What have they done to your arm? I am sorry, I was wrong." She pulled in closer to him for protection, her hands in front of her eyes, not wanting to face the inevitable, wishing she was anywhere but here. "I am so, so sorry" she whispered as a tear slid down her cheek.

"Well, lookey here" a man's voice boomed out. "It is only a couple of children."

Pocahontas peeped out from behind her fingers and saw a group of men in long coats standing above her and Kocoum, the fire-stick was still smoking. They all had amused looks on their faces.

"Put the gun down Christopher, you are scaring them. It looks like the boy has a bit of a flesh wound" one of the men said. "We better look after them, or we might make enemies of their parents - we don't want a repeat of the Chesapeake tribe. These are to be our new neighbours, we must let them know that we are friendly or they will not cooperate with us."

When the gun was safely put away, and the men's faces continued to show amusement rather than aggression, although she could not understand what they were saying, Pocahontas got her courage back and pulled away from Kocoum's protection. She jumped up, and pointed to Kocoum's wound.

"Look what you have done" she shouted at them, her eyes staring, colour flooding back into her cheeks. Kocoum could not believe her impudence.

"What is that child saying" one of the men was laughing. "She holds a lot of anger for such a little twig. Either she is very courageous or very stupid!"

Pocahontas *was* scared but did not want to show it. Kocoum's wound didn't look too bad, but that wasn't the point. The Longcoated men were meant to be friends, and so far she had not seen any evidence of it. She looked at Kocoum, doubt creeping into her mind. She hoped he wasn't right after all. Maybe they did eat people.

As she was pondering, one of the men walked towards them, put his hands together and bowed. He then smiled and held his hand out in friendship. It was a universal greeting.

Kocoum, raised himself off the ground and walked towards him taking his hand slowly, his arm still dripping with blood.

The Longcoat pointed at the ships, smiling.

"I don't think we should go Pocahontas" said Kocoum. "They might kidnap us."

"I won't be able to get any information unless we go Kocoum. Their eyes look kind. They don't look angry or mean now that they have lowered that fire-stick." Without waiting for his consent, she got up and started to follow the Longcoat. Kocoum tried to grab her arm to stop her, but he winced from the pain of his wound. He had no choice but to follow her - he couldn't let her wander off with these strange men alone.

The strangers took the children back to the ships. Pocahontas was excited as she gingerly climbed up the plank that connected the ship to land. This was such a fun adventure. One of the men sat them down on some boxes on the deck. The Longcoat murmured something to them and left them.

"Kocoum, this is amazing" she said.

"It will be amazing if we get out of here" he replied, shaking his head.

"Oh don't be an old stick in the mud. They are going to bind up your arm. Anyway, it doesn't look that bad to me." She looked sulky. They were given some biscuits and water, and Kocoum's wound was dressed. Pocahontas and Kocoum sat for some time, eating and drinking food that they had never tasted before, watching the Longcoats who continued to unload provisions and set up shelters for themselves. The Longcoats seemed to have almost forgotten the two children were there.

Pocahontas was getting fidgety. She knew there was more information that she needed to gather before they went back. She had to show her father that she was doing everything she could to save the tribe. She turned to Kocoum, innocence on her face. "I am just going to have a look around" she said.

Kocoum sighed. "Why don't you just sit still for once Pocahontas?"

With that she winked at him, stuck her tongue out at him, jumped up and raced around the deck, looking over the side, and prancing up and down as if she owned the ship. She was so excited to be on the large ship.

She noticed out of the corner of her eye, that there was a way to go down inside the ship. She looked around, holding her breath. Should she go and see what it was like? It might make them angry with her, and she didn't want to spoil things. But it was her only chance, and she had to take it, it was too good an opportunity to miss. She scrambled down the steps onto the deck below. It was dark, and she made out shapes of big tree trunk like things pointing out through holes in the side of the ship. Large balls were stacked next to them - it was really strange. As her eyes got accustomed to the dim light, she saw in the corner, a door with bars on it. She wandered over and looked inside.

Suddenly she felt dizzy. She knew this feeling from before. Everything before her became hazy and the ship faded from view...she shivered... the coldness of the Hobbomack overtook her and she was back in her Dream Vision...

... One of their number smiles at me,
   I know his name is Smith...

As the image faded, there before her was the man who had appeared in her dream. He didn't look very well. His hands were tied, and he was rolled up in a ball in the corner. His beard was long, and his eyes were closed. He looked very dirty, and she could smell an awful smell as if he had messed himself. She held her nose and continued to watch him.

He must have heard her, as his eyes suddenly opened, and he stared at her. His blue eyes met hers and she blinked, making sure that she was seeing correctly. It *was* him. Despite the filth, she could see his sandy coloured hair and stocky build. She did not know what to do. He was obviously a prisoner - but why? In her dream he was one of the leaders of the Longcoats, someone to make friends with and to trust.

"Pocahontas... Pocahontas... " It was Kocoum, he was calling to her down the steps from the top deck. "You must come back, they are going to notice that you have gone down there, and it could make trouble for us."

"Alright, Kocoum, I am on my way." She had one last look at the prisoner, who gave her a weak smile and grunted. She scrambled across the deck and ran up the stairs, glancing behind at the "cage" that contained the man she believed to be called Smith. She was full of questions. Trying to figure the whole thing out. She was certain that the prisoner was the man from her dream - but maybe she had been mistaken. She must have been. She ran across the deck and sat next to Kocoum as if she had been sitting there for hours. He looked at her, questions written all over his face.

"Well... ? " he said.

"Shhhhh... I will tell you about it later" she whispered, staring straight ahead, trying to get her thoughts in order.

They sat together in silence and after a while, Pocahontas noticed a group of the Longcoats huddling together earnestly talking and pointing at them. She started to worry. She hoped that they were not planning to kill them or kidnap them, or throw them in with the prisoner. If they were capable of doing that to "Smith", they might do it to her and Kocoum. Their faces seemed very serious, and it looked like they were holding something secret.

Kocoum seemed oblivious to any increased danger, and his face was blank with boredom. "I think we ought to head back now, Pocahontas, we have seen all there is to see here" he said lethargically.

"Yes, I think that is a good idea" said Pocahontas glancing furtively at the huddle of men. "It will be dark soon." She added.

As they got up to leave, one of the Longcoats rushed over "Wait" he shouted, his brows drawn together.

Pocahontas wasn't sure what he was saying, but it sounded like a threat. She realised that Kocoum had been right, these men wanted to kidnap them and ransom them. They would tie them up and throw them in a locked room like the "Smith" man and they would never get out. They had only been pretending to be nice. What would Powhatan say? Oh this was so bad, it was all her fault, she should never have suggested that they come. She should learn to listen to Kocoum. They were going to die.

She got to her feet and started to run towards the gangplank. She looked behind her to see if Kocoum was following her and beckoned him frantically.

"Kocoum, I think they are going to kidnap us" she shouted as she gathered speed. "They have a prison underneath with a man tied up, and they are going to do the same to us. Maybe they will ransom us" she cried.

Before Kocoum could respond, the Longcoat who seemed to be called 'Newport' came towards him, smiling as he blocked the exit path. He had something shiny in his hand and was holding it out. Kocoum looked down and saw some coloured beads that were more beautiful than any that he had seen before. Newport indicated that he should take them. Kocoum took them and turned them around and around in his hand, fascinated by their sparkling colours. Newport put his hands together and bowed, smiling at Kocoum, who only then realised that he was being given a gift of friendship.

Pocahontas watched the scene unfold and started to relax. Newport was clapping Kocoum on the back and smiling at him. Kocoum seemed pleased with whatever it was that he was given, and he waved for Pocahontas to come back and see. She tiptoed forwards, gingerly placing one foot in front of the next, judging the situation moment by moment, until she stood beside Kocoum and glanced quickly down to see what he was holding in his hands. She did a double take. She then relaxed when she realised that they had indeed, given Kocoum the most beautiful beads. She squealed with delight.

"Wow Kocoum. Those beads are very beautiful. Are they giving them to us?"

"Yes, Pocahontas, they are ours to keep. It looks like you were right, they are trying to be our friends. We must go now though, as we have a long way to go before nightfall."

They said their goodbyes and set off, hand in hand up the hill. Pocahontas took one last look back at the Longcoats and waved frantically, jumping up and down. She could see them waving back and smiling at her.

As they walked back, Pocahontas skipped and jumped, doing cartwheels and handstands, stopping every now and then to look at the beautiful beads that Kocoum was carrying.

"Oh Kocoum, that was so exciting. I knew they would be friendly" she said, laughing with glee.

Kocoum was solemn.

"What's the matter Kocoum?" she sensed that he was worried about something.

"I am just dreading facing everyone and telling them what we have done. Your family are going to be very angry with me for letting you do such a dangerous thing. It was fine in the end but it could have ended differently." His lovely brown eyes were furrowed, and he kicked a rock into the undergrowth, frustration showing all over his face.

"I am sure it will be alright" she said, taking his hand and looking at him smiling. "I have lots of things to tell them."

He looked down at her. "They won't be angry with *you*, they never are. It will be me that they blame. I am the warrior that allowed you to go into such a dangerous situation. Imagine if they had killed us with those fire sticks? As it is, I have a very sore arm.

"… but they didn't kill us Kocoum… and we have very good information to give to Powhatan. We know that there are three ships, where they have docked, how many people there are, what weapons they have and that they have a prisoner. That is very valuable information… and we have these beads, so we know that they are friendly." Her eyes were wide imploring him with her elaborate hand gestures.

35

"We'll see... " His long face did not change. She could tell he was not convinced. She was not entirely convinced herself, but it had been worth it.

As they walked hand in hand back to Werowocomoco Village, Pocahontas saw Matachanna running towards them, hair flying and eyes staring.

"Where have you been Pocahontas? What has happened to your arm Kocoum? We have been worried sick." Her eyebrows were drawn together, and she grabbed Pocahontas by the shoulders and looked into her eyes. "Well?" she said.

"Oh, we have had the most wonderful adventure Matachanna" said Pocahontas. "We watched the ships of the Longcoats come down the river. We even met some of them and they gave us these beautiful beads." She was stuttering with childish excitement trying to give as much information as she could in the shortest possible time.

"What do you mean child? What did they do to Kocoum? Look at his arm. I can see it is bleeding through the rags that are binding it.

"Oh, that is nothing Matachanna. They shot at us with their fire-stick - but they missed obviously!"

Matachanna was almost lost for words. "They *SHOT* at you?" Her voice was hysterical. "Kocoum, what do you have to say for yourself? Are you badly hurt? How did this happen... Where are these people? Who are these people that did this?" Her questions came like arrows and pierced Pocahontas's enthusiasm.

Kocoum looked at the ground, speaking in a whispering monotone. "I am not hurt badly Matachanna. The Longcoats were friendly really. It was just that because we hid behind some logs, they weren't sure who we were."

Pocahontas could tell by Matachanna's face that she was not impressed. "Kocoum, you are obviously not responsible enough to look after Pocahontas. I would not be surprised if her father bans you from being with her." Matachanna placed her hands on her hips, staring at the pair of them.

"Oh please Matachanna, don't tell Powhatan. I could not bear to be parted from Kocoum." Pocahontas had never considered that this might be the consequence of their adventure. She would die if she could not see Kocoum, he was her soulmate, and she could not live without him. She looked over at him. He looked so forlorn and sad. She knew it had not been his fault, it had been hers AGAIN. He had been right; he would get the blame. It wasn't fair.

Matachanna's face softened. "You had better get that arm seen to as soon as you can Kocoum. You don't want it to go bad. Now off with you, while I deal with this little madam, and I don't want to see you again until Powhatan has spoken to you, do you understand?"

Kocoum nodded, gave Pocahontas the beads and slowly walked away, looking back at her and giving her a weak smile. Pocahontas stood looking after him, the wind knocked out of her sails, finally realising that there could be dire consequences for her impulsivity. But Manito Aki had been with her on this great adventure - she was sure.

Everything started to fade and the Vision came again...

We are all as one,
   all creatures of the spirits...

TEENAGE LOVE: June, 1607

As the young trainee warriors finished their training, and started to drift away, Pocahontas dared to creep closer to where she could whisper to Kocum without anyone seeing.

"Kocoum... Kocoum..." she whispered.

He heard her and looked around to where she was crouched. "Go away Pocahontas. You know I am not allowed to speak to you" he said, whispering, looking over his shoulder, not meeting her gaze.

"No one will know Kocoum. Please just come and see me for a few minutes?" she pleaded.

He knew she would never give up. It was an annoying, but endearing trait and one of the many things about her that confused him... and he was confused. When his heart ruled, he fought to catch a glimpse of her laughing face as she helped Matachanna. But when his head ruled he never wanted to see her again. Damn it! She was his soulmate, but at times her convictions and her confidence pushed him off balance. She was, undoubtedly, a remarkable person even at such a young age, but her strength triggered insecurities that he never realised he had. Powhatan had been very clear, Powhatan knew and he must obey.

He had thought avoiding her would ease his turmoil. But she still took over his thoughts when he was off guard, and when he started thinking about her, especially looking at the half leaf that she had given him... he was lost. Seeing her here, out of the blue, jolted him.

Pocahontas grabbed his hand and he hesitated, pulling back, but eventually sighed and allowed her to drag him behind one of the Yehakins on the edge of the settlement. He noticed that she was shivering even although it was a June evening, so he placed the skin that he used for keeping himself warm after training around her shoulders and they sat down, huddling together for warmth. Again... he was lost.

"I am sorry Kocoum" she said. "I just got carried away that day, and I didn't listen to you. I won't ignore what you say ever again."

He looked at her earnest face. "I know you will do it again, Pocahontas. You just can't stop yourself... " He looked away shaking his head. "I do not blame you. You are strong and brave, and you must never change."

"So, does that mean you forgive me?

"There is nothing to forgive. I take responsibility for what happened."

"Kocoum, you know that Powhatan has forgiven us - don't you?" Wide eyes, pleading eyes.

"He has forgiven *you* Pocahontas. But he was really angry with me, and he still is. I don't blame him. He is right, I should have been stronger, and stopped you going. I am a disgrace and I am not supposed to see you." He hung his head and looked at the ground. "Now I must prove that I am a strong warrior."

"But you don't have to prove anything to me, you will never ever have to prove anything to me."

She was doing it again. He hugged her in close to him, to keep her warm, giving himself a moment to think. He paused. She held her breath, waiting.

After what seemed like an eternity, he took her hand and looked into her eyes. "You know, maybe once I fooled myself into thinking that we could be together, but what happened has made me see that I am not good for you. I must let you move on in your life without me." Kocoum continued to look at the ground. "As painful as it is for me, for once I have to do the right thing. I really should not have agreed to even talk to you today. I am beginning to regret it already."

She pulled away from him, her eyes wide. "NO - you don't regret it. You know you don't. I can tell." Pocahontas screamed. Her eyes wide with... was it anger, or was it fear?

He pulled her back towards him and put his hand over her mouth. "Be quiet, if I get caught talking to you, I will be in even worse trouble" he said.

She shook herself free. "So you are going to avoid me forever?"

"I have to Pocahontas. Just imagine how it made me feel when your father accused me of putting your life in danger. He was right – we could both be dead."

She shrank back, his words hitting her in the face like a wet blanket.

" I must do this for Powhatan and for you." He hugged her closer, and as he did so, he impulsively leant down to give her a farewell kiss on the cheek and immediately regretted it. She moved suddenly, so that their lips met.

He did not want to stop. They stayed for several moments, kissing and hugging each other and enjoying the closeness, until reason took over. The voice of Powhatan rang in his ears. He pulled away. She moved to kiss him again, and this time as their lips touched, he could not help himself, his tongue gently searched her mouth. Lost to everything but her for one glorious moment before he came to his senses.

He wrenched himself away, breathless. "We cannot do this Pocahontas. Powhatan is right. I am not the best man to look after you" he whispered.

He got up to go, but she rushed after him and took his hand. She stood on tiptoe to look into his eyes as she brushed away his tears. "We are meant to be together Kocoum, and it is no good you trying to fight it." His shoulders hunched in defeat as he looked at her with sorrow. "I am not good enough for you Pocahontas. Powhatan told me as much" he said.

She pulled away from him, her eyes flashing. "Who do you think you are, dictating to me? Don't I have a say?" she shouted, desperate. "You don't understand, I have seen us together in my visions - we *will* be together."

Kocoum's face turned red as the tempo between them rose, and the tender moment turned to angst. "Your bloody Visions. I am sick of your bloody Visions. They are fanciful dreams that mean nothing Pocahontas. Look around you - you are the daughter of The Great Powhatan, and I am just a disgraced warrior. We cannot be together, and the sooner you realise it the sooner you can move on to someone who deserves you."

He wanted to run, to be anywhere but here telling the girl he loved that she must find someone new. He looked at her sad face and the bruising to his heart increased further. His head told him that she was young, she would get over it, and thank him one day - his heart was crushed.

She was looking at the ground, biting her lip. He had floored her, and he was not proud. He took her hand. " For now the matter is out of our control anyway. I am going away for nine months for my Huskanaw[1]. We must see this separation as a sign and accept that we must part."

There was nothing else to say, she pulled her hand from his, avoiding his gaze. He watched her as she got up and marched away, dropping a brown and yellow piece of leaf as she went.

Kocoum and I walk hand in hand...
but the world is covered with blood

It was summer, and she lay in the long grass, looking up at the infrequent puffy white clouds skidding across the blue sky. The sun beat down making her feel lazy and sleepy as her mind drifted.

Her life had changed so much. One could say in the space of a few weeks she had had to grow up and start taking responsibility for so many things. She was no longer a carefree child whose behaviour affected no one. She looked at Badger, who crouched next to her, as ever. He understood. At least on this painful journey of life she had her Badger Guardian Spirit as company. Otherwise, it would have been unbearable, especially without Kocoum.

Kocoum... there was no turning back time. She had rushed back to the scene of her breakup with him, hoping to find Hurit's leaf, but it must have blown away - perhaps a message from the Gods? She had looked at the spot where she and Kocoum had huddled together and yearned for it to have turned out differently. Maybe if she had not walked away she could have made amends? A pang of regret pierced her like an arrow through her heart.

The bitter image of her and Kocoum in a world covered with blood still haunted her, and its meaning escaped her, but her dreams rarely made sense to her... in fact, when she thought about it, much of life did not make sense to her.

She had not seen Kocoum since that day. He had gone to his Huscanaw without saying goodbye. She could not get away from the gnawing ache of her loss, and she could not see it ever getting better.

Powhatan, had begun to trust her to start forging an alliance with the Longcoats. To try to focus her mind away from thoughts of Kocoum, she had put her heart and soul into it, making daily visits to the colony which had diminished in size and threat with starvation and disease. They were in a perilous situation. John Smith, thankfully, had been released from prison after a misunderstanding and with his leadership and her help in providing food, some improvements had been made, but they had a long way to go if they were going to survive in the long term.

John Smith – he was such a nice man. She thought of him and smiled. He was like an uncle to her, and with her frequent visits they had become good friends. Learning each other's language had become such fun, and it was something that pulled them together in one another's affections. The only thing that marred their relationship was the constant unexplained flashbacks to her dream vision:

He glances up and catches my eye, pleading...
   his head goes down...the block is cold, the axe is sharp

It was John Smith she had seen.... What did it mean? Why did she keep getting these messages about the ones she cared about?

She sat up, troubled by her thoughts yet again. Badger walked over to be near to her, to comfort her.

She stared at the sun as it went behind the clouds.

When would the warmth of the sun sun come back into her life?

[1] Male coming of age training and ceremony

ARCHER'S MISTAKE: August, 1607

The sun's heat was sweltering. In any other situation, the blue skies and the lapping water would have been a wonderful experience, but they lay, vomiting, sweating and thirsty. John Smith smelled the stink of dead bodies and illness and knew that they were literally dying for lack of food and fresh water. There were only ramshackle buildings, meagre shelter as there were not enough able-bodied men to build. No crops would grow in this intense heat, and the water was stagnant. Large blue bottle flies hummed happily and hungrily around the weeping eyes and vomit of the emaciated bodies. John shook his head. This was the "land of plenty" overflowing with succulent fish, plump birds, and fertile land? This is what they had been promised. What had happened?

John had been held captive since the fleet of three ships had left the West Indies, so he had had no input in any of the planning and organization of the Colony until now. Since they had reluctantly released him from the brig, he had become increasingly frustrated at the incompetence of his colleagues. He looked around the settlement. They had camped in completely the wrong place, they had handled the relationships with the native Indians badly, and now they were paying the price.

Archer had always been his main enemy and had been instrumental in his unjustified incarceration on-board ship. It was Archer had who had accused him of mutiny, when he had only been trying to give them the benefit of his vast experience. Didn't Archer realise that he had been a soldier for many years? He knew his stuff when it came to managing people and his only fault was that he was not afraid to challenge authority. His skills and knowledge had not counted for much amongst these arrogant sons of the aristocracy. Yes, he was only a Yeoman's son, but he had guts and balls - that is why the Virginia Company had put him forward as a member of the Council in the first place. It would have been a vastly different scenario if *he* had been allowed to manage the situation - they would not have set up camp in a swamp for a start!

Edward Wingfield, who had been appointed leader was weak and self-serving, and his cronies, Bartholomew Gosnold and John Ratcliffe, were no better. Gabriel Archer was the worst though. John was sure that he was a secret Catholic, and he was determined that he would expose him when the time was right, but there were other priorities. Survival.

They had released him from prison eventually on 28th May, 1607. John smiled – the hypocrites had released him and immediately sworn him in as a Council member - something the Virginia Company had directed them to do months previously, but which they had chosen to ignore, as it suited them to have him out of the way and not interfering with their quiet life. He laughed when he thought of it. Only when things were so tough that they really didn't have a clue what to do and they needed his input did they give him the status that had been originally intended.

Christopher Newport was an old seasoned sea dog and reasonably competent alongside the ineffectual Edward Wingfield, but he had set sail back to England, when he found things difficult, under the guise of getting further supplies. Needless to say, they had not seen hide nor hair of Newport since he had set sail 19th June, 1607. So, they had been left under the leadership of Wingfield and his band of incompetents, and only recently had John been reluctantly included.

The truth was that the Colony was in serious trouble. There were only 38 men left, and most of them were suffering from illnesses - salt water poisoning and parasites had taken the rest. It would not be long before they were all dead. He had to do something; he was the only one who saw the reality of the situation.

There was one ray of hope, and as he looked up, he saw her coming. There was no doubt about it she was a very special child - only eleven years old, but she had the courage and maturity of someone a lot older. He remembered when they first landed, how she had come down to the hold and seen him as a prisoner. Amazing that one so young had dared to explore the foreign ship. John respected her. She came each day with food from her tribe, hoping to make friends with the English, or the Longcoats as he realised they called them. He was the only one who had responded positively to her and she had indeed made a very good friend in him. It was extraordinary, that at such a young age she seemed determined to forge an alliance with the English, and she had started with him. The others laughed at him, but he took her very seriously - she was the Chief's daughter and could have a lot of influence, despite her tender years. John Smith was a hardened soldier, but when it came to children, he had a soft centre. It was his greatest sadness that he had fathered no children of his own.

He watched her as she approached, her long black plait hanging down her back, and her little skinny naked body running towards him. She was always accompanied by at least five warriors for protection, as she was the favourite daughter of the Great Powhatan. Looking at her, he knew that she was going to grow up to be a very beautiful woman.

As she approached, she looked around her at all the sick and dying men. John saw the look of sadness in her eyes as she stooped to offer water and corn to a man reaching out to her as she passed. Not only was she intelligent and brave, she was sensitive and kind. When she stood up, she started walking towards him. He held out his hand to her and she took it and sat down on the ground next to him. She beckoned her warriors over, and they presented him with several containers of corn and some berries.

"It is only corn and berries, but it is all that we have at this time of the year."

He bowed his head in thanks.

Pocahontas took a bunch of the berries and made a large gesture of putting one in her mouth. "Mecher" she said looking at John, her big brown eyes wide and serious.

"Eat" he replied, taking one of the berries, copying her and eating it.

She held up one finger in front of his face, laughing when he crossed his eyes. "Nekut" she said.

He grabbed her one finger pretending to bite it. "One" he said.

She pulled her finger away from him, and put up two fingers. "Ninge" she said, looking very serious.

He grabbed her fingers again and said "two". He lurched towards her and grabbed her little body and threw her up in the air, and she squealed with childish delight, the horrors of her surroundings forgotten for just a moment. He set her down on the ground, and she pretended to run away from him, hiding behind a pile of wood. He ran towards her and grabbed her again laughing. She was such a perfectly delightful child, he thought.

Archer came swaggering over to him. Sadly, he was not one of the men that had died, thought John.

"Well, well, well… what have we here then John? Taken yourself a little Indian Squaw, have you? Surely, they are only good as servants? Savages, I say old boy… dirty and ignorant. I am sure they are crawling with bugs. Don't know why you bother. All we need to do is to defeat them - we just want their land and their food; we don't need to make friends with them or learn their language. Come on John, wake up. They are Heathens for Goodness sake."

"You really have no idea at all Archer, do you? You really *do* think that you are superior, and superiority will always win. It is interesting that your tactic so far, has been to intimidate everyone - perhaps that's what they teach people at law school. It hasn't worked though, has it?" Archer typified the attitude of most of the colonists. Archer, Wingfield, Gosnold and the rest were deluded in their importance. This was the sole reason they had not even started to plant and grow crops or forge decent relationships with the Indians. It was below them. There was a limit to what he could do on his own to develop the Colony, but meeting with Pocahontas was a small part of that. At least he was learning the language of their neighbours, which he considered to be fundamental if they were going to have any success in taking these lands.

John could see Pocahontas moving way from Archer towards her warriors, gauging the aggression in Archer's voice and sensing danger. Archer swaggard towards Pocahontas, glaring at John, his face showing the determination of making a point. John moved forward to intercept, but the warriors preempted him and were already there, placing their large painted bodies between Archer and Pocahontas, their spears pointing towards his throat.

Archer tried to wave them away, laughing as if they were flies. Then he held his fist up towards them in defiance trying to hold on to some kind of dignity. John could see the tension in the bodies of the warriors, their muscles were rippling in anticipation and their eyes were staring at Archer. They were not going to take much more from this little cockroach who was threatening their beloved Princess. Archer was so stupid; he did not realise the danger he was in. He had completely misjudged the situation. An upper-class idiot who thought he ruled the world, thought John.

John realized that he had better do something, more for peace, than to save Archer. He bowed to the warriors, smiling in apology, hoping to avoid a nasty confrontation that would spoil all the hard work he had done building up a relationship with the tribes. He could not imagine the damage that would be done if anything happened to Pocahontas.

The warriors nodded in recognition of him but started to walk towards Archer pushing him roughly to the ground, where he lay shouting and protesting in the dust like an upturned bug.

"How dare you, you filthy Heathens. I am a citizen of the Crown" he shouted. The warriors looked increasingly angry, not understanding a word that he said. Archer finally realized the danger that he was in as he looked up at the long sharp spears that were almost touching his face. He froze, his eyes looking from side to side with panic..

"John do something." He pleaded. His demeanour now that of snivelling coward.

John laughed and gave him a swift kick in the backside watching the dust fly out of his filthy stained trousers. "That will teach you to be more courteous to ladies" John mocked as he smiled at the warriors who were all starting to relax as they saw John's total disrespect for the idiot on the ground, who quite obviously was no longer a threat, but a joke.

Pocahontas started moving towards Archer. John rushed forward to intercept her but she brushed him aside, pulling her leg back as far as she could to give the helpless Archer another almighty kick. He cried out in pain. For good measure, as she stood looking down on him, she spat in his face. Archer spluttered trying to wipe the spit that was mixed with sweat and mud. "You little… you little… " He struggled unsuccessfully to regain his dignity.

John looked at her and gave her a wink. My Goodness, for an eleven-year-old she had spirit, he thought. God help us when she grows up…

SMITH'S JOURNEY: December, 1607

John knew it was down to him. Things in the settlement were at crisis point. He did not really care if Archer, Wingfield and the rest perished, but it was a point of honour that he had to try his best to save the other poor innocents of the Colony who had trusted the Virginia Company to look after them. The leadership had been disgraceful. The Colony had no food and no one was doing anything about it. Pleasant though his meetings with Pocahontas were, he knew that the Powhatans were not going to be able to help for much longer, as in this drought ridden land, they had their own people to feed, and there was not that much food available.

The English needed to trade with other tribes, and they needed to explore more to do that. It was too late to plant this year, and if they planted next year, harvest would be at least nine months away. Also, if there was a North West passage, his ego dictated that he needed to be the one to find it.

He had decided to go on an expedition up the river that they called Chickahominy to see if he could find other Indian tribes that he could trade with. So far, he had been very successful. He had met with the Chickahominy who had been very grateful for the beads and trinkets that he had brought with him. They did not come under the leadership of the Powhatan, so he was not afraid of stepping on Powhatan's toes. John felt that he had become quite a hero with the Chickahominy although he could tell that they too were starting to grow tired of his constant demands for food. This was his fourth visit upriver to trade with them.

This time, he decided that he was going to go further up the river. His adventurous nature was egging him on to find new and exciting lands. Maybe there were other friendly tribes that he could get food from? Maybe there were more rich and fertile lands that they could cultivate. He was excited at the prospect and rowed further and further up the river. To travel into lands that had possibly never been trodden on by white men gave John a thrill. The eeriness of the dark forest stimulated his enthusiasm as he breathed in the damp pine scented earthy smell of his surroundings.

He had two men with him. George Cassen was a labourer, one of three brothers that had come to Jamestown, and Thomas Emry, who was a carpenter. Both men shared John's love of adventure and had volunteered eagerly to come on his mission. To be on the safe side they were accompanied by two Chickahominy guides. The Chickahominy were used to tracking in forests like these.

As they went further, the river started to get shallower and shallower and narrower and narrower as John had feared it might. The forest was dense and damp with small streaks of sunlight jumping in the shadows as they penetrated the forest canopy. John could see progress was going to be tough the further they went. There was a reason these parts had not been explored before.

"Looks like we won't be able to go any further. There are fallen trees up ahead, and it is becoming too difficult to navigate these shallow waters with the canoe" he shouted. "I will take an Indian scout with me, and we will go up ahead and see what the land is like. We will come back for you, and if we find it is better further up. We can go on, but otherwise, we might have to turn back." His men nodded in confirmation. "Stay here, keep your matchlocks poised and shoot if you sense any kind of trouble. We will return and help if we hear your shots. We are probably trespassing, so we have to be cautious." John gestured to one of the Indians and together they climbed up the riverbank and headed toward the denseness of the forest.

His heart was racing. This was what he thrived on - new experiences and adventure. It was a stormy day, and the treetops high above him were swaying in the wind. They were walking through muddy, squelchy terrain, and he could smell the mud, mingled with pine needles as they navigated through the trees. What was going to be around the corner? He was free, he was in control, unrestrained by pompous English aristocrats for once. He heard a rustling in the trees and stopped in his tracks.

Suddenly, he looked up and without any warning, he was confronted by ten warriors painted with red pucceen, faces menacing, all pointing arrows at him. His adrenaline started pumping as he tried to think. There had been no shots from the men that he left behind. That could only mean one of two things.

He had to act quickly, he knew his life was in danger. He pulled the struggling Indian guide in front of him using him as a human shield and started walking backwards, hoping he could get far enough away to start running. The Indians were coming towards him, aiming at him but not shooting, aware of the Indian in front of him. These were not Chickahominy though. Chickahominy would not behave this way towards him. They must be Pamunkey - under Powhatan's jurisdiction. He was surprised they were being so aggressive, but there was no ignoring the fact that their eyes were murderous, and he sensed that they wanted him, dead or alive.

He started moving backwards faster and faster, still holding on to the Indian, unable to see where he was going. Suddenly he felt himself stumbling and then sliding... sliding. He could feel himself starting to lose control. The mud had turned into a bog, and it was swallowing him and the Indian thick and fast. He felt the cold slimy mud holding him like a vice and he struggled for his life, trying to find anything he could to grab and pull himself up, but his struggling only seemed to pull him further into the clutches of the sinking mud. He let go of the Indian, and his gun, concerned only with keeping his head above the mud. His arms were waving frantically in the air, and he began to realise the futility of his struggle. He would have to be pulled out by the Indians or he would drown in the mud. The next few seconds would tell him which way it was going to go.

One of the Indians walked forward and pulled at his arm as he struggled. He relaxed slightly, realising that he was being helped. He was not sure whether death through drowning in the mud might have been the better option. But then again, as they were rescuing him, they must want him alive… but maybe only for the joy of torturing him.

He put his dripping muddy hands in the air in surrender as he spluttered and spat the dirt out of his mouth. The Indian that had pulled him out, tied his hands behind his back. John felt sick. He had no idea what they were going to do with him. These Pamunkey were so unpredictable. These must be Powhatan's men. The warriors were painted in the same way as the warriors that brought Pocahontas to the camp. But why were they attacking him? He thought he had started to make inroads in the relationship with Powhatan. If torture was not their goal, maybe they wanted to keep him alive to get information from him. He had to play along with them and see where he was taken. Not that he had any choice in the matter.

The Indians roughly pushed him and his Chickahominy guide forward, walking him towards the way that he had come. As they came through the trees, he saw the canoe that he had left behind. His face fell when he saw George and Thomas and the other Chickahominy guide lying with their mouths open wide, gaping holes in their throats so deep the white bone beneath was revealed. Their heads hung limply, almost disconnected from their bodies. There was a pool of blood in the bottom of the canoe that he could see getting larger and larger as it drained out of the bodies. The eyes of the freshly dead men were staring, the panic and disbelief at the moment of death frozen on their faces. Large blue bottled flies feasted hungrily on the fresh bloody meat. A stench of death permeated the scene. John looked away in horror, retching at the spectacle. Maybe these Indians *were* savages, or maybe it was that men in general were savages given the opportunity? He remembered many scenes when his own men had carried out similar atrocities. They just needed an excuse - did they have an excuse to do the same to him? Surely if they wanted the fun of torturing him in the same way, they would have done it by now? He heard them laugh as they pushed him to walk faster.

He was made to walk for what seemed like several hours, with his hands tied behind his back, stumbling from time to time as fatigue and hypothermia were seeping into his aching bones. Each step was torture for him, as he forced himself to limp onward. At last they came to a small settlement, and his captors pushed him into a nearby teepee, grunting at him. He stumbled inside, and only then, realised how hungry he had become. December was not a friendly month in these parts, and the dampness of the mud that clung to his body made him shiver. The warmth of the teepee seemed to defrost his senses and he fell onto a deerskin blanket that was on the ground.

Groaning, he wrapped himself up in the blanket as he took in the seriousness of his situation. He knew that he was in no fit state to try and escape, he was weak with hunger, cold and fatigue. He was starting to feel his body as the warmth hit him, but with the feeling came the pain. All he could do for now was lie wrapped up in the blanket shivering and stare up at the ceiling, catching his breath and his thoughts. He was still very unsure of what the motive for all of this was. Why had they not already killed him? Maybe he would be better off dead. He thought back to George and Thomas. A horrible end to two young men who had courage and a sense of adventure - maybe his end would be the same.

After what seemed like hours, he heard someone walking towards the teepee and saying something to the guard waiting outside. The flap was lifted, and an elderly Indian Squaw entered, nodding at him. She brought twigs and wood and started making a fire in the centre of the teepee. She glanced at him from time to time and murmured to him - but he couldn't understand what she was saying. When she had lit the fire, she signalled to him to come closer. He jumped at the chance for warmth and came forwards rubbing his hands together over the fire. The smoke rose and escaped through a hole in the roof.

The woman bowed and walked backwards to the exit. He breathed a sigh of relief. They were actually looking after him. That must mean that they wanted to keep him alive! A moment later, another slightly younger squaw entered. She held steaming food in a large container and she brought it to him, bowing and smiling. He took it from her gratefully and started eating the hot venison stew with gusto, feeling the juices dripping down his chin, and the warm meaty gravy burning as it went down his parched throat. He hardly tasted the food as he was eating it so quickly. The Squaw then left and reappeared with a container of water and three loaves of bread that she put down on the floor beside him. He nodded and smiled at her, not breaking off from his frantic and clumsy attempts to get the meat into his mouth as quickly as he could.

When she had gone, and the meat, bread and water had all been finished, he sat back and enjoyed the warmth of the fire. His thoughts started to go wild. They had not killed or tortured him - but maybe they were fattening him up for the pot. Maybe they were cannibals. They were very vicious the way that they had tortured his men, so it was not out of the question that they might be in the habit of eating people. This was not good. He must try to escape when he felt better, and he had managed to see the lay of the land outside. If only he had been able to learn more of the language from Pocahontas, he might be able to overhear what was being said.

He started to drift off to sleep but was woken by heavy footsteps coming towards the teepee and he shook himself awake violently, ready for combat. The flap opened and there stood the leader of the warriors that had captured him. He was an exceptionally large man, with huge presence. When he entered the teepee it was like he took over the whole space, but he did not appear aggressive. Who is this? John thought. He sat down cross-legged opposite John and put his hands to his chest and bowed his head in greeting.

John did the same. The warrior pointed to himself. "Opechancanough" he said. John then knew who he was. He had heard stories of Powhatan's younger brother. Indeed, a fearsome warrior and someone that was exceedingly respected in the area. He had the reputation of ruthlessness.

John pointed to himself "John Smith" he said, and bowed and smiled, hoping to indicate friendship. John gestured with open hands and raised eyebrows trying to communicate the question of why he had been captured.

Opechancanough nodded. He drew in the dirt of the teepee, indicating where they were. "Rasawrack" he said. Then he drew a line to indicate another village. "Werowocomoco, Powhatan" he said.

John then realised. They had captured him to take him to Powhatan. He still didn't know why. It could be to kill him, or to torture him for information about the English invasion. Whichever it was, he could not imagine a good outcome.

NIKOMIS: December, 1607

At last it was the mid-winter festival of Nikomis. It was celebrated every year, but this year was going to be extra special. Everyone knew that the great change was coming, especially after Pocahontas had told the Quiakros of her Dream Vision. Of course, she had not been told the detailed meaning of her dream, but maybe today things would become clearer to her.

At Nikomis, the Great Woman that fell from the sky infiltrated the minds of the Chosen Ones - maybe even Pocahontas, now that she was seen as a Beloved Woman. Hopefully more of the future would be revealed in the Visions and Messages that were received today so they could prepare themselves for the changes that were to come.

Nikomis knew everything, and her grandsons Okee and Ahone had protected the Powhatan Nation for centuries. This particular festival was to be the biggest and best tribute to them for years. Fear of the future compelled them to seek the certainty of answers that the Gods might give them.

They had hunted for deer for weeks and made bread for days for the feast that would take place after the ceremony. Before the ceremony, much to Pocahontas's dismay, they had all fasted for several days in honour of Nikomis, Okee and Ahone.

Pocahontas was especially excited as it was her first Nikomis since she had had her Dream Vision and became a Beloved Woman. She was looking forward to having a big part in the ceremony, and, whereas in all previous years she had had to sit far away with the children and not able to see what was going on, this time she was going to be a large part of it. She was going to dress up in full ceremonial dress, and her hair was going to be adorned with beautiful white feathers like The Woman That Fell From The Sky and she would sit proudly with the other Beloved Women. At last she had a place. She felt the butterflies in her tummy and took a deep breath, glancing at Badger and sighing. Why could Kocoum not be here to give her support too?

Preparations were all nearing completion and she was sitting patiently whilst the younger girls painted her arms and legs with ornate pictures of flowers and animals. Her soft deerskin dress had been laid out ready for her to slip on.

Her stomach gave a very embarrassing growl to accompany the butterflies. Hunger was essential to the process as, together with the burning of apook, chanting and the beating of drums, it made the head swirl and the body tingle, preparing the mind and body for the state of spiritualism that overwhelmed everything at the ceremony of Nikomis.

Pocahontas thought of the mountains of deer meat dripping with juice making spitting sounds over the fire pit outside as it was slowly cooked in preparation for the end of the fast. Her stomach growled even more, and she tried to put it out of her mind.

Kanti, her favourite little sister, started to plait Pocahontas's hair creating individual strands with turkey fat. These strands would hold the white feathers symbolic of a blessed woman. Pocahontas's face was flushed with excitement and she could hardly sit still. Kanti was only ten years old and she and Pocahontas had been close since Kanti was a baby. Kanti was probably the closest sibling that Pocahontas had apart from Matachanna, and she had asked her in particular to do her hair on this special occasion.

Kanti stopped for a moment to wait for Pocahontas to settle down, sighing. "You are so fidgety Pocahontas. How do you expect me to do a good job when you are jiggling all over the place? By the way" she said, "I just saw the warriors dragging in a Longcoat to see Powhatan. He looked really terrified" she said. She hoped that if she could get Pocahontas's interest, she might sit still. "I wonder what they could be doing with him?" she went on nonchalantly as she separated Pocahontas's hair into more sections, dipping her fingers into the slimy turkey fat.

Pocahontas was immediately alert, her body tense, jerking away and turning to stare at Kanti. "When did you see this? What were they doing? Who was it?" Her voice was hurried and her eyes wide. The whole episode sounded strange. Why would Powhatan do this?

Kanti looked startled at the intensity of Pocahontas's interest. "Whoa… whoa…I was just trying to make conversation to make you sit still. I don't know anything. I just saw the poor man very distressed being taken into Powhatan's Yehakin. I assumed the Longcoat was coming to be part of the ceremony" she said, her eyes focused on Pocahontas's hair. "Please sit still Pocahontas, I have to start all over again now."

"Sorry Kanti" said Pocahontas. "No, I'm actually not sorry. Before I can sit still, I have to know everything about the Longcoat that you saw."

Kanti shrugged her shoulders. "I think someone called him 'chawn' or something like that. Please can I do your hair now? I am going to get into real trouble if your hair looks a mess for the ceremony." Pocahontas stood up. "Kanti, this is really serious. I think I know the man that you saw. His name is John. He is a friend."

Kanti rolled her eyes. "He can't be your friend Pocahontas; he was a prisoner."

Pocahontas paused and then put her hand on her forehead "Oh no - you were right in what you said before, they have brought him to take him to the ceremony of Nikomis. You know what that means don't you?" Kanti thought Pocahontas's eyes were going to pop out of her head. Her speech was rushed and almost incoherent. The image came back…

He glances up and catches my eye,
  pleading...
  his head goes down...
  the block is cold, the axe is sharp

"Yes, I know what that means Pocahontas she said nodding her head slowly. "But it is just what happens. It is really nothing for you to worry about."

Pocahontas jumped up, and started to run towards the door, loose feathers that should have been in her hair were sent flying.

"Where do you think you are going Pocahontas - you need to stay here until it is time to go to the great hall for the ceremony...and your hair isn't even done!" screamed Matachanna, unable to contain her disbelief.

"No, I am really sorry Matachanna, I can't stay. It is a matter of life and death... " Pocahontas shouted over her shoulder as she lifted the flap and ran out into the frozen air.

—————————

Pocahontas ran towards the Yehakin where she knew her father was preparing himself for the Great Ceremony. There were warriors standing outside. When they saw her approaching they drew aside and let her enter.

As she went in, she saw her father sitting quietly with his eyes closed, gathering his thoughts for the coming Nikomis. She tiptoed up to him.

"Powhatan... Powhatan... " she whispered.

He opened his eyes and looked at her. "My child" he said, as he beckoned her to come forward to him.

"Father - you have one of the Longcoats held captive?" she asked. She was breathless, and her face was red and moist.

"Yes, that is right. He is John Smith." He nodded smiling and raising his eyebrows.

"Why are you holding him captive before the feast of Nikomis? He is my friend." Her eyes were wide and her chest heaved up and down.

"I know he is your friend. I know that when I send you to the camp with food for the Longcoats, that you meet with John Smith. Do you not think I know everything?" He smiled, shaking his head.

"So, if you know he is my friend, why have you captured him and held him prisoner?" She frowned.

"The Quiakros are very wise men. They considered your dream very carefully and they believe within it were messages from the Gods – you saw John Smith at the festival of Nikomis."

She saw it again in a flash:

... the block is cold, the axe is sharp

Her eyes opened wide and her stomach turned over. "No" she cried. "You cannot kill my friend because of *my* Dream Vision. That would be like *me* killing him!"

Powhatan took both of her tiny hands in his. "Pocahontas, calm yourself little one. You are only the Messenger; you have no say in what you are shown and neither do we. We do not know what will happen to John Smith, we only know that we must re-enact the Vision that you saw.

"But of course we know…. If his head is placed on the block, he will be killed!"

Powhatan shook his head. "Listen to the Spirits, my child. At the ceremony, answers will be given. John Smith will be transformed. The Gods will decide whether he will enter a new world by becoming my Nantaquoud[1] cementing his place and the place of his people in our tribe, or he will cross over to the next world. Either fate is good. We must wait and see what Nikomis desires. Neither you nor I know until he stands before me in the ceremony, what path will be chosen for him."

"How can it be good if he dies?" Her tears were falling in a steady stream down her face.

"Death is only a transition, Pocahontas. It is not to be feared. You must place your faith in the Gods to know the true way forward. Whatever happens today is part of a greater plan that we cannot know."

She looked at the ground, her mind in turmoil.

He continued. "I know it is difficult for you to understand, but you must trust me to do the right thing. You must go now. It is not long before we must start the ceremony of Nikomis. Look at the state of your hair." He touched her unruly locks. "Go back and get yourself ready, my child of mischief. Whatever happens is meant to be and is dictated by the Gods." He nodded his head, his feathers fluttering with the movement.

She dragged herself out of the yehakin, clenching her fists. The cold air hit her face as she left, but she barely noticed. What could she do? Was the answer in her dream? She tried to think back, but no answers came. She would have to rely on the judgment of the Gods to save her friend. She would have to place her trust in the Gods - she had no control, something that was hard for her to accept.

She ran back to the Yehakin to finish the preparations for Nikomis. Her heart was heavy, and her mind confused by what her father had said. If only she could talk to Kocoum.

Would the Gods show mercy and embrace John Smith as part of the tribe? They would if they believed his people to be friends. She was so sure that John Smith was a friend, but what about his people? She thought back to Archer - he had been cruel and unkind. It was obvious that Archer thought of her people as little more than animals - maybe he was more representative of his people than John. Would the Gods see the cruelty in Archer's eyes reflected in John's eyes? Maybe he would be judged by the traits of his people rather than on his own merits. How did the Gods see him?

The more she thought about it the more the interpretation of her Dreams seemed to change. What was she to make of these Longcoats? One thing was certain, her destiny was to save her people. From what, she was not yet sure.

"Pocahontas, Pocahontas... " Someone was shaking her, bringing her back to the moment. It was only dear Matachanna.

"Oh, sorry, Matachanna" Pocahontas said, trying without success to draw her mind back to the present. What had happened to all the excitement that she had felt when she first woke up this morning?

"Pocahontas, will you please pay attention to what is happening. For goodness sake." Matachanna was starting to get cross with her.

"Oh, ok Matachanna" she said nodding her head in agreement and looking around to see what everyone else was doing. They were now starting to form a line to go into the Quioccsan. She ran to sit down so that Kanti could quickly do her hair. It was not the best of jobs, but it would have to do. She ran over to join the line of people queuing to go in, her head bowed, thoughts still running around her mind. What was John Smith doing now? Was he alright? Were they taking care of him? Her stomach was still churning without food, and she felt a little faint, but the wafting smell of cooking meat turned her mind to the ceremony ahead.

As she entered the Quioccsan with Badger by her side, she was overwhelmed by the spectacle. Of course, this happened every year, but this year things were bigger and more spectacular than ever. Coming in from the cold December day, the heat was the first thing that she noticed. The fire in the middle was burning fiercely, and the smell of apook was spicy and warm in her lungs. There was the fresh fragrance of pine and wood. In December, it was difficult to adorn the Quioccosan with flowers, so the Squaws had used what they could find, and long branches of pine mixed with duck feathers and flaming torches were dotted around the huge hall. Her body started to respond to the fragrance and the warmth, and she could feel herself absorbing the atmosphere of the room. There was no doubt that the spirits were watching them, she could feel their presence as she walked past the huge red and black pillars with the carved faces of the Gods observing their every move.

The throne of the Great Powhatan was empty, awaiting his arrival. It was a long bedstead upon which were placed twelve mats. There was a squaw at both ends, and ten of his best men seated on mats on the ground each side of the fire. Behind the men, were many young women their faces painted red, adorned with chains of white beads. The bedstead had been decorated with pine as well as berries and beautiful feathers. Large raccoon skins were thrown over the back of it, and cushions made of hide and feathers were placed to make it comfortable for the Great Leader when he arrived.

The room was filling up, and as the Sunks, Sunsquaas, Beloved Women and Quiakros took their places they began chanting words of respect to Okee and Ahone. Drums were sounding a rhythmical beat. The noise got louder and louder as more and more people joined the throng.

Pocahontas was starting to feel overwhelmed. The smell of the Apook, her fear for John Smith, her hunger, the steady beat of the drums and chanting were pulling her out of consciousness. Her head began to swim with dizziness. She let herself drift, surrendering to the feeling, aware but somehow unaware, as if she were floating on the ceiling, looking down. Everything was hazy as she saw the Great Powhatan enter the Quioccosan in full ceremonial dress, his neck covered with many chains of great pearls. Everyone stood up. The chanting stopped. He walked to his throne, raised his arms, and chanted the great prayer of Ahone. He then lay down on his side facing his people, and everyone followed by sitting.

Pocahontas heard the chanting begin again, and the warriors were on their feet with their spears, banging them on the ground and shouting a war chant, looking towards the exit. At that point the flap opened, and two warriors dragged John Smith into the Quioccosan. She saw him looking around, his eyes wide and his face drawn, a damp patch started to appear on the front of his trousers, his fear deepening as he saw the sacrificial stone platform that was placed in front of Powhatan.

Pocahontas welled up inside - feelings of fear mingled with apprehension. Her dizziness deepened and she felt her body go limp, on the verge of fainting. She could see the aura around John Smith. She felt the pulsing energy in the air. All the eyes in the room were straining to see what was going to happen. Everyone knew that the greatest gift the Powhatan people could give to Ahone and Okee, was the sacrifice of a human being. Powhatan had not made any promises about the fate of her friend, so she had to believe that whatever was to happen would be the right thing. She trusted in Powhatan and the Gods, but at the same time prayed for John's survival.

The Great Powhatan began to speak. Pocahontas tried to control her rushed and anxious breathing. Her chest rose and fell, and she felt the blood rushing to her face.

"My brothers and sisters, we have come here today to honour the Spirits. We know the great change is coming, and we have with us today, John Smith, who is one of the number that are bringing change to our people. All our actions today will determine how the Spirits direct our future. The world is unfolding before us - pure and beautiful. We must ensure that this beauty is never defiled - we must teach our brothers how to nurture the world, how to live as we do." He stopped and looked at the smoke rising. He signalled for his warriors to bring John Smith in front of him.

Pocahontas's heart was beating, and her mind was swirling. There was nothing she could do to save John Smith. His fate had already been decided by the Spirits, and she was powerless. Her breath became faster and faster as she watched through a haze of hunger and apook induced stupor as the warriors made John Smith kneel before Powhatan with his head on the stone platform. She could see John Smith trembling - even though he was a strong and able soldier, there was nothing that he could do to change this situation. He was tightly bound. He could only succumb to what he was being told to do, even if it meant succumbing to his death.

He glanced up and caught her eye, pleading.

Pocahontas closed her eyes; her body racked with emotion. There was nothing she could do. She heard John Smith cry out, and her body would take no more - hunger, apook and the emotional tension of seeing her friend in danger took its toll. She passed out as she heard the word 'Nantaquod' ring through the Quioccosan.

[1] son

TROUBLE IN JAMESTOWN

He had thought that he was finally going to meet his maker. He had never felt so much fear in his life - not as a soldier, not even when he had become a slave in his misadventures in Turkey. He had tried extremely hard to maintain his composure. Maybe there was an afterlife? Maybe it was the beginning and not the end?

When his head was placed on the cold hard stone, his heart was beating so fast that he thought it would explode. He had looked at Pocahontas, then closed his eyes and waited for the axe to fall, imagining the short sharp pain as his head was severed from his body... nothing came.

He waited, trembling. Each passing second a lifetime. Each breath savoured as if it was his last.... finally opening his eyes when the axe did not fall. Through blurry tear drenched eyes he could see Powhatan, smiling and raising his hand in the air. He heard the chanting and smelt the pungent tobacco smoke. His heart was beating. Was Powhatan waiting for a Divine signal before dropping his hand down to signal his death?

He felt his hands being freed and he lay there for a moment, breathing heavily and trying to understand. One of the warriors pulled him up to a very shaky standing position and he stood in front of Powhatan, head bowed. He did not know what to feel - was relief too premature? Powhatan then beckoned him forward and embraced him. Powhatan whispered "Nantaquoud". Then he knew - he was being bestowed the honour of becoming a son to Powhatan. His eyes welled up with tears of relief, and he felt like he was going to faint.

It was only when the dancing and clapping had started, and the warriors laid down their spears, did he realise the importance of what had just happened. He had been accepted. He had succeeded. He was alive!

The next day John marched back to the settlement accompanied by four of Powhatan's warriors, his mind going over what had happened over the past few weeks. The agreement to give guns and tools to cement their relationship was tricky. The English didn't want the Indians to have guns that could be used against them in battle should things turn nasty again, which was bound to happen. He had a good idea of how he could get out of this - more lies and more deceit.

He shook his head thinking of Pocahontas, whose views of the world were so innocent, trusting and kind. He almost wished she did not trust him so much; he really didn't deserve it. She had never known anything but her tribe and the Spirits that watched over them. She honestly believed he was her friend and that the Powhatan and English could co-exist. He sighed. There was little possibility of that. The Virginia Company wanted money and to get money they had to develop land. The land belonged to her people. Yes, these lazy bastards had not been highly successful so far, but with time he was sure that they would be, and it was his job to ensure the Powhatan were crushed into submission. How could he live with himself?

At last after four days of heavy marching, a weary John and four Powhatan warriors (one carrying food, one carrying John's belongings, one a guide and one a lookout), reached Jamestown. John could see that things were the same as when he had left them.

"Ahoy there Archer - I can see you are busy as usual" John shouted throwing a stone in Archer's direction.

Archer looked up. "Ahoy there yourself. I see you have been collaborating with the enemies again Smith. I assume you have some corn for us at least?" Archer jumped up and swaggered towards John and the four accompanying Powhatan warriors. "Look ye here - John the returning 'Hero'" he shouted across to his companions. "He has brought us some corn, and some savages to torture." Archer did a double take as his devious piggy eyes took in the party of Powhatan that had accompanied John. "Hang on… where are your men? Where are George Cassen, and Thomas Emry? Have you lost them John?" Archer raised his eyebrows and smirked.

John shook his head and sighed, an unwelcome picture of the mutilated bodies flashing before his eyes. "Sadly, they did not survive, but I can tell you everything once I have given these warriors what they want in return for the corn that they have brought us."

"Of course - you have to get your priorities right, don't you? Make sure the savages are looked after, nothing else matters." Archer shrugged and walked off towards his colleagues.

John indicated to the warriors to follow him as he walked toward the large bronze Saker cannons that had been taken off the ship. The warriors walked around the cannons, touching them and looking down the barrels, their faces were filled with childlike fascination. John, finding the few Powhatan words that he knew, said that he would show them how the cannons worked. At this, the warriors vigorously nodded smiling.

John walked over to one of the cannons and indicated that he needed them to help him move it into position, pointing away from the settlement toward the trees. He called one of the lads over from the fort to help him clean, and load the gun with stones, for demonstration purposes, before attaching the long fuse wire ready to light the powder.

He pointed to the Indians that they should put their hands over their ears - but they ignored him and just nodded and smiled. He shrugged. This will be interesting he thought to himself.

He walked over to the long wire and lit the end. They all watched in

69

suspense as the spitting fire gradually crept up towards the gun. The gun jerked aggressively with a tremendous noise, louder than any thunder that the Powhatan had ever heard as smoke filled the air. The stones were propelled violently forwards and clattered against a tree in the line of fire. Snow and icicles were thrown into the air with torn shards of wood from the tree. Birds screeched in alarm as they took to the skies. John watched with some amusement as the Powhatan screamed and ran, eyes wide, hysterical with fear, away from the smoking cannon.

Silence followed. Gradually the Powhatan returned shaking their heads, clearly shaken up by what they had witnessed. John smiled at them. Today was not the day that they were going to take guns, he thought thankfully. Instead he gave them bags of trinkets that brought a smile to their faces. The cannons would have been far too heavy for them to carry, and anyway he had managed to scare them away from the idea of going near them. Job well done, he thought.

The Indians thanked him, bowed and turned to walk back to the tribe. John sighed with relief - he had had a stressful few weeks, and he just wanted to settle down with a bit of food and some sleep. At least he had the corn that Powhatan had given him, he was sure the English stores would be just as empty as when he had left.

Archer appeared again, meandering over with his filthy toothless grin. "So, John... I think, now that your entertainment session is over, we need to find out what happened to your men, don't you?"

John sighed. "For God's sake Archer, if you must know they were both killed along with one of the Indian guides. It was a horrible situation and there was absolutely nothing that I could have done to save them. I feel sick about it. Only by the Grace of God was I allowed to survive."

"That's just it, John. It is all very strange that your men were slaughtered, and you, on the other hand seem unscathed."

John stood and thought for a moment. He knew Archer would stoop at very little to bring him down. "I left them as the water was too boggy and shallow for the boat, and I continued on foot, hoping to find a different way through. They had instructions to alert me if they were in trouble. What none of us realised was, that the area was overrun with Pamunkey. They didn't have a chance." John found himself justifying himself and kicked himself for stooping so low.

"So you were saved and they were not…that seems strange. Are you starting to get a little too close to these Heathens? So close that you put them before your own men John?" Archer was starting to raise his voice. The others were crowding around now, interested to see what was going on. A chance to put down John Smith was not to be missed.

"You ungrateful bastard. You are out to get me Archer aren't you?" John's face was puce with rage as he marched towards Archer.

Archer saw the anger in John's face and walked backwards. "You are a waste of space John Smith. Not even a gentleman. You do not deserve to be here" he mocked. John could not contain himself any longer. The stress of the past few weeks had built up to uncontrollable rage verging on madness. He pulled back his arm and punched Archer with a force that surprised even him. He watched as his nemesis doubled over, landing on the hard-frozen earth, groaning.

"I have been up the river three times to get corn for you lazy sons of bitches. You would have starved like the others have, if it wasn't for me. You do nothing, absolutely nothing. At least I make expeditions upriver and I also try and make relationships with the Powhatan in order to do trade. Now you are accusing *me* of letting my men die. I cannot believe this. You have let hundreds die through incompetent leadership." He looked around at the assembled group, who watching Archer lying in agony, were clearly not sure who's side to take. Finally, Edward Wingfield stood tall and puffed his cheeks out.

"I have often wondered about your dysfunctional alliances John. I am afraid you are getting too close to the Heathens, and this latest incident is stark proof that your priorities are questionable." He put his hands on his hips and stared at John.

Bartholomew Gosnold stepped forward. "I think this could be termed high treason. The matter is exceedingly serious and we need to think about your future John. Those men were in your care - it is indeed suspicious that you come out of it unscathed - in fact so friendly with the Indians that you are giving them a show of the cannons!"

Archer struggled up from the frozen earth, his face contorted with hate. "I think this man has been heading towards treason for some time. Now this has been confirmed, I think we ought to seriously consider his position. The sentence for treason is death."

Once again John was seized, his hands tied behind his back and he was thrown into the hold. How ironic, he thought to himself as he lay on the stark wooden floor yet again. *I have just managed to cement the relationship between the colonists and the Indians in such a way that we could move forward, taking their land peacefully. These idiots have no idea about anything, about politics, about surviving or about moral justice. What hope is there? Maybe now I will not live to see the disaster that is surely going to happen. Maybe these idiots are so lazy and unintelligent that the Powhatan people may defeat them after all, despite our advantage of superior weapons.*

He wished with all his heart that they would.

2nd January 1608

The ship appeared around the headland. It had taken much longer than expected. Many lives would have been saved if Captain Christopher Newport had returned sooner. The surviving men standing on the shoreline were clapping and cheering in anticipation. More supplies from London to supplement the corn John Smith had managed to get from the Indians was essential. They had been clinging on to life, and now help was at hand.

Newport, in his dashing navy uniform walked down the gangplank, his stump of an arm visible to all. He was used to it now, but his image had certainly been dented when he lost the arm in battle. He had had to regain his status and prove that he was still capable in this male orientated hierarchical environment and hence he made his stance appear erect and commanding. He looked down at the rabble of men in front of him. A poor sight indeed. Was all this effort worth it? Did these people really deserve to be successful?

One hundred more settlers, full of anticipation for their new futures and pleased to be back on dry land, walked down the gangplank, following Christopher Newport. Their faces fell as they saw what they had come to. Hopes were dashed as images of warm houses, soft beds and a hot meal were quickly erased from their minds. They all knew that the supplies that they had started the journey with had all but been used, or were riddled with maggots. They were hoping this new land of plenty would at last feed their hungry bellies.

"It's good to have you back Christopher." Wingfield, as leader approached with arm stretched forward to shake Newport's only hand, face beaming.

Newport avoided the outstretched hand. "I see not much has been made in the way of progress." Newport's face was stern, no hint of a returning smile. He looked around him at the group of unsophisticated huts, the skeletal, sickly and idle colonists smiling and cheering, and he felt his heart sinking.

"I have brought you more colonists - but they need feeding and shelter. I hope you are able to look after them?" This was not looking good, he thought.

"Have you brought us any supplies?" Wingfield held his breath.

"Sadly, we have used everything up. I was relying on you to provide from the harvest and the fishing that you have done" said Newport. He could see from the sorry state of the Colony that this was not going to happen, and his anger was rising.

"Of course, of course" Wingfield lied. "Everyone can find a hut and make themselves at home. We will find something to eat in due course." His heart was sinking. 100 more mouths to feed, when they were struggling to feed themselves, what were they going to do?

"Where is everyone?" Newport asked looking around at the sparse numbers.

"I am afraid this is all that is left. There are only 38 of us, the rest have died." Newport noticed that at least he had the grace to look ashamed.

"What the devil have you been *doing* Wingfield?" Wingfield shuffled around and looked at the ground, then searched the watching faces for the rest of the members of the Council, all who were similarly looking at the ground hoping not to be summoned to account.

"Come and relax Christopher" Wingfield pointed to a ramshackle hut, completely ignoring the jibe. "I can tell you what has been happening since you left."

Newport followed Wingfield to the hut, accompanied by Gabriel Archer, John Ratcliffe and Bartholomew Gosnold. All the men looked very serious. They knew they had to get their stories right, not that they had done anything wrong, of course.

Newport looked around the assembled company his eyes taking in every emotion that they were disclosing and some that they were not, as they shuffled uncomfortably in front of him like naughty children. "So what has been happening? Have you managed to start growing crops or trading with the Indians?" Eyebrows raised. Expectant.

Wingfield cleared his throat taking the lead. "Well, Christopher, there has actually been quite a lot of trade with the Indians. Our stores at the moment are better than they have been for quite some time." His mouth smiled, but his head was hammering with fear. "I do have to reassure you that we have worked very hard at this." He smiled again raising his eyebrows, looking around at his colleagues who were all nodding vigorously in agreement, the same vacant smiles on their faces, the same churning stomachs.

"I see... So, the Indians are establishing a good relationship with you then?" Newport felt suspicious. He was picking up vibes that they were not telling him everything. Their eyes were shifty, and Wingfield had his arms crossed defensively across his chest, despite the attempt at bluster.

"Well, yes - things have been much much better" said Archer, trying, but failing to sound certain.

Newport scanned the group. "Better eh? Where is John Smith?" He asked, his voice becoming louder as he stared at each one in turn.

"Well, unfortunately John has been a bit of a problem again and we have had to arrest him. He has been locked up." Archer was taking pleasure in announcing the news of his old rival. His body tensed as he stared at Newport as if ready for confrontation.

"I see. That seems strange, when he was the one that seemed to be making the relationships with the natives and doing the most trade the last time I was here. What happened?"

Archer cleared his throat. "John was fraternizing with the Indians far too much. He frequently met with Powhatan's daughter, Pocahontas, and was very aggressive if anyone else came near. I for one, was nearly attacked by Pocahontas's bodyguards and John did nothing to protect me. Even worse than that, he went on a trading expedition recently and deserted his men leaving them to die whilst he went to the Indian camp and had a feast with them. Three men were killed. It is outrageous and clear to all of us that he is crossing the line. It is treason at the very least." Archer stood his ground, self-righteousness oozing from his pores, pleased that he had made his case so well. A sick condescending grin on his face.

"I see" said Newport, still looking them up and down with a pensive gaze. "So.. who is it that has secured the stores that you have at the moment?"

Wingfield looked around furtively at his accomplices. "Well...John Smith did... but we could have done it - he just wanted to get together with the Indians for a feast." His words were rushed, as he fought to think of excuses.

Newport could see their faces changing. They were no longer sure that they had the upper hand and they were physically squirming. He knew the story just didn't add up, and they were scared. "I think I need to hear John Smith's version. This is very irregular. Bring John Smith to me." He commanded.

In a few minutes, John appeared. His hands were tied behind his back and he was filthy, smelling of excrement, not having been allowed the dignity of managing his toileting. His beard was unkempt and his cheeks were hollow. He looked at Archer as if he could kill, and then moved his gaze slowly to take in Christopher Newport shaking his head.

"My God John, what the hell has happened to you...?"

John sat alone with Christopher Newport in front of a roaring fire. He had washed and dressed and had consumed a decent meal of the corn he had traded for - something that had not happened for several days. His head was in his hands and his shoulders slumped as he stared at the dirt floor.

"I am not sure that I can go on for much longer Christopher. They are out to get me, and this time it was serious. If you had not arrived when you did, they would have hanged me, I am sure of it. It's so ironic, when I am the one that has made the relationship with the Indians and have made an amazing breakthrough with Powhatan.

They don't want to know though. They just like looking for bloody gold, paralysed with the thoughts of riches, sitting on their behinds all day smoking. It is pathetic Christopher. They have a misguided illusion that the Indians will provide them with food, despite the disrespect that they show them." He gave a low chuckle. "I think the time has come for me to leave them to it. I have done the best I can, but they are determined to break me."

Christopher Newport leant towards John.

"I understand your frustration John..." he ventured.

John sat up and looked him full in the face. "You understand... you understand... don't patronize me you son of a bitch." His voice was raised."They have nearly killed me twice. Third time lucky, is it? It isn't *your* life that is on the line here. You have the luxury of escaping back to London whenever you want to. At this rate I will be joining you in a coffin... ." He lowered his head and looked at the floor.

Newport sighed. "Just calm down for a minute John. Tell me exactly what you have done since I have been away. Surely you don't want all that hard work wasted now? In the state that we are in at the moment, I cannot see the Colony surviving without the goodwill of the Indians. We have little food, we will not be able to start planting for months and I have brought another hundred mouths to feed. We need to take action.."

"All of that is true, but Archer and Wingfield have no comprehension. They are complete idiots with not a brain between them. How the Virginia Company even considered putting them in charge is a mystery to me. They continue to treat the Indians like savages with absolutely no respect. No effort is made to forge relations and at the least provocation they shoot at them for sport, laughing amongst themselves about how clever they are.

Archer takes delight in insulting the Chief's daughter - who is only eleven years old for God's sake. He would be happy to kill as many as he could if he had the balls. I promise you, none of them have any idea of intelligent war tactics or that we are actually the inferior force in this contest. An inferior force trying to conquer a superior force without goodwill - laughable really." He smirked, shaking his head.

"Leave them to me John. I understand what you are saying. The Virginia Company will not be happy to hear what has been going on, and I will make it very clear that things have to change. I can't see Wingfield lasting anyway - they need a new leader."

"I am not sure you will be able to do anything, but at least it is worth a try" said John.

"Just tell me what you have been doing" said Newport sitting up straight and taking a deep breath.

John looked at the floor. "For what it is worth, I had made extremely good inroads with negotiations with the Powhatans, until it was thrown back in my face." John squared his body and took a deep breath, recounting the tale of his near death experience and his new relationship with Powhatan.

"That is better than we could have hoped for John. What did they want in return" said Christopher eyebrows furrowed.

"They want guns and tools. Obviously, we do not want them to have guns - so I was able to stall them for now." John's face fell as he thought about it.

"What is the matter - we have them where we want them, don't we?" Christopher's eyes were wide.

"I know, it couldn't be better. They are being friendly and giving us all the help we need... but I know, in time our goal is to take their lands and convert their people to a religion they do not understand. They seem to be innocents, unaware of our intentions. My previous enemies have not been friends. I am not used to kicking friends." He sighed.

Newport's eyes widened and affability left his face. His role as Commander rather than friend returned. "No, no John. I don't agree that they are our friends. They are *pretending* to be our friends. They know damned well that for now we are not in a position to harm them. Look at us. We are a ragtag bunch of inept ruffians - you have said as much yourself. What harm could we do to them? On the other hand, Powhatan has seen our weapons, he has seen our tools, and he knows that we are very advanced in comparison to them. Do you not think he wants some of that to maintain his power over the other tribes... and possibly us? I would not feel too sorry for them - he is being a very astute negotiator, actually. He may be a savage, but even savages have an instinct for survival. He may not know the extent of our plans, but he is not being completely altruistic about our being here. If it helps both sides for you to be close to them, then what is the problem?"

John sat up straight and looked Newport in the eye. "The problem is deceit. We are going to grow in numbers eventually as more and more ships come with more and more people, and the Powhatans will be driven out, losing their homes and their way of life."

"That is as may be John, but it is your duty to carry out the orders of the Virginia Company. You cannot let sentiment get in the way of the goal. I am surprised at you. Maybe the others were actually not far from the truth - maybe you are getting far too close to the Indians. You need to pull back and remember why you are here.

I understand you have had frequent sessions with Pocahontas. It has been useful that you have been learning the language, and she is a charming young child. Do not be flattered by her or her people - you are a soldier, not a saviour." Newport's voice was rising, and the colour was coming into his cheeks. "For God sakes man, do your duty" His brows were drawn, his eyes staring. "I can only think that it is the hunger and isolation over the past days that has got to you." He said with irritation in his voice.

John rolled his eyes. He knew there was no point in his argument. What did he expect Newport to do? There was no way that the Virginia Company was going to pull back now. Their only concern was money. He should not have even mentioned it, but he had felt very emotional after his starvation in the cells. Maybe Newport was right. Maybe Powhatan had thought this through and wasn't as benevolent as he had first thought.

Powhatan had killed many Indians in other tribes in his quest to gain control of the area - he was no Saint. God damn it... there was nothing he could do anyway. He had to continue what he had started. He, of all people, knew that it was a luxury for a soldier to have sentiment. What was happening to him?

He sighed, shaking his head, pausing. "You are right Christopher. I do not know what came over me. My past few days have crushed the enthusiasm I had to make this Colony work. I don't think you can blame me though, considering what I have been through."

"I will give you the benefit of the doubt John. I am going to trust that you will do the right thing for the Virginia Company if I release you from the clutches of Wingfield. Do not let me down." He looked John straight in the eyes, looking for affirmation. John nodded.

"You can trust me. Please forget my outburst. I am sure that if we can exploit the inroads I have made, we can really make headway." He returned Newport's gaze unflinchingly.

"Well, as it happens, I have brought back some trinkets from England for Powhatan. The timing could not be better after your recent inroads with them.

I have a coronation robe to make him believe that we honour him as a King. After all, these savages love their trinkets and ceremony. They are a bit primitive really, aren't they?" He smirked, superiority flooding his face.

John looked at him. He realised the depth of his ignorance. He had sworn alliance to the cause of the Virginia Company, but was his heart really in it? Powhatan has more heart and soul than Newport has in his little finger, he thought. There was no point in trying to educate Newport or any of them though. There was a monetary mission to complete and honour and justice could not compete with that. He only half heard Newport continue with his "wonderful" plan.

"... I also have a lovely white greyhound dog to give them. I don't suppose they have ever seen such a beautiful dog, so that will impress too, I am sure." John nodded with lips pursed.

" Oh, and another thing... I have with me a young man, Thomas Savage, that I propose lives with Powhatan. Hopefully, Powhatan can let us have one of his young men in return - that way we can learn each other's language and cultures, so that we can communicate.

I will go to the camp to honour Powhatan. This will convince him that our motives are honourable. You must come with me. Do not give up now. This will be a cementing of the Indian and the English peoples that will hopefully end any aggravation between us and allow us to make a lot of money for the Company without too much bloodshed."

John looked straight ahead expressionless.

RIVALRIES: February, 1608

⁓᳆᳆᳆᳆᳆᳆⁓

Pocahontas looked into her big brown eyes. She was so beautiful. She had never seen a dog that was so elegant and kind. The beautiful creature nuzzled into Pocahontas's neck and whimpered. Her fur was as white as snow, and her nose black as the blackest burnt wood. John Smith and Christopher Newport had brought her to Powhatan as a gift, and Powhatan seeing Pocahontas's face when she saw the dog, said that she could have her. Pocahontas knew immediately that this beautiful white creature would always be her best friend just like Kitchi had been. Nowadays Kitchi spent all his time hunting with the warriors as she always knew he would once he grew out of puppyhood. Their time together was always going to be short. He was needed to do a job, not just play with her. She had missed him terribly. No dog could replace Kitchi in her heart, but maybe this beautiful creature could fill some of the lonely days without Kitchi... and Kocoum.

What should she call her? It had to be something that signified the growing friendship between her people and the Longcoats... I know... Waki Qiwebis means Peace - I shall call you Waki for short. She threw her

81

arms around the dog's neck and gave her a squeeze. "You are Waki" she laughed. "Waki, Waki. You will bring Peace to all of us. I just knew the Longcoats were good. How could someone like John Smith do anything to hurt us? You are really one of them, I suppose - and I know you will always love me." The dog lay and looked up at her adoringly. Pocahontas stroked her pink tummy as Waki lay on her back with her legs in the air. Pocahontas suddenly thought of Kocoum. What was he doing now? He was in the middle of his training - she wondered if he was alright. Maybe we can be friends again when he gets back. She knew he would love Waki as much as she did and imagined the three of them playing together.

"Well hello!" John Smith's voice boomed out as he walked into the Yehakin where Pocahontas cuddled up to Waki. "I see that you have made a good friend of the greyhound" he laughed. "I have brought another friend for you as well... "

Behind John, Pocahontas could see a young man who was about her age. He had beautiful golden hair and blue eyes, and he was grinning at her from ear to ear. He was very tall. She had a sudden intake of breath. She had never seen an English boy like this before. Yes, she had seen some of them at the camp, but they were very ordinary dull and dirty. This one was vastly different. Their eyes met and there was silence.

"Are you tongue tied Pocahontas? - I have never known that before, I must say. May I introduce you to Thomas Savage. He has come to live with your people to learn your language, so he can translate for us. Powhatan is sending your brother Namontack back to our fort, so that he can learn our language. We are determined that our peoples will become friends and live peacefully together. You and I have started the process, but this will be even better. As you know some English already, I think you would be the best person to take Thomas under your wing and start teaching him, the way you have been teaching me."

Pocahontas blinked, trying to take in what John was saying. She had to spend time with this boy - she was not sure she could even *speak* to this boy, and she had no idea why. Her face had turned red, and she knew that they could both see she was flustered. The more she tried to hide it, the redder she became. What was happening to her? She had to look away to try and regain control.

"Are you alright Pocahontas?" said John, his eyebrows raised, smiling.

"I am very pleased to meet you" said Thomas, struggling for composure when he saw the most exotic and beautiful young girl he had ever seen.

"I would be most grateful if you could help me to learn your language." He put his hands together in front of his chest and bowed, his large smile getting even bigger as he glanced at her long shiny dark hair and dusky skin. His heart beat faster.

Pocahontas took a long deep breath and gazed at Thomas; her eyes wide. "Sir, I would be very pleased to teach you my language." She managed a tiny smile, and bowed in return, her hair catching the light as it tumbled like a curtain before her.

March, 1608

Kocoum had seen Pocahontas with the English boy on several occasions from afar since he had come back from his Huskanaw training. They looked like they were having fun, laughing and playing together as if no one else existed. They often visited Jamestown together, taking corn to the Longcoats and visiting John Smith. He thought back to when he and Pocahontas had gone to Jamestown that first time. How close they had been only a year ago. He closed his eyes and imagined her small hand in his. Her words came back to him again and again… "We are meant to be together Kocoum…" It was no use though, so much had happened in a year - the ceremony of Nikomis, her friendship with John Smith and his own training for the ceremony of Huskanaw, during which he had been isolated from the tribe for several weeks. He had made the ultimate sacrifice and rejected her. He had made fun of her Visions and told her that they could not be together. Sadly, it seemed as if she had taken him at his word.

Now, he was back it was obvious how things were. She looked at Thomas Savage in the special way she used to look at him. He had thought that her smile was only for him - he was so wrong. He had glimpsed them running together in the fields with that damned white greyhound, laughing and obviously happy to be together. She even seemed to have forgotten Kitchi. Admittedly, Kitchi was a working dog with no time to run around and play any more and he had been away, so they hadn't had much of a chance to sort things out between them.

After that day when they had kissed, before he went away he had avoided her, too full of emotion to face her. He had to admit that his longing for her had not disappeared as he hoped it would. Huskanaw was supposed to erase all previous memories, but it had not worked for him. He missed her, but he had burned his boats when he had shouted at her to leave him alone. She had not forgiven him, and he would never stoop so low as to ask her to.

He thought about "Savage". Ah yes, he didn't speak Algonquin. But even that advantage was being eroded as the two of them spent intense hours exploring and learning each other's languages. Kocoum felt useless and stupid by comparison. Everything was against him.

To overcome his heartache at leaving Pocahontas, he had put his very soul into becoming the best warrior that he could. Casting aside fear, he had performed the most perilous tasks in his training, putting himself in danger and outdoing the other trainee warriors, just to put her out of his mind and to prove himself to Powhatan. Maybe at some level he still had hope, but he realised now that Thomas Savage had arrived, his hope was futile.

Lost in thought, he suddenly saw them coming towards him and tried to turn the other way. "Kocoum, Kocoum…" she shouted, waving at him and jumping up and down.

He hadn't spoken to Pocahontas since his return, and he had never spoken to Thomas Savage, nor did he want to. He turned and pretended not to hear.

"Kocoum - what is wrong. Come and meet Thomas" Pocahontas shouted louder.

He knew that he could never walk away from her. He turned, his face sour, ready to brush them off. He had better things to do than make conversations with a little girl and a stupid Longcoat invader.

Her face was pleading. "Please don't walk away Kocoum. I have not seen you for ages, don't you want to talk to me any more?" Her eyes were like dark brown shining pools of light.

If only she knew the truth, he thought. He turned around. "Oh it's you, Pocahontas" he said dismissively, his eyebrows drawn together and his mouth unsmiling. "I thought you were busy with the Englishman and had no time for your own people." He nodded with contempt in the direction of Thomas, his eyes hard and staring.

Thomas ignored Kocoum's body language and smiling, put his hand towards him in friendship. "Hello Kocoum. Pocahontas has told me so much about you. I understand that you are a great warrior, and that the two of you have had some very exciting adventures." His blue eyes were smiling.

Kocoum looked at Thomas. His face revealed his confusion. He understood very little of what Thomas had said, but his hand was being offered in friendship. Did he really want to be a friend? What should he do? A Powhatan never turns away from the hand of friendship. He grudgingly offered his hand in return, but did not return the smile. This was a rival - he was not going to be a friend. He knew that Pocahontas would not forgive him if he was aggressive towards this stranger that seemed to be making such an effort to be his friend. He knew they would never really be friends and that Thomas Savage didn't care. He just wants Pocahontas, thought Kocoum, and the smiles belie the truth. Pocahontas, smart as she is, is naive in so many worldly ways.

Thomas looked at Pocahontas, putting his arm around her. "I don't think he understood me. Of course, I forgot, he doesn't know any English, does he? Can you tell him what I said?" he asked. His face showed his condescension as he smiled a smile that was too exaggerated to be genuine. Then he gave Kocoum a cheeky wink and stooped to kiss Pocahontas on the top of her head.

Kocoum could bear the taunting congeniality no longer. His mind was racing out of control. That bastard touching her had done it. Maybe he had lost Pocahontas, maybe she had chosen this 'savage' over him, but how dare he flaunt it so openly? His breathing became rapid as his heart beat faster. His eyes were staring, his body was tense and throbbing with anger. All he could see was the 'savage' slobbering over Pocahontas and laughing at him.

It was as if his mind was out of control, his body propelled him forward, all his warrior training, and none of the restraint training for the past nine months coming to the fore. He threw back his fist and with strength that he didn't know he had, he punched the unsuspecting Thomas in the stomach.

Thomas spluttered, trying to catch his breath as he fell heavily on the hard frozen earth. He lay sprawled on the ground looking up at Pocahontas with pathos and disbelief, blood dripping from his mouth where he had bitten his tongue. He clutched his stomach as if in extreme pain, theatrically bringing his knees up to his chest, groaning. He furtively glanced at Kocoum giving him a sly wink.

How could such a kind and gentle friend act with such aggression? Even although they had parted on difficult terms before he went away, there was no excuse for his treatment of poor Thomas. She could tell by his face after he had done it that he knew he had behaved badly. He had immediately turned his back on her and walked away, unable to look her in the eye.

Since that day, she had not seen Kocoum. She no longer sought him out, having seen a side to him that she did not know existed. What was he thinking of? Her instinct told her that he was not thinking at all and that he was probably as shocked by the incident as she had been, but her loyalty to Thomas would not let her take Kocoum's side or try to reconcile with him. If he wanted to apologise, that would be a different matter. She would welcome him with open arms - but there had been no sign of him for weeks. Perhaps he was not sorry? When she thought about Kocoum her stomach did a somersault and she felt slightly sick. So she tried, without success to blot him from her thoughts.

HEROINE: May, 1608

Fate had taken a turn for the worse. Any of her fanciful thoughts of an alliance between Powhatans and Longcoats had disappeared dramatically and forcefully when hostilities increased again between the two peoples. It had recently become so serious that her father had sent Thomas back to his people in disgust, so she did not even have his company anymore.

Thomas had proved to be a good friend to her. Even after 'the incident' he had not spoken harshly of Kocoum, and for that she respected him. He was not like Kocoum - but maybe that was a good thing – the feelings between them were not intense. He was more like a big brother. He laughed with her and played with Waki and they had had lots of fun together. They had often visited Jamestown and had long conversations with John Smith. Thomas had gone.

Kocoum had gone.

She could not visit John Smith.

It had all gone so horribly wrong. How had this happened? Christopher Newport had sailed back to London in April and with him gone, the

Longcoats seemed to have lost all restraint. Even John Smith had not been able to contain the violence. *His* concerns lay more in ensuring they had enough food than in monitoring their behaviour. Colonists had been firing guns at Powhatans for sport, laughing and creating havoc. Powhatan was furious. After all he had done for them: welcoming John Smith into the Powhatan fold, giving them land, providing food when possible – it had all been in vain, and he was at a loss to know what more could be done. In the first instance he had sent Thomas to Jamestown requesting restraint, but this had been ignored. Consequently, the Powhatan warriors became very angry and felt at liberty to steal anything they could get their hands on, and molest any Longcoat stragglers wandering outside of the fort. This had further heightened tensions.

The Longcoats had taken Powhatan hostages in retaliation - where upon the Indians took Longcoat hostages. In reprisals the English burned some of the buildings in a nearby Powhatan village. Tit for tat they had achieved nothing but destruction and it was escalating out of control. But what could she do? They were all acting like children instead of working together the way that they had envisioned after John Smith's life had been saved. She had to make things better - that was what the Manito Aki wanted from her. She had to make them understand. But how? She was only a girl - it was insane to think that she could make any kind of difference. But if she didn't, they were headed towards slaughter on both sides, and the peace represented by the lovely Waki was going to die.

She was heading towards Jamestown accompanied by six warriors and Rawhunt, who was a special adviser to her father. Rawhunt had one arm smaller than the other, and he was thought to possess special powers. Powhatan had sent him to negotiate the release of the warriors that were captive and to try one last time to re-negotiate the peace that they seemed to have lost. She was to translate. Powhatan was giving her this chance to prove herself, and she must not falter.

She stood in the small smoky room in Jamestown beside Rawhunt. She had seen the captive Powhatan warriors in the corner of her eye as she came in. She was shocked to realize that one of them was Kocoum. Why didn't her father tell her? How could she maintain composure. If only she had been warned that it was her best friend that she was fighting for. She gritted her teeth and tensed her body, holding everything she was feeling firmly in check. Her face was straight, no sign of emotion, and her head was held high. She was immaculate with her hair in a long plait hanging down her back. A soft leather shift covered her small body, framed by a mantle of feathers that Powhatan had given her to keep her warm. White feathers adorned her hair as befitted a Beloved Woman and she stood as tall as her twelve year old self could, grasping at dignity, eyes forced front so that she did not meet Kocoum's pleading gaze. She had a job to do.

Rawhunt started to deliver the speech that he had been given by Powhatan. Pocahontas translated.

"Dear friends. We are sorry for any misunderstandings between our two peoples. Our aim has always been to have peace between us at all costs." Rawhunt and Pocahontas both bowed and put their hands in front of their chests - the prayer position of good will. "We are mere men, as are yourselves, and we understand the reckless emotions that sometimes are released with the frustrations of our time. We must all, however, understand that in order to gain the most from each other, we must remain friends and work together. The Great Powhatan wants this more than anything. However, we must use restraint when our men are intent on succumbing to baser instincts. Powhatan is releasing the hostages that were taken, and he would urge you to do the same so that we can return to the peaceable relations that we worked so hard to achieve." Rawhunt bowed his head. Pocahontas also bowed her head and looked slightly to the side, quickly glancing at her friend, eyes meeting for one glorious second, an arrow in her heart.

She walked forward. She looked up and saw Thomas Savage smiling at her to encourage her. John Smith was also part of the audience. How had he let his men get so out of control? She felt small and helpless, her friends were watching her, and the life of her dear heart was at stake. She was determined to carry on, remembering that her duty to the Manito Aki was her prime concern, but now Kocoum's life was also in the balance, her determination knew no bounds. She must do this. She thought of the large brown eyes of the wonderful Waki, and remembered the significance of her gentle friendship. What she was going to say now would make a difference to the lives of many people, not just the captive warriors standing before her. She knew this with the certainty of one who could see beyond what others see. Badger stood watching her. Was that pride on his face?

She took a deep breath and paused, shaking inside. She looked at Kocoum. She looked at Thomas Savage. She looked at John Smith and finally Gabriel Archer. The look was not that of a child, it was of a stateswoman.

———————————

They carried her high on their shoulders back to Werowocomoco. She had been a triumph. She laughed and cried at the same time, relief sweeping her body as she realized what she had done. The whole audience - Longcoats and Powhatan had stood open mouthed as she made the speech of her life that had made them all humble and ashamed at what had transpired between them. Even Gabriel Archer had clapped her when she had finished. She knew that it was not really *her* that had given the speech - she was the voice of the Manito Aki. Nevertheless, her heart was singing with pride. She had secured the release of the warriors, including Kocoum, and the Longcoats had agreed that things would continue on a better footing between them all from now on.

They had all loved her.

The Powhatan warriors carried her into the Quioccosan, chanting and laughing. Kocoum clapping the hardest, jumped up to touch her. As she passed him by, high on the shoulders of the warriors, their eyes met for one precious moment. His look told her all she needed to know.

A large fire was burning in the centre and the girls were dancing around it clapping and twirling. Waki was running around darting between the dancing squaws, playfully nipping at their heels. The warriors stood in a circle around the edges, their spears banging on the ground in time with the loud drums that were beating in unison, causing dust to fly. The apook was burning in the fire, and the strong scent mingled with the smell of the venison roasting, crackling as the fat spattered into the fire. It was heady, an assault on the senses - sounds, smells, vibrations and energy all mingling to a climax of delight.

Powhatan sat on his large throne smiling from ear to ear as he clapped along with the drums, his eyes were wide, feathers on his headdress fluttering with the movement. He could not stop looking at his beautiful and extraordinary daughter. She had earned the name Amonute - her name as Beloved Woman, and he had known she would do it - but there had always been a nagging doubt as she was so young. No doubt existed now - it was as the Gods had prophesied. She was a rare Miracle sent from the Heavens as had been foretold even before she was born. Her name would never be forgotten. She had more work to do, and now he believed she would do it.

Pocahontas felt overwhelmed and started to feel as she had done at the Hobbomak when she had her Dream Vision, everything began to take on an eery light as she started to float...

"I am rising... I can see the joy that is below me... Waki... Waki...Ah - there she is with Badger. We are riding together, and we can see the land before us - an adventure.

two boys, two men, two cultures.... I stand in the middle, one on each side.

Ahone and Oke? Kocoum and Thomas? Longcoat and Powhatan? Symbols of peace or war? They are fading, my hands are reaching out to touch them, but I cannot reach...

Two babies... one fair, one dark. Always two... two men, two cultures, two babies... my heart aches, but I do not know why... I need them.. Oke and Ahone, so precious to The Grandmother Who Fell From The Sky... am I the Woman That Fell From The Sky?

Badger shakes his head. The same... but different.

BROKEN PEACE: October, 1608

I t was one of those bright early winter days. The watery sun was suspended in a clear blue sky, the trees newly naked, reached like fingers pointing skyward. She sat by the bay, shoulders hunched as she watched the circles surrounding each thrown stone move symmetrically outward in the water. Order. Each circle was the same - each stone plopped and moved the water as it should. If she concentrated long enough, maybe her mind would be free of the chaos of the rest of her world and become as ordered as the circles in the water.

Her mind kept sending her images that seemed to make no sense – nothing made sense.

How quickly the words of men morph from promises to lies. Last May, a mere five months ago, the stones that she threw in the lake made the same sound, made the same shape in the water as they did now - Nature continued with little regard to Man. Nature could be relied upon. The word of Man could not.

She had been overwhelmed with joy, she had made those older and more important than her see sense. She had resolved the differences between her people and the Longcoats. But it had not lasted long. What had happened? She remembered how it felt to be high on the shoulders of the warriors, laughing - seeing Kocoum gazing from the crowd. Triumph. Joy. Love.

However, the truth of the situation started to become clear as hostilities unfolded again gradually but consistently. Colonists continued relentlessly and aggressively to take food from Powhatan women and children. Powhatan continued to ask for swords and guns that were not forthcoming. The peace that she had thought she had won, had been very short lived. A distant memory. She sighed. Promises turned to lies.

No - men could not live together when they were competing for resources and struggling to survive. Men had to kill, she thought, her eyes welling up with frustration. Who was to blame?

John Smith had tried. Powhatan had tried - or so she had thought. Each wanted survival - that was undisputed in her mind. But doubts on their motives had started to worry her as the months moved on from that joyous day, and violence started to raise its ugly head bit by bit, overcoming any progress that she had made.

Powhatan did not want war. He knew that the Longcoats had guns and weapons far superior to those of the Powhatan nation. 100 warriors had been turned back when they had confronted only a handful of Longcoats firing the huge fire-stick. That had really been the turning point for Powhatan.

She shook her head. She couldn't blame him. She was coming to understand that he was a man like any other, and he wanted his people to survive, as she did. In this new and changed world, he knew that they would not survive unless they were on an equal footing with the weapons that the Longcoats had.

Maybe he was not so benevolent after all - maybe he had been as cunning and political as the Longcoats had been, enticing them with food and mock friendship to get at the guns. He was not stupid or naive, he was following the way of the Gods to protect his people as best he could.

As for John Smith. He was her friend. Why had he allowed his men to attack the Powhatan and take food? Why had he not followed through with his promise to share guns with them? Surely he understood that despite their guns and firepower, his people were struggling to survive without the Powhatan providing them with food? As more and more ships had arrived bringing more and more people, but no supplies, food had become scarcer and scarcer and the more colonists there were, the more squabbling for food. Ships always seemed to come at the beginning of winter when it was not possible to harvest or plant enough food. They had camped in a completely unsuitable place; they had not worked to grow crops and they were still on the edge of starvation. The Colony was a place of squalor. Were they completely stupid? Powhatan had offered them so much - and they had gladly accepted, and then as good as spat in his face. She threw a large stone into the water and watched it splash. If anyone were to blame, they were.

Maybe she had been completely naive in believing that two cultures could co-exist amicably. She threw another stone so hard that it splashed her. The cold water was unpleasant, but she sat, feeling the droplets as they dried on her body - allowing her mind respite from the constant analysis of a situation that she still felt was her duty to solve. But how?

And what of Kocoum? He had looked at her so adoringly in May - hadn't he? But he had made no effort to see her again. The pain of his absence returned. Maybe she was deluded in believing that everyone loved her including Kocoum. That myth was being dispelled very brutally. Was it just an illusion? Her stomach turned at the thought of her arrogance. No, the reality was that she was a twelve year old girl who was quite ordinary. She had achieved nothing so far.

She had thought that Kocoum might break the silence between them after that glorious day, but he had not, and her own pride dictated that she avoid him. She was not going to stoop to that level. He had to approach her first.

Thomas had been allowed to come back when things between the Indians and Longcoats seemed to be going well. So, for the past few months her loneliness had diminished. She often held hands with him playfully as they walked around the village testing each other's language. He was very kind, and she liked being with him - with his blond shiny hair and blue eyes that smiled at her as if she was the most beautiful girl in the world. At least with him she felt special, but the way things were going with the hostilities, he was sure to be recalled to Jamestown again and then she would be completely alone again.

She threw another stone into the water and rearranged her thoughts. Ah… it suddenly hit her, maybe if she married Thomas, that would be the way their peoples would finally come together in peace? Maybe that is what Manito Aki wanted, maybe the Manito Aki had kept Kocoum away. Maybe it was all part of the plan.

It wouldn't be bad being with Thomas. Maybe she would have lovely blonde, blue eyed babies. Would they be girls or boys? She smiled and threw a smaller stone, watching the spray in rainbow colours as it fell on the water, breaking the shiny surface with tiny droplets. She sighed, as her mind fluttered back to Kocoum, an ache in her heart, her stomach fluttering as she remembered his one kiss. Just one kiss, all that time ago - how could it have had such an effect on her?

Maybe she should go and see him? Maybe she should tell him how much she missed him? No - she couldn't, it would be just too humiliating if he told her to go away. She could not bear the embarrassment…but maybe it was worth it to feel his hand in hers again? No, No, No - she yelled at herself inside her head, throwing a handful of stones into the water with as much force as she could muster, the resultant splashes almost drenching her.

She heard the crunching of stones behind her, and turned, looking with surprise at his approach.

"Hey, hey, hey Little Mischief. Why so violent?" he said smiling and putting out his hand to help her up.

She looked so lovely, he thought as he sauntered towards her holding his hand out to her.

"Hello beautiful friend" he laughed.

96

Pocahontas looked behind her and saw Thomas Savage. His blond hair sparkled in the sunshine, and over the summer the sun had created a sprinkling of freckles on his nose. Ignoring his outstretched hand, she beckoned him to sit next to her. She felt her face flush as she remembered her presumptuous ideas about marrying him, and quickly re-directed her mind.

"I am so fed up doing nothing when our people are tearing each other apart" she said, her eyebrows drawn as she threw yet another stone into the water, the droplets sprinkling upwards like a rainbow in the early winter sun.

"There really isn't anything that you can do Pocahontas. You have tried and tried, and against all odds you made such good progress with the peace between our peoples in the beginning. I think men have a need to be dominant over rivals, something that even you can't sort." He smiled. "Not that I am referring to Kocoum in any way!" He took her hand in his. "I do have some bad news though." His smile had disappeared, and his shoulders were hunched.

She looked up at him, eyes wide with expectation, fear showing on her face at his sudden and uncharacteristic change of mood. "What is it Thomas?"

He looked at the ground, she could see that he was trying to hold his feelings in. "Your father has said that I must go back to Jamestown again. He was very nice to me, and he told me that he realised that nothing about the recent hostilities is my fault... but he thinks it better that I am with my own people. This time it is for good." He was taking long breaths, trying to calm himself down.

She saw sadness in his face and read it in his eyes. She instinctively reached for his hand. "I knew this was going to happen, Thomas. What will I do without you?"

He felt her touch like a lightning bolt and pulled away. "You must know my feelings for you Pocahontas..." He looked her squarely in the face, his usually smiling expression replaced by sorrow. "...we are from different worlds. I would be willing to sacrifice my world to be in yours, but I don't think that is fair on you."

"Thomas we have such a very special bond. Why couldn't you stay...?" she took a long intake of breath, her eyes wide with anticipation, "maybe we could get married?" She looked at him from under long dark eyelashes, pure sincerity etched on her face. "That's the answer! That's the answer! If we got married, there could be peace between our people.... What do you think?" Her eyes were wide and she was breathless, taking hold of his hand.

He paused, looking at her, his heart breaking inside. "Your life belongs to Kocoum" he sighed. "That is the reality."

She dropped his hand and turned and looked out over the water, lost in thought. "Kocoum doesn't care about me any more though Thomas."

"Is that what you truly think? Why does he look at you the way he does? Why did he react so badly when I touched you? Why, when we are together do you always talk about Kocoum? I was horrible to him and made him angry on purpose, and I am really sorry. I didn't realise the damage I was doing. It was just a joke at the time, but I see now how cruel it was to both of you." Thomas could hardly get the words out for the emotion that he was feeling. He was throwing Pocahontas back to Kocoum. He knew it was the only honourable thing to do. How could he keep this beautiful butterfly when he knew she did not really belong to him? He had been a pig when he had provoked Kocoum and he knew it. It had had the desired effect though - but as time went on, he had come to realise as he spent more time with Pocahontas and began to really get to know her, that he had damaged something beautiful between her and Kocoum. He was trying to put it right, even although he was probably going to regret it for the rest of his life.

He stared at the ground. "I don't love you, anyway Pocahontas. You are not of my culture and I need to find a nice white English girl to warm my bed." His words were fast and hard, like an arrow to her heart. "I could not bring you to Jamestown as a wife. Everyone would think I had married a savage." He threw a stone into the water and watched as it sank.

His words stung her. Then she gathered herself up and stood in front of him, gazing down, hands on hips. "I don't believe you mean that Thomas. I think you *do* love me, like I love you."

To hear that she loved him, made his heart lurch. He knew that she didn't really know what she was saying though. He wished with all his heart that it was true, but she was such a kind person, she would say anything to relieve his suffering. The few times he had seen Kocoum and Pocahontas together, he had seen the look that passed between them. He had witnessed how Kocoum had looked at her on her triumphant day, when she had negotiated with the Longcoats. Of course, he could give in now and take her in his arms and ask her to be his wife when she was older - but it would not be right. He stood up shaking the thought away. He bent down and kissed her cheek.

"I do love you Pocahontas, you are right, but I am not the only one that will love you." He put his finger under her chin and tilted her face upwards to look in her eyes, pausing.

"I know that in the life that you are to lead, many people will love you. I am not a mystic as you are, but even I know that your destiny is not to be just with me. Listen with your gift, listen to the wind in the trees and the birds in the sky. They will all tell you what I am telling you. And maybe one day you will cement peace between our peoples."

She threw her arms around his waist burying her head in his chest, feeling his heart beating and the solidness and heat of his body. He was so precious to her. His arms encircled her small body in response. "*Please* don't leave me Thomas. I don't know what I will do without you." The tears were falling down her cheeks and her body was shaking as she clung to him, not wanting this moment to end, cementing forever the feeling of his strong body. She was going to be so alone now.

They stood. Neither wanting to pull away, both knowing that they had to, and this time it would be forever.

Badger had a tear in his eye.

TRAGEDY: January, 1609

Thomas had gone again, leaving her sad and lonely. Over the past few months conflict with the Longcoats had escalated exponentially, and now it was so bad that the whole tribe were having to escape into the forest. She watched them pack up everything. It had to be done overnight with speed, so that the Longcoats were unaware that they had gone until they tried to come back for more food. She saw them silently dismantling all the Yehakins and marching all the stores to the new location in the woods. Powhatan was tired of the constant begging for food that had now escalated in some of the villages to rape and violence if the Longcoats did not get what they wanted.

Powhatan wanted to show them that they could not survive without help. January was not a good time for food - the Powhatans resorted to eating berries and whatever they could find as the ground was as hard as stone. The Longcoats had no knowledge of what to do, and Powhatan had given up on common sense negotiations and advice. Pocahontas had tried to convince him that they had to continue with peace talks, but in the end even she could see the futility. The English had proved themselves to be mean and stupid. Powhatan had warned them that his people would disappear into the woods so that they could not do any further trade, but they had not believed it, they continued with violence and aggression.

Pocahontas knew that they would be disappointed when they discovered their food supply had fled. More Starvation was on its way for them, and Powhatan was past caring. Perhaps it was the best way to get rid of them, as it was clear that they were intent on staying and taking all that they could get. She couldn't blame Powhatan. His people were under threat of violence when the Longcoats did not get what they wanted, and he knew that any retaliatory violence against the them would amount to massive slaughter of Powhatans because of Longcoat superior weapons. Powhatan now had to starve them. He had tried everything else and failed. Even honouring John Smith as his son and Werowance had proved to be a futile gesture treated with contempt.

It had come down to a competition between Powhatan people and Longcoats for survival and Powhatan was determined that his people were not going to be displaced.

...I stand in the middle, one on each side....

She was The Beloved Woman. Maybe it was her fault? Maybe she should have tried harder? Maybe there was something that she could still do? Maybe she should go and appeal to John Smith to come and try and make peace with her father? She had not seen John for a while as her father had stopped her visiting Jamestown when the violence had escalated. John Smith was still her friend - he would listen to her. The violence was not down to him. She was sure of it. Why had she not thought of this before? It was very obvious really. She had to act fast though.

Having pieced her thoughts together and making a plan of action, she started the journey. She scrambled through the undergrowth, determination to succeed outweighing any consideration of obstacles that might lie ahead.

It was late afternoon and the light was starting to go. She stumbled and then quickened her pace concentrating on the ground in front of her, realising it would be much more difficult to find her footing when darkness completely descended. Her breath was like cold smoke and she pulled her mantle of feathers tightly around her to keep in what little warmth there was. The evergreen trees that surrounded her swayed in the wind, giving off an eery sound as if they were lonesome spirits. She had taken Waki with her, and she saw Badger following her every now and then - nothing bad would happen when those two were watching over her. Pocahontas looked upwards for a moment. The Gods would always look after her - they had told her this in her dreams.

... Manito Aki tells me it is the Gods and Nature
that will save the day
but my name will go on...

Waki could run like the wind with her long elegant legs, but she slowed down to keep Pocahontas's pace, instinct telling her that her friend relied on her. Her thin white velvet-like form darted in and out of the bushes, her large brown eyes that were like dark liquid, watchful for danger, never lost sight of her mistress for a second. Waki was kind and gentle, but she could fight like the fiercest warrior if needed. Her long nose housed large teeth capable of ripping enemies to shreds in seconds.

At last, as the moon started to rise, Pocahontas saw the buildings of Jamestown appearing through the trees. She slowed her pace, creeping like a mouse.

Standing outside the palisade surrounding the settlement, she recognized the ugly form of Gabriel Archer. He wove backwards and forwards singing an out of tune song, hiccupping every now and then and laughing at himself, almost falling over with jollity. He staggered towards a bush and pulled out his penis ready to relieve himself, and then caught a glimpse of Waki's white form out of the corner of his eye. Pee went all down his trousers as he instinctively grasped for his gun.

"Bugger my mother, look what you have made me do" he hollered, chuckling to himself. "Wha goes there?" he slurred, stumbling. He stopped, righted himself and peered through the dusky light. "A white deer eh...? ah... that will make a tasty meal."

After several attempts he found his gun and aimed it in Waki's direction.

"Stop!" Pocahontas shouted as loudly as she could sensing his incoherent stupor. She ran and placed herself in front of Waki. "Don't shoot. I am the Beloved Woman and daughter of the Paramount Chief Powhatan of Tsenacommacah. I command you to put down your gun at once." Her legs were shaking and her stomach was turning, but she made her voice sound authoritative. The only way she was going to get out of this was to make sure that she reminded him of her position.

For a second, he paused scratching his bald head and scrunching up his eyes and peering even more in the direction of where the voice was coming from, disbelief on his blank face. He moved as if in slow motion holding his gun high. As quick as a flash, Waki sped towards him, jumping, and clasping her teeth around his wrist. He pulled the trigger but was falling backwards with the force of the large dog who was growling like a wolf, worrying his arm. He cursed with the pain and kicked out at Waki, who seeing he was now of no threat, whimpered with the inflicted blows and ran back to her mistress.

Pocahontas in her eagerness to protect Waki, had lost her footing and fallen backwards hitting her head on a large stone. As consciousness started to leave her, she looked up and saw in the distance, the figure of John Smith standing on the platform of the palisade above her, silhouetted by the moon. She reached her arms up towards him as she saw him turn away.

She felt the world began to swirl and the pain in her head intensified, blood pouring from her wound, she was aware of being lifted into someone's arms. Everything was hazy as she saw Badger's face getting fainter and fainter....

She passed out.

I see him - John Smith standing there looking at me, holding his hand out to me and whispering - but I cannot hear... he is fading...

The stillness of the night is shattered into a thousand burning pieces. His world turns orange red and black. Gunpowder flash. Thrown like a feather on the wind. Piercing throbbing pain. Water cold as ice, red syrup swirling in the moonlight. Sinking into the black silvery depths. Life in the balance. I feel the arrow of grief pierce my heart. I cannot breathe. John is in danger...

HUSKANASQUUA: (1610)

Her head throbbed. What had happened? She had woken up the next day in her bed with little memory of events after she passed out. She remembered having seen John Smith in the distance, but then everything had disappeared from her mind except her terrifying vision of the gunpowder flash. Something had happened to John and she knew it was very serious by the vivid images that haunted her.

How had she got back to the village? It was a complete blank. Everyone was too busy with the final bits of packing up to give her any time to talk about her escapade. She had asked Matachanna who it was that had brought her home, and she had just shaken her head as she bandaged her wound, and said that it was one of the warriors who had been patrolling the area. Powhatan had reinforced his dictate that she should never go back to Jamestown as it was far too dangerous. Matachanna had made clear her displeasure and then landed her with hundreds of jobs to do, despite the fact that her head ached, and nothing more was said. One thing was clear - her mission had failed.

Just as the tribe were all packed up and ready to go, Pochins had arrived with two bits of devastating news. Firstly, John Smith had been in an horrific accident. Pocahontas listened to the details of the explosion, but she didn't have to listen too hard as she had already seen what had happened in her vision. No one who saw what happened believed that he had survived. The pumping blood and the gaping wound told the whole story, and she had to hold her breath to stop herself from crying out in anguish. He must be dead. Her friend was dead. She had to turn her head away to hide the tears that were falling. They saw him as the enemy, but to her their relationship had symbolised peace - and now he was gone.

His second bit of news had turned her stomach, and broken her heart still further. Pochins told them of the massacre of her Uncle Wowinchopunck's tribe. 70 Longcoats had stormed the village, killing indiscriminately. They had captured one of Wowinchopunck's wives and two of his little children. The children were taken into the forest and shot through the head; their tiny bodies thrown in the river. Their mother was taken back to the fort raped, and when all had had their pleasure, her throat had been cut... and they call us savages, Pocahontas thought. How did men do such things? To the Powhatan people, women and children were sacred and not to be harmed. She pictured the faces of the little boy and girl - only five and seven years of age as they stared down the barrel of a fire-stick screaming for their mother, who stood, feet and hands tied watching as her babies were jolted backwards by the force of the shot, their innocent blood spattering on the ground.

Pocahontas imagined the unimaginable as their mother faced multiple rape, tied down like an animal. This is what happened without John Smith's influence and it was the last straw for Powhatan, there was to be no going back now. It meant war.

This was the finality Pocahontas had been dreading. She thought of Thomas Savage who was still at Jamestown. She remembered him with sadness and joy in her heart. They were destined never to meet again after these atrocities. They had been so close. But he had been right, their friendship could never have been more than friendship. They came from different worlds. But how she would have liked to have seen him again.

Friends were hard to come by.

She thought often of the things that he had said about Kocoum, but she had not seen Kocoum at all. She had heard that he was now a great warrior - he had obviously moved on from their childhood friendship of stolen kisses and held hands. He was probably even married now. She reached for Waki and threw her arms around the patient dog, who looked at her with large brown eyes and pushed her head under Pocahontas's arm, nuzzling her.

"Oh Waki. Why have things gone so wrong?" she whispered with a pleading voice. "I think I have been forgotten by everyone, and I will never be able to save our people... I am not such a Beloved Woman now, am I?" She fondled Waki's soft velvet ears and buried her face in her neck. "You and Badger are my only friends. Even Kitchi is too preoccupied these days."

At that moment, Waki saw a rabbit and with the wind behind her, tore away from Pocahontas's embrace disappearing into the undergrowth. "Even you have deserted me... " Pocahontas shouted after the disappearing dog, her face crumpling with despair. She looked in the undergrowth – Badger still lurked -that was something at least.

Pocahontas started walking towards the Yehakin in the new village in the forest. At fourteen, she still felt like a child, but her body had changed. She now had the curves and breasts of a woman. Her monthly bleeding had started, and her position within the tribe was changing to take on more senior tasks. People looked at her differently now, although she felt exactly the same and struggled unsuccessfully to let go of her mischievous and childlike ways.

Today was the day of her Huskanasquaw, the ceremony that recognized her transformation from child to woman. Why would one celebrate such a thing? Even the celebrations had not gone as planned and her heart was not in it. The Quiakros had told her father that she may be valuable to the Longcoats as a hostage, being the daughter of The Great Powhatan and a Beloved Woman, and so everything that she did had to be very low key, with little publicity. Hidden away like a prize, unable to live a free life. She was watched day and night in case she was kidnapped.

The Quiakros said that, if kidnapped, the ransom would be high. She didn't really believe she was valuable, but she had to go along with it. John Smith would never have contemplated such a thing, but now it seemed that he was dead, and the likes of Archer would go to any lengths to crush her people.

So it was to be token celebrations this evening. She could not get very excited though. Yes, it would be lovely to dress up and have feathers in her hair and dance the night away. But she didn't have anyone that she liked to dance with. Her father had made several suggestions of young warriors as her suitors, but they were all ugly or smelly. She would rather be alone than with anyone like that. No mind, she had to go anyway. There promised to be a reasonable feast at least - Matchanna would see to that, even though there would not be very many guests.

————————————————

The Quioccosan looked beautiful. She smiled. Even though it was not as grand as might be expected, under the circumstances, her friends and family had gone to great trouble to make everything look lovely for her Huskanasquaw. Maybe she was a little bit special after all. She glowed inside as she looked around at the effort that had been made just for her.

The smoke from the fire was comforting and Matachanna rushed over and grabbed her hand, her face beaming with excitement.

"Oh Pocahontas - you look so lovely." She smiled at her younger sister. "This is a great day for you, and the start of the rest of your life. You can leave your childhood behind and look forward to a wonderful future."

Pocahontas thought about her childhood. No one had had a better childhood than she. She had been embraced by the tribe, and despite having never known her mother, she felt an abundance of love. Matachanna had been the closest thing that she had had to a mother. The laughter, the kisses and the cuddles had always been there - her naughty behaviour was always embraced as eccentric and cute. Would that change, now she was a woman?

She wondered what was to come. She had thought that maybe from a cute and funny child she would evolve to become a heroine and make peace with the Longcoats. But her success with the Longcoats was now a distant dream to her. She had to be satisfied with being just an ordinary girl, with an ordinary life, whatever that meant.

She spotted Waki and Kitchi in the corner. They had also been adorned with flowers and feathers, and were hopping and skipping between people looking for food. Waki's long face ended with a glistening black button nose which nudged and pushed, her pink tongue lolling as she made her presence known in the crowd of thronging humans. Kitchi's tail swiped everyone as he bounded through the crowd. Badger, as ever was minding his own business, but watching her every move. Pocahontas smiled. Her three true friends.

The music and the drums started up and the girls began their Medewewin[2] dance, their painted bodies swaying as they sang, while everyone clapped. As ever, the fragrant apook permeated the air - a smell that always made her body limp and at peace. Her father sat on a high altar seat watching the proceedings. He stood up and raised his arm for silence. Everything stopped. She looked up at his brown face that had become gnarled and lined with the worries that had been placed on his shoulders. He was such a good and peaceful man, in a violent and aggressive time, she thought, her heart breaking for him. She remembered the irony of his words - 'a stranger is only a friend you have not met yet.' They had met so many strangers that had not been friends that the saying was now tarnished with blood. Her eyes moved to the fire. We both tried, she thought wistfully.

"Come to me Pocahontas." He had a smile as large as his face, which was rare these days. He looked towards the assembled crowd. "These celebrations are for my lovely Matoaka, who has chosen the name of Pocahontas as her Huskanasquaw name. The first Pocahontas was Matoaka's mother, the woman that I have never stopped loving, even though she has crossed over into a different world.

Our daughter, Pocahontas now enters the tribe as a woman - a treasured woman, who is also one of our Beloved Women. Her mother is watching her and smiling." He pointed to the sky and nodded as if he could see someone watching. He beckoned Pocahontas to come closer to him.

She stood before him. He wrapped his arms around her and kissed her on the forehead. "My special girl" he said. She could feel his large body shaking with emotion as he pulled her closer to him as if he never wanted to let her go. Gradually he released her and held her by the shoulders looking into her eyes, savouring their closeness. As their moment of intimacy ended, he reluctantly turned her around to face the crowd of well-wishers, sharing her with them.

"Please celebrate the coming of age of Matoaka, our Pocahontas" he shouted, his face full of joy. He dipped his finger in a cup of deer's blood placing a mark on her forehead and bowing, his hands at his heart. She curtsied and bowed to him, smiling.

"Now go and enjoy yourself young woman, enjoy tonight, and enjoy the rest of your adult life" he said. She turned and walked towards the clapping crowd. They all patted her on the back as she moved through them. Gradually they all moved away, dancing and singing, enjoying the festivities.

She stood by herself, watching, lost in thoughts of all that had happened in her short life, wondering what the future held.

She felt a hand being slipped into hers. She held her breath, wanting it to be him but not wanting to look in case it was not. Her heart was beating as she looked slowly up at the man standing next to her. He was not looking at her but she felt his closeness - he was the person she knew most in the world, the person she most wanted to stand next to her. No words were needed. They stood, neither seeing or hearing the celebrations any more, each feeling only their hands touching - every fibre of their being focussed on exploring the union of their hands. The warmth, the solidness, the softness and the pulsing heartbeats meeting as one.

As they stood, they were alone amongst a crowd of swirling beating bodies. They were in a Utopia that no one else could see. She felt the heat increasing as he held her hand more tightly, the vibrations streaming through her body. Pleasurable agony that she had never experienced before. It was not the heat from the fire or the pulsing of the drums, it all came from his touch. She was no longer aware of anything else. She wanted to stay there forever. She did not even want to look at him or move in case the feeling stopped. She needed this moment to last forever.

Breathless, silent tears of joy slid down her moist face as finally he looked down at her, his eyes pleading and tender. "I have had to wait a long time to see you, never coming near you. Your father was testing my love for you. But I have waited and watched you. Who do you think carried you with a bleeding head from Jamestown? Now, if you will have me, I will be yours for ever" he said.

In that moment she knew that he would be the love of her life for eternity.

[1] Female coming of age ceremony
[2] Medicine Dance

A NEW LIFE: 1611

~⦕∾⦖~

S he looked down at the snuffling little creature at her breast and felt
the gentle tugging as he relieved her of the excess milk that caused
her breast to ache. She needed him as much as he needed her, the
flow of milk soothing her body as he sucked. She scanned his beautiful
velvet face, his dusty pink cheeks, his tiny fingers that caressed her chest,
little fingernails, perfect toes, and the soft downy black hair on his head.
She bent over him breathing in his sweet baby scent and kissed the top
of his head while he suckled. He was such a miracle. She never thought
she could love anyone as much as she loved his father until she met little
Kocoum, or Ko-kee as they called him.

This love was different, but no less intense. She would protect this little
one to her death. He was innocent and helpless. She drew him closer to
her, and he grunted rhythmically with pleasure as the milk flowed into his
little heart shaped mouth. He stopped every now and then and looked at
her, then fell asleep again. She tickled his chin to wake him - he needed to
take more milk, she had so much to give. He suckled again, happy to take
what she had to offer, until he fell asleep again, baby dreams floating across

his smiling face.

She watched him as he slept. He did so look like her beloved Kocoum. He was handsome, like his father. His coming had increased her closeness to Kocoum, if that were possible. Over her pregnancy Kocoum had been excited, but worried. He was a warrior, and he had to protect her in her vulnerable state. Everything she needed was provided - even if she didn't really need it, she thought, and smiled. He had fed her the richest milk and he had provided more food than she was capable of eating. He constantly felt her swollen belly, and bent down to kiss it.

When it was time for the baby to come into the world - only two weeks ago, she thought poor Kocoum was going to faint with worry. He danced up and down until the Sunsquaas ordered him out of the Yehakin. It had not been an easy birth, but when Kocoum had heard the little plaintive cry of his son, he had barged into the Yehakin, eyes wide and body shaking with excitement. He had come to her and wiped the sweat from her brow, bending down and kissing her on the lips.

She remembered the moment the Sunsquaa had approached him with his son. He had been so tender. He had looked at little Kocoum with sheer amazement written on his face. He had touched the little body and held out his hands to hold him. He held him so gently - Pocahontas would always remember the gentleness of her strong warrior husband. He gazed at the baby, walked over to Pocahontas, and lay him next to her. "We made this perfect creature together Pocahontas." He had laughed. "Can it be true? Is this the most extraordinary miracle that ever existed?" He punched the air. He had lain on the bed next to her turning his gaze from her to the baby. So much joy.

Pocahontas was pulled from her thoughts by a commotion outside the Yehakin. It sounded like one of Powhatan's scouts had come back with news of the Longcoats. She idly wondered what the Longcoats were up to now. Everything on that front had been a little quiet for a while. She knew that there had been some terrible times for them. She remembered visiting a few times at the time of John Smith and seeing the distressing scenes, but that had been quite a while ago. Her father had stopped her going soon after that. Now there were reports of even more extreme hardship, although she could hardly believe that anything could have been worse than what she had last witnessed. There was a rumour that they had even resorted to cannibalism at one point - one man killing his pregnant wife, discarding the baby and chopping his wife up to eat her. Having seen the extreme suffering that she saw on the last day she had visited, she could imagine that to be true. She had heard that even Gabriel Archer had succumbed to death from starvation. She looked down at the sleeping little Ko-kee and her stomach turned to think of such suffering.

She had heard that now they had a new Marshall of the Colony, Sir Thomas Dale. They said that he was determined to make a difference and to try and instil a work ethic in those that were ablebodied, to turn the Colony from a graveyard to a self-reliant, going concern.

Powhatan's men always kept a close watch on the Longcoats, and tales had filtered back of the cruelty of Thomas Dale. Corporal punishment was now rife in the Colony as Dale was not going to allow a repeat of the insubordination of the past. He ruled with fear, but maybe he had to save them from themselves, she thought.

She shuddered as thoughts of Thomas Dale brought faint unbidden images into her mind.

A small room.
I am crouched down on the floor...
darkness....
humiliation...
searing pain...

She stopped. Concentrating. Hoping the images would become clearer so she could understand. Her body tensed and she had an intake of breath. She wasn't sure what it had been, but she knew instinctively that whatever it was she had seen signified something bad.

Her Visions had not come to her for many moons, so this surprised her. Maybe her Dream Visions were starting again. Maybe this was a warning.

Now her focus was on this tiny little being in her arms. Her whole world had changed at his arrival.

Please Okee, please protect my little Ko-kee and Kocoum, the love of my life. She closed her eyes, hoping for an answer, but she got none.

Pocahontas heard the loud footsteps of Kocoum running toward the Yehakin and then she knew.

"Pocahontas... Pocahontas... " he cried, breathless, his face contorted..

"I know Kocoum" she said calmly. "I know". She gazed at the sleeping innocent cradled in her arms, running her finger down his soft cheek. "I know" she whispered, her face drained of colour. She did know. This was the beginning of the end.

"We must leave at once Pocahontas," Kocoum shouted. "You don't know, you don't understand. The Longcoats want you. The Quiakros have seen it in their Visions. They know this to be true. You cannot argue." He was breathless, red with panic, sweat running down his face. "Pocahontas, please listen to me... you must get your possessions. We must take Little Ko-kee and leave at once. Your father wants you to go as soon as possible, he met with the Quiakros and they are frightened for you." He started to shout.

"Where will we go Kocoum? Wherever we go, they will find me. Maybe I should just give myself to them."

Kocoum ran over to her and grabbed her by the shoulders. "Pocahontas, don't say such a thing. I will die before I let them take you."

"That is what frightens me more than anything" she said putting her head on his shoulder with the swaddled baby between them.

I am looking into Kitchi's eyes... the world is covered with blood...

LAWS DEVINE, MORAL & MARTIAL: May, 1611

~⊙⊙⊙~

Thomas Dale was determined to secure order in the Colony, having only recently arrived as Marshall, and had implemented a strict regime - 'Laws Divine, Moral and Martial'- that he carried out to the letter with cruel satisfaction. He was determined that under his command, the sloth and disorganization that had almost destroyed the Colony, would now be eradicated. His name would become synonymous with success, regardless of the distress caused.

"Right Argall... " He looked at the colleague sitting next to him at the head of a large table in the room they had set up as a court of law. Samuel Argall was a man of high breeding related to the previous Governor, Lord De La Warr. He was a ship's Captain who had made many voyages to Jamestown and mixed regularly with the Great and the Good. Argall had been involved with the development of the Colony since the start of the project. He shared Dale's vision for the Colony, and Dale respected Argall for his social standing and his experience.

Dale was enjoying the power that he had in the Colony and relished showing it off to Argall. He looked in Argall's direction. "I see you have brought before me some dissenters. Tell me of their crimes." He nodded arrogantly in the direction of a group of filthy whimpering prisoners who were cowering in the corner. Dale was unsmiling, his ginger hair and beard clipped to perfection and his clothing immaculate.

"Well, my Lord," Argall sat upright. "Our first miscreant is Gabriel Smith" he said looking at a list in front of him. "Gabriel Smith - please will you step forward so that we can see you."

A young man of about nineteen stepped forward. He had blonde hair and bright blue eyes, a good-looking lad that now stared with terror at the two men sitting at the desk. "I am Gabriel Smith, Sir" he whispered.

"Speak up man - we can hardly hear you" Thomas Dale bellowed at the young lad.

"Yes sir" Gabriel said, standing upright, determined to give a good impression.

"It says here Smith, that you stole two pints of oatmeal. Is that correct?" Argall looked him in the eyes, waiting...

"My sister needed food to feed her three children as her husband died working with the work gangs. They are only babies, so my sister cannot work." His eyes were pleading, and the sweat poured down his face. "Please Sir, I will work every day to pay back what I stole - it was just that her children needed the food right away as they were going to die without it."

Thomas Dale had a self-satisfied look on his face. Another victim for him to taunt, he thought to himself. "I take that as a 'yes' then. Do you not understand that if you steal from someone, it means that someone else cannot eat? If everyone just took what they needed, where do you think we would all be? Chaos, that is where we would be. You have committed a gross crime against this society that is punishable by death" he shouted, banging his fist on the table.

"Please Sir... Please... No...My sister's babies will certainly die if I am not there to provide for them." He started to cry.

"For goodness sake - be a man Gabriel. Your sister will have to find a more honest way to feed her children in future. Everyone must find an honest way to make a living. There are absolutely no exceptions to that rule in my Colony."

Gabriel collapsed on the ground, weeping. "Please, please... I will do anything" he cried.

"I think you have done enough" said Dale smirking. "I sentence you to have a needle stuck through your tongue so you cannot eat, and I want you to be chained to a tree until you are dead. I want everyone in the Colony to see what happens when people steal." Dale stopped for a moment, deep in thought, imagining the scene of the lad gradually getting thinner and thinner, his good looks ravaged with starvation. He had the power to do this. He smiled. After all, it was for the good of the Colony. "Take him out of my sight, guard." Dale motioned with his hand, as if he was getting rid of a fly. He poured a glass of wine from the flagon on the table and raised it as a toast to Argall. "Bring on the next case Samuel." He smiled, his eyes sparkling at the morning's entertainment.

Argall glanced down at his list. "Anne Laydon, please come forward" he shouted.

The room went silent as a young girl stepped forward. She was at least eight months pregnant, and crying with fear, her large round belly protruding from a body that was thin and scrawny. Tiny stick-like legs and arms, and long dirty hair.

"What has this one done Samuel?" Dale's eyebrows were raised with surprise as he took a sip of wine and licked his lips.

"Anne Laydon - it says here that in your profession as a shirt maker, you made shirts that were too short, deceiving the purchasers and charging them the regular price despite the fact that you had used less material. What do you say?" Samuel Argall could see that everyone in the room was shocked that this young woman was standing before Dale in such a delicate condition.

Her voice was sweet and soft, her mouth turned down with fear. "I am sorry Sir. It is true that my shirts were slightly too short. I am new to making shirts and the pattern that was given to me was an old one. I would never deliberately deceive anyone or try to make more money than I am owed. The older ladies trained me and told me what to do. I was completely ignorant of any crime." She held her hands on her extended belly, and looked up at the table where the two men were sitting, moist brown eyes under long lashes. "Please Sir, this is my second baby, and I need to be there to look after my child. My husband also works hard day and night building for the Colony. He never misses a beat of the drum when he is chopping the wood. We are honest and hard working people." She tried to smile, but could see that Dale was distracted, looking at some commotion at the back of the room. She feared that he had not even heard her words.

"What... oh yes... You know that women are not exempt from punishment in Jamestown? I need all women to understand that they must behave as well as the men. I must make an example of you Anne, I am afraid. It is a shame that you are in the condition that you are in - but that is no excuse either. We can't have all the women getting pregnant just so that they can rob and steal from people and escape the consequences, can we?" He grimaced, pouring himself another goblet of wine. "Let's see... I think a flogging in the centre of town will probably do the trick. I think a hundred lashes." He was distracted again by the commotion in the back of the room. "What the devil is going on there?" he screamed.

"Sir, it is Anne's husband that has come to plea for her" said someone at the back of the room.

"Oh, I see. How noble of him" he smirked looking at Argall and raising his eyebrows. "No, actually... How bloody rude of him to interrupt the proceedings. Who does he think he is barging in here and interrupting my court. My Court! His wife can now have two hundred lashings, and he will be burned alive. I think people will remember that they cannot influence my decisions or interrupt my court." He turned to look at Argall. "I am not sure I can stand much more of this Samuel. I am getting bored. How many more people have we got to sentence?"

"There are at least ten more Sir Thomas" said Argall.

Dale sighed. Let me look at your list. He held out his hand, impatience written all over his face. Argall passed the list to Dale. Dale scan read the names and the misdemeanours.

"Oh for goodness sake – there is little need for me to go through each one. They are obviously guilty or they would not be standing before me. Hang them all tomorrow at ten o'clock. … you can do her flogging after that." He pointed at the girl standing before him.

The room erupted. All those sentenced shouted words of protest.

Anne Laydon fainted. Her small four-year-old daughter, with long dark pigtails broke away from the crowd and ran crying to her mother's side.

Dale stood up. "Silence!" he yelled. The room stood still.

It was his eyes that everyone noticed most. They were pale blue, staring and as expressionless as a snake. The only sound in the room was the tiny four year old girl, sobbing as she stooped beside her mother. Dale focussed on the child. Time stopped. What was this mad man going to do next?

"Bring that child to me" he said. The child clung to her mother who had roused herself to consciousness.

"I SAID, BRING THAT CHILD TO ME!"

One of the clerks pulled the little girl away from her mother, who collapsed, crawling forwards, nails digging in to the dusty wooden floor, stretching out to reach her child as she was taken. "No, please….No…" she cried.

The child was placed next to Thomas Dale, her face red and tear stained, rigid with fear as she tried to turn towards her mother. The whole room was silent; no one dared breathe.

When Dale looked at the child before him, the trace of a smile whispered across his face.

He took hold of her little hand and looked at it, pondering. The whole room waited, most wondering whether Dale had finally lost his wits, fearful that the child would be harmed. He paused for what seemed an eternity.

"Innocence" he murmured. "Pure innocence…. Where does it go?" he said to himself, his voice quiet and wistful. It was almost as if he had forgotten the room full of people that were on tenterhooks as he looked at the shaking little person. It was as if he had gone to another time and place

– remembering his own innocence long since eradicated by a cruel world that he was intent on crushing.

Someone in the room coughed.

Dale jumped as the moment of reflection vanished alongside his moment of humanity.

"Take her away" he shouted at the waiting clerk. "This is no place for children!" He got up from his chair. Knocking over his goblet of wine in his haste, he headed through the crowd towards the exit. The people parted as he passed, growling obscenities as he went.

———————

The next day Anne Laydon, bloodied and bruised from her 200 lashes, hardly able to move, was frogmarched to the scaffold and made to watch her beloved husband screaming with agony as his body, that she had loved for so long, went up in flames before her. She cried hysterically and tried to hide her face, but each time she tried she was beaten, so in the end she stood silent and motionless, all feeling dulled within her, as her waters broke and contractions started to bring her baby into a world that was not fit nor ready to receive it.

The crowd watched the spectacle of cruelty and destruction. Those trying to get on the good side of Dale cheered, most stared at the ground frightened to show the horror that they felt. Dale looked with pride at his handiwork, his blue eyes hard and unblinking – the colony was going to be crime free if he had anything to do with it. He was going to make his name through discipline.

He then looked into the crowd and caught sight of a small girl in tears watching the destruction of her family. She was like a broken doll. His blue eyes started to water as he turned and walked away.

ROLFE'S DREAM: September, 1611

John Rolfe had first landed in Jamestown on the 'Sea Venture' in 1610. This grand ship, the leader of a seven ship convoy, commanded by the most eminent leaders, Sir Thomas Gates, Sir George Somers and Captain Christopher Newport had been caught in a hurricane, blown off course, and separated from the other ships in the convoy. As the 'Sea Venture' started to sink, and prayers were said for their souls, they hit a reef off the island of Bermuda and were saved. After ten months of living in a plentiful paradise they built two smaller ships, 'Deliverance' and 'Patience' from the wreckage of the 'Sea Venture' and set out for their original destination of Jamestown.

John looked back on his time spent with the three hundred survivors in Bermuda. He and his pregnant wife Sarah, had embarked on the journey with high hopes, until the hurricane changed their lives forever.

Sadly, their baby girl, Bermudas was only strong enough to survive for two weeks after being born on the island. He remembered little Bermudas, and blinked the moisture from his eyes. Her soft white hair, blue eyes, and tiny little toes. How she had aired her lungs when she had entered the world! He would give anything to feel her little fist clutching his finger. She was so young when she died, he never saw her smile - he could only imagine what her laughing little face would look like now. His joy at the thought of her, turned immediately to sadness when he remembered her inability to feed, when Sarah's state of mind prevented her from giving her daughter the milk she needed. Bermudas had become frantic and desperate for survival, face red, screaming and screaming, thinner and thinner, her lusty cry turning to a whimper as she became weaker and weaker.

A little abandoned lamb without a mother to feed her properly. It had broken his heart. How cruel that Bermudas had been taken before her life had even started. There had been nothing that he could do. Buried and left in a little grave on Bermuda, weeds growing into her tiny casket forever. He had never lost the feeling of helplessness and hopelessness.

His wife Sarah was so very young, and had been tormented by the traumas of the journey and the loss of their baby, and John had been unable to prevent her taking her own life. He was still haunted by the look in her eyes as she threw herself into the swirling angry sea as they set sail for Jamestown from Bermuda, leaving him all alone.

Death had seemed to be a part of his life, he thought with bitterness. The pain of losing his wife and daughter brought back memories of his best friend in the world - his twin brother, Eustace. He had been powerless to save Eustace too. His stomach churned at the memory of Eustace's hand slipping from his as he fell from a cliff top, crashing downward and turning into a bloody mangled form on the ground below. He saw Eustace, Sarah and Bermudas every night in his nightmares. He would never forget them, and he would never forget that he had been powerless to save them. He had been a failure.

He had thought Jamestown might offer him some solace. He smiled at how naive he had been. He remembered arriving at Jamestown on 24th May 1610, during a time that had become known as "The Starving Time". He had not forgotten the skeletons that greeted them on the dock, flesh being picked off bones and eyes gouged out by the birds. Flies swarmed everywhere, and the stench of death permeated the air, to the point that most people retched and vomited as they stepped onto the ground that they had eagerly waited to see for months. Men, women, and children were dying - there was no discrimination. John had come from the paradise and sadness of Bermuda, to the horrors of Jamestown.

His most vivid memory was of seeing a young native girl, the first Powhatan that he had ever seen, tending to a young child, trying as best she could to relieve a little suffering, putting a cup of water to the child's mouth. Thoughts of Pocahontas had haunted him since that day. She had been so young, beautiful, and compassionate in a place of ugliness and cruelty.

The Colony had eventually been saved by a whisker as Lord De La Warr arrived just in time to provide enough food for a few weeks. It had not been an easy time. It had been touch and go for the survival of the Colony, and whilst things were improving, hardships remained.

John smiled at an irony – he had set out to find a better life and the only potential positive was a few measly tobacco seeds that he had brought from Bermuda. Dear old Sir George Somers had encouraged him to start cultivating them back in Bermuda. He had come across them by accident. It was an act of fate that these rare Spanish seeds had ended up in his possession. Without knowledge and skills the tobacco had been promising, but not up to the required standard. He knew there were possibilities - but he was powerless to do more.

Smoking tobacco had saved his sanity. He knew he was addicted, but the fragrant leaves allowed him to float away from his troubles on a cloud of beautiful fragrant grey smoke. He would often just sit by himself inhaling and tasting. It was very rough, and he kept experimenting with different methods. Nothing so far had improved the results. The Powhatans had been curing tobacco for generations – if only he could see their methods. However, it was forbidden for anyone in the Colony to trade or talk to Powhatans - all negotiations had to be done through Gates and Dale. John shook his head. To the powers that be, there were so many things of greater importance, but it was his only chance. Maybe it was their only chance too - but they did not realise it yet.

There had been talk of a new town at Henrico - a much better location for growing crops. If only he could get Gates to allow him to go there and plant his seeds, he might have a chance. He looked down at the few plants that he had managed to cultivate. Straggly and pathetic in unsuitable ground. That had been part of the problem for the Colonists generally.

There had to be a way. If he stayed on the right side of Thomas Dale, he might be able to realise his dreams.

ARGALL'S PLANS: September, 1612

"So, Argall, you seem to be doing well with these bloody savages - fourteen hundred bushels of corn from the village of Pasptanzie, that is good going."

"Thank you Sir Thomas" he said. "I need three hundred of those bushels for my men though. We can't expect them to feed the whole Colony and not gain anything for themselves, can we?" Argall raised an eyebrow. He knew Dale of old, and he knew that Dale would take the shirt off his back if he wasn't vigilant.

"So, what are your plans now Samuel?" He neatly changed the subject giving no commitment.

"I believe that the most pressing matter is getting more corn in before the winter sets in. I have built up relationships with several of the tribes along the Potomac, and I think I can persuade them to do more trade." Argall had many plans in the back of his mind. He looked at Dale wondering whether he should divulge his ideas. Was Dale to be trusted? He sat in the large armchair opposite, letting the heat from the smoky fire permeate his body. Dale was a man of action. Under Gates and Dale the Colony had changed completely since the starving days of 1609.

He thought himself like Dale in many ways. He remembered all the personal successes he had had in his career. He was thought of as a genius who did things properly - everything by the book. He was a man of perfection, well known and liked at the English court, well respected both there and in Jamestown for his attention to detail and his ability to think things through. If things needed doing, he was the one that people turned to for help. He had experience, he was intelligent, and he worked hard.

He was not ruthless like Dale. But, he thought, Dale gets things done, he just uses different methods.

Argall's real strength was as a people's person. He was good at negotiating; he understood the motives of people and the way they thought. He always focused on the goals of his enemies and he was able to manipulate and deceive with a smile on his face, maintaining the facade of a gentleman.

His aim now, was to replicate the work of John Smith. He had tried to make relationships with the natives in order to overpower them. Sadly, the Virginia Company and Smith's own greedy and inept colleagues had not had the foresight to recognize Smith's devious genius. But Argall did. Why fight for corn when you could smile and take it anyway? He thought with horror of the tactics of De La Warr and Percy - why would you attack an Indian tribe, set it alight, kidnap the queen and her two small children and then shoot the children one by one in front of their mother? Barbaric, he thought shaking his head.

No. Kidnap was a better idea. People did not have to get hurt, but each party ended up getting something out of it without violence. It had been preached as a manipulative tool many times by the Virginia Company, but the Colonists had been too stupid to realise its value and continued trying to suppress with violence and brutality.

On his last trip down the Potomac, he had heard rumours. Rumours about the daughter of the Great Powhatan. Now that was very interesting. She would be a great prize. What better way to get Powhatan to do what the English wanted, than to kidnap his most treasured possession? That would certainly make Argall a hero. All these years, all these leaders, De La Warr,

Smith, Percy, Gates, Dale - none of them had really been able to conquer the Powhatans. Now he had a plan that would do it. A plan that could end the hostilities, a plan that could mean a stop to all the Indian attacks. It could mean that more corn could be had, and eventually more cultivated land taken over by the English (with a smile, of course). He would be a hero for certain. It was genius.

Should he divulge this to Dale? Should he just keep it to himself, and do the deed? He did not want Dale taking all the glory after all. He couldn't contain himself though. It was just too good to hold in. He reigned his thoughts in, looking at Dale sitting and staring at the fire.

There was a knock at the door before he could say anything more. "Enter" shouted Dale imperiously.

The door opened, and in came young Thomas Savage with a jug of wine.

"Excuse me Sir," Thomas bowed. "Would you like some more wine?"

"That sounds a good idea Thomas, please fill us both up" said Dale lifting his cup off the table and moving it towards the young lad. Thomas filled both their cups to almost overflowing.

"Thank you boy - you may go now" said Dale as he nodded indicating Thomas's dismissal.

Argall lent forward and took his cup of wine. "I have been thinking about the next step with the Indians" he said, frowning. He took a sip of wine.

As Thomas Savage made his way out of the room, Argall pointed at him "That young man spent a lot of time with Pocahontas, didn't he?" The door closed as Thomas left.

"Yes, I believe he learned a lot of the Algonquin language through his time living with her people. It made him a very valuable person to have with us. Why do you ask?" said Dale, intrigue etched on his face.

"We need to get these savages under control" said Argall.

"Indeed... ?" Dale was fully focused now, Argall could see by the way he had replaced his cup on the table and was looking straight at him, waiting to hear what he had to say. He was extremely interested.

"Pocahontas is Powhatan's most coveted daughter is she not?" Argall was taking pleasure in eking out his proposal.

Dale nodded. "Get on with it Argall" Dale spluttered.

"On my last trip up the Potomac, I heard rumours that Pocahontas was no longer with her father, but that she had moved with her husband and new baby to live somewhere up the Potomac. I think she is probably hiding. I know the tribes in that part of the world very well." He sat back in his chair, watching Dale's response with relish, eking out his idea, playing with the obviously intrigued, Dale.

"So, what is your intention then Argall, get on with it" Dale's face showed irritation at being made to wait.

"To sail up the Potomac again, to do more trade, obviously... but also to keep my ear to the ground to find out exactly where Pocahontas is."

"Who cares?" said Dale dismissively, picking up his wine again and shrugging his shoulders.

"Powhatan cares" said Argall, eyebrows raised, looking condescendingly at Dale. "If we were able to find out where she is and kidnap her, we would have a precious bargaining lever, wouldn't we?" He looked at Dale, pleased that now he was the one with the power and the ideas, he was the superior one.

Argall smiled, winked, and raised his cup of wine. He could see that Dale was pensive. He did not jump at the plan - no, he did not want to appear too eager, and too pleased with someone else's idea. Dale was not a man to give credit where credit was due. He preferred to take it himself. Nevertheless, Argall could see that Dale's mouth was turning into a slow and calculated smile as he thought the idea through. There was no way that he could dismiss this - it was too big an opportunity.

Dale raised his cup to touch Argall's, spilling the wine with the force of the toast, and bursting into uncontrollable raucous laughter. "You rascal Argall - what are you waiting for?"

SANCTUARY DISTURBED: 1612

P ocahontas missed her tribe, having escaped on that dark night when
Kocoum had been so sure that she was going to be kidnapped. She
thought of her friends there. She had treasured her time with her
family and their love and help with her new baby. However, she understood
why Kocoum had brought her up the Potomac to his brother's tribe, as it
was so far away from her village, making it difficult for her to be found by
enemies. There had been Prophesies from the Quiakros that the Longcoats,
determined to overpower Powhatan at any cost, might kidnap the Chief's
treasured daughter. She knew in her heart that they must be right, she
had seen it in her dreams. Kocoum had been frantic to protect her and
Ko-kee. However, she knew that no matter where she was, she was not
going to escape the Longcoats. She might as well have walked to Jamestown
and given herself up - that way she might have saved any confrontations.
But Kocoum would not allow that. He guarded her day and night and had
warriors patrolling along the river to be alert for any strangers heading
towards the village. So far there had been no sign of anything suspicious,

but it was only a matter of time. She was going to try and enjoy as much time with her little family as she could before the inevitable happened.

Japasaw, Kocoum's brother, and Winanuske Japasaw's wife, had been very nice to her since her arrival, but it was not the same as being with her own family. She missed Matachanna's fussing around her and Ko-kee, although, she had to admit, there had not been a moment in the day when Ko-kee was not being held or fed or played with. The young girls of the tribe had been enchanted by his large brown eyes and smiling face as he tried to walk and talk.

She looked down at him. He was almost a year old now and was starting to try to toddle around. She had made him a pair of soft skin moccasins - tiny little shoes to protect his small soft feet from the stony ground. She smiled. How beautiful every part of his body was - but especially his little feet and toes. He had chubby brown thighs and a round belly with a round button in the middle. How perfect he was, she sighed. What was going to happen to him? What was going to happen to the love of her life, Kocoum, when the Longcoats came?

She looked across at Kocoum, the man she would always love. His brown eyes took on a softness that was there only for her and his son. He was smiling with pride as he held Little Ko-kee's small hand. He suddenly took the baby by his torso, throwing him up in the air. There was a look of panic on the little boy's face for a second as he flew through the air, before he shrieked with pure delight. Landing safely on his feet, Ko-kee looked expectantly at his father with a cheeky smile. "More, dada... The tiny mite giggled and made to toddle away. Once again Kocoum caught him and grabbing his little body, threw him even higher. "There you go, my little man" he said, his eyes sparkling.

He looked over at Pocahontas and gave her a wink and the biggest most beautiful smile. "We've done well, you and I," he said. They were a picture of pure joy - her two boys. Her two loves. Her heart was bursting. She took in every detail of the picture before her, not knowing how long it would be before she would be taken.

She held out a little fur toy for Ko-Kee. When he saw it, he grinned from ear to ear. Letting go of his father's hand, he ventured into unknown territory across the space between his mother and his father. "Whoops"! Pocahontas laughed as his little legs wobbled and he fell on his padded bottom, looking startled. "Whoops" he said and laughed, looking around to make sure that his mother and father were watching his efforts.

"Come on, Ko-kee, my little Biibiins." Pocahontas whispered the special name she had for him, reaching out to him. Up the little baby got, putting his chubby hands on the ground, lifting up his bottom and heaving himself up with a great deal of effort, never taking his eyes from hers. She watched as he very carefully lifted each foot and placed it on the ground, step by wobbly step until eventually he threw himself into her arms laughing and gurgling with baby delight. "Djoodjoo, Djoodjoo…" he gurgled his name for her.

She felt his little round plump body shaking with mirth and held on to him tightly as if to cement the feeling of his softness into her mind forever. Each joyful moment had to be savoured. He was so precious, and so innocent. He had never known cruelty or hardship - and she prayed to the Manito Aki that he never would. She knew that if Kocoum had anything to do with it, he would be safe forever. Kocoum would put his life before his son's. But she was not sure that Kocoum would be around to protect their son. He was as vulnerable as she was, despite his strength. There were forces greater than love at large. She did not like to close her eyes at night for fear that she would see too much of the future. She had already seen far too much. She shivered.

If only John Smith were alive - she knew her family would have been safe. But he was long dead.

She looked at Kocoum. Her strong and proud warrior husband. Whenever she looked at him, he stirred her. His dusky skin was gleaming, and his torso, devoid of hair in the Powhatan tradition, showed strong rippling muscles, his eyes an iron will. The other side to him - his softness and gentleness was a rare gift bestowed on very few and she treasured every second with him. Her stomach did a somersault. How long could she hold on to them? How much longer before the big change came?

Waki whimpered. "What is it Waki?" Pocahontas looked towards the trees. Waki's white head was tilted to one side as if looking at something strange in the undergrowth. Kocoum jumped up, picked up the baby, thrusting him into her arms.

"Quick take Ko-kee inside. I will see what Waki is so worried about." His eyebrows were furrowed, and he grabbed his bow and arrow, at the ready to defend them. "Quick, Pocahontas" he shouted.

She turned and ran as fast as she could towards their hut. The stones hurt her feet as she ran, but she knew that any moment, could be her last moment of freedom and she ignored the pain. She dived into the hut, clutching her little baby.

"There, there, Biibiins - Djoodjoo is here." She ran her hands over the baby's silky dark head, and pushed his face into her chest, feeling his heart beating against hers. She waited. Please Manito Aki, please don't make it today. She whispered. She kissed the baby's head and hugged him in tighter to her.

She waited in the silence. Outside she could hear the rain starting to fall. Large drops beating on the roof of the hut. She could smell the damp rain-filled air as it seeped through the sides of the Yehakin. Drip, drip, drip,... went the rain. But where was Kocoum? She could hardly breathe with worry. Ko-kee wriggled and pulled away, wanting to find his father. She pulled him back towards her, and he started to whimper seeing the tragic look on her face. She knew that he could feel the vibrations of her emotions as she looked at him, she had tried to hide them, but it was impossible.

The thunder crashed and the lightning flashed, lighting up the inside of the Yehakin for several seconds. Pocahontas felt so alone, even Waki was not there. Her world was going to change, and maybe this was the start of it.

She heard people coming at speed towards the door of the Yehakin and held on tightly to Ko-kee shielding him from whoever was going to burst through. "Hush little Biibiins, Djoodjoo is here." She buried her head in his silky dark hair and held her breath, bracing herself for what was to come.

They stood before her - two very wet drowned rats of men, looking cold and pathetic. Two men that she cared about. She relaxed, let Ko-kee get off her knee, and she ran towards Kocoum, throwing herself against his wet body, feeling droplets of water fall onto her neck from his long dark hair. She burst into tears, her body trembling, relief flooding through her as his arms wrapped around her. She felt small, helpless, and safe. She stood for several minutes, just enjoying the feeling of safety, the feeling of Kocoum's body against hers once more. Then she pulled back to look at the man standing alongside Kocoum.

"So, what are you doing here Thomas Savage? You gave us quite a fright." She walked over to him, and hugged him, noting how he had filled out since she last saw him. She looked him up and down. He had the same white blonde hair and blue eyes, and he still smiled at her as if she were the most beautiful girl in the world. His eyes were sad though, and although she could tell that he was happy to see her, his face was ravaged with worry. Something must have happened at Jamestown, something that would impact upon her. She knew that he would never let her down. He was her friend forever, even though they were on different sides of this stupid war between the Powhatan and the Longcoats.

"You have come many miles, my friend" she said as she touched his cheek and looked into his eyes. On foot it must have taken him a long time to get to here, across some very difficult terrain.

"I have been traveling for days Pocahontas. I had to see you. You are in danger, and I wanted you to have as much warning as I could give you." He looked deeply into her eyes, and glanced over at Kocoum who was standing guard by the door. Ko-kee wandered over and looked at Thomas with wonder.

"Hello little man" Thomas said. "Come and sit on my knee." He picked up Ko-kee, who smiled at the stranger, sensing that he was a friend. "I see you have more to protect than just yourself now." He glanced at them both, worry on his face.

134

He continued. "We have some very ambitious leaders at Jamestown now Pocahontas. Thomas Dale and Thomas Gates have made sweeping changes to the way things are done. To their credit, the settlement is run with precision, and the lazy ways of the past have been stamped out. The Colonists are now planting and building and working very hard to make a success of it. Thomas Dale, rules with fear though. Dale is ambitious - and it seems that one of his barriers to success is the constant aggression between your people and ours. He wants it to stop at any cost.

He has on his staff a Naval Captain called Argall, who is well respected and very competent. He turns his hand to anything and he is usually successful. The other day, I was serving them both wine, and as I left the room I heard Samuel Argall mention your name. Of course, I was very curious, so I listened at the door. It seems that Argall has a very good relationship with your brother Japasaw, Kocoum. He said that he had done lots of trade with him, and that they were on exceptionally good terms." He took a deep breath. "Argall has been traveling up and down the Chesapeake doing as much trade as he can. He has also been trying to find out where you are. He wants to capture you and use you to bargain the release of English prisoners and guns. He heard from a scout that you may be up here."

Pocahontas looked at Kocoum. She knew that this news was going to come sooner or later. It had taken some while though. At least she had been able to enjoy some time with her family.

"How long have I got Thomas?" she whispered.

"I am not sure Pocahontas, but Argall will be setting out soon, so I don't think it will be long. They see you as a precious bargaining chip to broker peace with your father."

"Well, peace is what I have always wanted" she said.

"I would not trust Thomas Dale, or Samuel Argall for that matter. Nothing will be as simple as just taking you and returning you so that everyone can live happily ever after. Thomas Dale cannot do anything without a touch of manipulation and cruelty." He shook his head, remembering the glint in Dale's eyes when he watched the men at the gallows struggling for their last breath. There was definitely something wrong with the man. He was a sadist. Thomas Savage could not bear to think of his beloved little Pocahontas under the power of such a man. "You must hide, Pocahontas. You must leave as soon as you possibly can. Leave your baby with the tribe, he will be well looked after - but go with Kocoum and live in the woods where no one will find you." He was leaning towards her, his face gaunt.

Pocahontas glanced up at Kocoum. What could she do? She knew that they would find her wherever she went. The thought of leaving Kocoum and Ko-kee broke her heart, and she felt a tear slide down her face. She glanced over at Ko-kee, who was playing happily with Waki in the corner. Such an innocent darling. Whatever happened, she knew that Japasaw and Winanuske would look after him. Hopefully the women from her own tribe would eventually come and get him. Her heart sank at the thought.

Kocoum, the love of her life. He would be in danger if she ran - she knew he would, because he would fight to protect her, and she knew that he could not win against their guns and their weapons. If she went willingly, there was a chance that they would leave Kocoum alone and he could be there for Ko-kee until she returned.

Maybe this was also her chance to broker a peace, and to carry out her duties as a Beloved Woman, whilst also saving her family. Her father had always wanted her to do her duty, and he had always told her that her name would be remembered for generations. Hiding away in the woods was not going to make that happen. She had hidden away from her duty for too long. She had to save her people. She and Kocoum had run away once but they could not spend their lives running.

She had to make it easy for them to find her - to take her and to bargain with her father. Thomas Savage and Kocoum would never understand. But she knew, she had a duty to do.

She looked at Thomas and Kocoum. "I know you are right. They *will* come to get me, and I thank you with all my heart Thomas, for risking your life to warn me. I cannot leave though. They will find me, and I must make sure that no one else is in danger by going peacefully. My duty is to the tribe and to the people that I love - the philosophy of my father and the Manito Aki." She pulled Kocoum and Thomas towards her, and the three of them in a circle hugged, each one with their own thoughts about the future.

Pocahontas glanced away from the embrace of the two men and saw Badger lurking in the corner. The look in his eyes told her all she needed to know.

UP THE POTOMAC: 1613

Captain Samuel Argall watched as the landmarks passed him by. He had been up this river many times trading for corn, and his relationship with Japasaw was one of friendship despite their differences. They had often sat down together around the fire, smoking the fragrant Apook and enjoying the juicy venison that the squaws so readily offered him. He always looked forward to seeing Japasaw, but this time, his visit was far more important. One could really call it 'State Duty', he laughed to himself. If Pocahontas were in or near Japasaw's village, he would find her. He was the only one that could carry this out. He was brimming with satisfaction knowing that Thomas Dale would be indebted to him.

He had the edge of surprise, and it was all going to be done without aggression and with polite friendliness. That was Argall's way, unlike the dislikeable Dale. He just had to find the Savage bitch.

They had sailed up Chesapeake Bay and were now navigating the winding Potomac. The village was a few miles up the river. He stood, tapping his toe against the deck, sighing with anticipation. Yes, he thought to himself, he was a genius. It had taken a while for people to realise it, but this was going to prove it to everyone.

It was Springtime and the leaves were starting to sprout on the trees. The pine evergreens standing tall and the smell of the pine enriched earthy undergrowth mingled with the salt water. It was damp and fertile land. The sounds of the birds and the water as it splashed along the side of the boat ploughing through the water breaking the mirror-like appearance as the water shattered into thousands of pieces, lulled him into a momentary sense of peacefulness. This land was undoubtedly, very beautiful.

As they neared a bend in the river, Argall thought it would be best to drop anchor and go on foot, exploring land he had never visited before. Maybe he could find some new resources. Maybe he could meet some passing tribesmen from the area that might be able to help him find Pocahontas.

They dropped anchor and rowed the smaller boats to the shore. The land was boggy and forested.

They walked for several hours through the trees, the cushion of pine needles making a fragrant carpet. Suddenly, Argall saw a clearing. The land started to open out to grassland. He heard a strange grunting sound.

"Stop." He signalled with his hand. "There is something up ahead."

"I will go ahead" he whispered.

Argall moved slowly through the trees, peering to see what was there. In front of him were a herd of large brown beasts, larger than Argall had ever seen before. The bigger of the beasts were at least as tall as a man with the large hump behind its head. It was solid and heavy like a large bull. The herd was grazing and moving lethargically, every now and again lifting their heads and looking around making grunting, sneezing, and snoring sounds. They had large woolly shoulders and huge black horns.

Argall turned around and signalled to his men to move forwards slowly.

"This looks like supper" whispered Argall, smiling.

As he stood there, a small calf with reddish yellow fur, having heard commotion in the trees started running towards him, with the curiousness of youth. Argall saw the calf running towards him and focussing on it, he did not see the mother charging from the side, grunting and puffing coming straight at him, until a second later.

When he did catch sight of it, Argall was frozen to the spot with fear. His eyes wide, it seemed like eternity before he heard the shot from one of his men, as the mother plunged to the ground, inches from him, dust flying. She was not dead, her eyes rolling, grunting and puffing she attempted to get off the ground, her legs weak, she kept trying, staggering clumsily until another bullet through her head finally caused her to lose her fight for life and crash heavily to the ground.

The calf ran towards the dead mother, nudging her with its nose, making an awful noise full of pain, trying to wake her up. The scene was tragic.

Argall turned to his men.

"Thank God" he sighed. "I was almost finished."

One of the men walked over to the corpse and raising his gun, shot the little red calf straight through the head. It fell heavily on the ground beside it's mother. The rest of the herd was long gone.

"As I said" laughed Argall. "Supper."

———————————

They sat around the fire, watching as the calf sizzled and spat over the heat. Argall was shaking his head staring into the flames, holding his arms out over the fire and rubbing his hands together. It was not warm in March, and the fire and the dripping meat were a comfort to them all.

He looked around at his companions who were all enjoying the warmth of the fire. "Well boys, you could have been having dinner without me… that was a very close call. Just a reminder that we must stay alert and look out for one another. We will have to take turns at night watch - we don't know who or what might be in the vicinity." In the night air his breath was like a cloud as he spoke.

As the meat grew crispy and tender, it was taken off the fire and large lumps were handed around to each of the hungry men who drooled and slobbered as they sucked up the delicious juices. Replete, they sat back burping and laughing, staring into the fire which was the only source of light that they had.

As Argall looked around the trees, an owl came swooping down, hungry, chasing a small rodent that scurried into the undergrowth. The large bird screeched as it lunged "Whocooksforyou...whocooksforyou..." They all jumped at the sound, looking around, conscious that there could be many dangers hidden in the pitch-black depths. They could only see to the extent of the firelight as it danced around the trees.

Suddenly Argall heard more movement - he sensed that there was something behind him. He turned and caught a glimpse of something through the deep black depths of the forest. It could have been a nocturnal animal, but he was on high alert. His men were laughing and talking and did not notice. "Shhhhhh... " he whispered. They all stopped talking and listened. There was nothing but the owl continuing to hunt for rodents and their own breath coming in white clouds as it hit the cold air. "I am sure I heard something" whispered Argall. "Everyone - get your weapons to the ready."

The men all reached for their guns, alert and watchful, silently getting up from where they were sitting, each moving towards the darkness, their bodies half crouching, ready to spring or shoot.

They waited. Nothing happened. They waited. Nothing happened. They breathed the silent cold air.

"We will have to be watchful, lads" said Argall. "But whoever and whatever it was, clearly is not intent on attacking us tonight. "I will take first watch with Robert Small" he said. "Everyone else tuck down and try and get some sleep as we have a hard day tomorrow."

Everyone started moving towards the fire. Sparks flew and the flames rose in the air as more wood was thrown on the burning crackling embers. They gathered the animal skin blankets around them and settled down on the hard earth for an uneasy sleep, grunting and groaning as they tried to get comfortable, which was an impossibility.

Argall and Small, took positions on opposite sides of the group, alert, watching the dark nothingness of the forest for movement. Several hours passed.

Suddenly they were surrounded.

Before Argall and Small had time to raise their guns, they were faced with twenty Warriors all with raised spears. They were frozen to the spot, knowing that there was nothing that they could do in the face of such numbers. Argall's men jumped up from a hazy semi sleep and looked bleary eyed at the frightening scene before them, confusion on their faces, looking to Argall for instructions."

Argall then noticed a white face amongst them.

"God's Wounds, it is Henry Spelman, as I live and breathe." He spluttered with surprise and walked towards the young man thrusting his hand out in welcome. Patting him on the back roughly. "What are you doing here?" His eyebrows were raised, and relief on his face, realising the invaders were friends.

Argall had known Spelman for several years, as he had been in the Colony since 1609, having been given to Powhatan as an interpreter like Thomas Savage. He had a good understanding of the Algonquin language, and had been a valuable asset to both sides for many years. At only nineteen, he was a plucky lad, who had, from an early age had to fend for himself, managing to find a place for himself within the Powhatan tribe, coming to prefer the native way of life to his own.

Spelman grinned. He had dark hair and green eyes, and from a distance could have been mistaken for a native. "Argall…I am so glad it was you… we have come from Japasaw up at Potomac, where I am now living. We heard there were some bison in the area. Just wanted to check it out when we heard a shot. Thought you might be hostiles."

"Well, we *are* hostiles - depending on who is approaching" Argall laughed. "But we are very glad to see *you*. We have an excess of meat as we had to kill two beasts earlier. Come and sit by the fire, and we will cook some more for you." Argall indicated to the fire. "They're Bison, are they? Never seen them before. The rest of the herd vanished back into the trees. You might be able to pick up the trail tomorrow when the light comes again. So… you are now living with Japasaw… "

"Yes, I *was* living with Powhatan, but when things turned bad with the English, I didn't want to stay anymore. It didn't seem safe. Thomas Savage stayed on with Powhatan - but I think he went back to Jamestown not long ago. Japasaw is an honourable man, and I like him. His wives are a nightmare though" Spelman sighed "they can't get it out of their heads that I am not a servant to be ordered around…but all in all, it's ok." He shrugged his shoulders.

"Talking of women" Argall took his chance. "I hear that Pocahontas is staying with Japasaw. What is she like? Is she still the little mischievous vixen that used to do handstands naked with the lads at Jamestown?" He winked.

"Changed days, I'm afraid Argall." Spelman laughed. "She is married with a little baby now. I often sit and talk with her - she does make me laugh though. She's one of the most intelligent women I have ever met. I think every man that meets her falls in love with her still. She's obsessed with Kocoum, her husband though sadly. Lucky devil."

"Sounds like you are one of the men in love with her lad!" said Argall.

"She's way beyond my reach. I am content just to be her friend." His eyes conveyed a deeper story.

"So, is she actually staying with Japasaw?" asked Argall, his voice starting to convey the urgency that he was feeling. He had guessed correctly.

"Not far from the main village - within walking distance" said Spelman. "Why do you ask?"

Having skinned the animals and banked up the fire with more wood, they all sat around for the rest of the night eating and laughing. Neither Argall nor any of his men had tasted Bison before, but the meat was delicious. It was reminiscent of the best beef, and there was too much to finish it all. Argall was impatient to get back to the ship so that he could visit Japasaw, so they bid farewell to Spelman leaving him with the rest of the meat, and headed to the ship at a fast pace to start their important mission. This was going to be easier than he thought.

After travelling up the river for several hours, they rounded the bend and he saw the village of Potomac in the distance, warriors were placed all along the banks. That is strange, Argall thought. They had never been security conscious at this village. Well, no matter, as soon as they saw that it was him, there would be no problems.

He stood on the bow, watching as the village drew closer, feeling the breeze on his face as they drew near. "Land ho" he shouted to his men. All the activity for landing commenced, men running backwards and forwards, shouting at each other, ready to steady the boat for a gentle mooring against the side of the riverbank.

Indians were poised with spears and arrows. They always had to keep a watchful eye. It would all change when Chief Japasaw appeared. He would let them know that they were friendly.

Sure enough he saw the flamboyant figure of Chief Japasaw walking down to greet him. He waved his hand, and Japasaw waved back at him smiling. A very promising start.

As he jumped onto the riverbank and his men tied the boat up, he rushed over to Japasaw smiling. He bowed his head in greeting and held out his hand. Japasaw offered his hand in return and they smiled at one another. Argall had a decent spattering of Algonquin, so he could converse with Japasaw adequately, although he thought on reflexion he could have done with the help of Thomas Savage, but for some reason Thomas was nowhere to be found when they had set off upriver.

"Welcome, my friend." The Indian chief smiled at Argall and waved to him to join him in the village. "Come and eat and drink with us. We can talk trade, and you can tell me all about what you have been doing with yourself." Japasaw was an amiable fellow, indeed, thought Argall.

As they entered the warm Yehakin with the fire burning in the centre, giving off a welcoming glow, Japasaw gestured to Argall to make himself comfortable on a seat covered with soft brown and white skins. Argall settled himself, looking around.

"May we speak in private?" he said to the Japasaw.

Japasaw looked surprised. "We have never had to have privacy before Samuel." He looked the other man up and down; Argall could see that suspicion was starting to creep into the other man's voice.

"No, it has never been necessary before. But for these negotiations, I need to speak to you alone. I cannot do so if not." He stared at the Chief, a fixed smile conflicting with the hard glint in his eyes.

Japasaw hesitated, looking at his warriors who were strategically placed around the Yehakin. "Well, as we are friends Argall... but I need to have my guards close at hand outside the door.

"Of course, my friend." Argall smiled, shrugging his shoulders casually.

When Japasaw's warriors had disappeared, the two men sat in silence for a few minutes.

Argall fixed his gaze on Japasaw, leaning towards him. "Japasaw, I must tell you that if I do not return to my ship, my men have strict instruction to kill all your warriors, rape all your women and burn all your houses."

Japasaw's mouth fell open, eyes wide at the totally unexpected statement. "My friend, what are you saying. There is no need for that. We would never harm you after so many years of friendship." His brows were furrowed, and the sweat started to appear on his forehead.

Ah, I have his attention now, thought Argall. He had a pang of guilt at his betrayal of a trusting friend, but he shoved that to the back of his mind. He had a job to do, and the job of a soldier was sometimes not easy. It would be more than worth it in the end.

"I understand that you are harbouring Pocahontas, the daughter of The Great Powhatan." he said .

"I cannot deny that she is staying temporarily with us as she is the wife of my brother, Kocoum." Japasaw's eyebrows were raised. He was obviously not expecting this.

"It is true that you and I want peace between our peoples, is it not?"

"Yes, of course that is true, Samuel. On that we are one." Argall lent towards the Chief rubbing his hands together, fidgeting with anxiety.

"Pocahontas is the answer." Argall said.

The Chief looked at him frowning. "I do not understand, Samuel" he said.

"If you give me Pocahontas, I can use her as ransom to get all our hostages back from Powhatan, and also to get more corn. Our commander will be very happy and the hostilities between our peoples will finally end. There will no longer be any need for these pointless acts of reprisal."

"But Samuel, I cannot do that, it is impossible. She is my beloved sister in law. In any case, I can give you as much corn as you need without such dire measures."

Argall sat up straight. His face took on a murderous look and his speech was low and menacing. "I *need* to have Pocahontas. If you do not give me Pocahontas, there will be no one left in your tribe by this evening. All will be dead, including yourself. I will then make it my mission to eradicate as many other tribes as I can on the way back to Jamestown, and I will take Pocahontas by force anyway. Is that the way to peace Japasaw? Is it?"

The Chief put his head in his hands. "But you were my trusted friend…" he murmured.

"It is because I am your trusted friend, that I am giving you this opportunity for all of us to achieve peace without any bloodshed." Argall said, his voice friendlier but measured. He did not want trouble. As he did not want to completely alienate Japasaw, he smiled at him, but the Chief did not return the gesture. His face was like thunder at the deception, and he got up and moved towards the door. "I cannot take any more of this" he said.

Argall jumped up. "Do not even think of alerting your warriors, my men are prepared with guns and cannons to kill everyone if they think there looks like trouble."

The Indian Chief stopped in his tracks. "I do not want one drop of blood shed." He shouted, glaring at Samuel Argall. He dragged himself back and sat down, staring. "You are a wicked man, Samuel. I do not trust easily, and it just goes to show that no Longcoat can be trusted. How do you expect me to get Pocahontas to go on your boat? I can hardly force her - the daughter of the Great Powhatan." He shook his head, disbelief etched on his face. "There were rumours of her kidnapping over a year ago, that is why Kocoum brought her here, to ensure her safety. He is very vigilant about her safety. He will not let you near her without a fight."

Argall leant towards the Chief and put his fingers together, deep in thought. "I take your point Japasaw. But I think that is really your problem. I can easily get my guns and my men and wrench her from the arms of her husband and baby, killing many of your warriors in the process. Or, you can come up with a plan to get her aboard my ship peacefully. I am offering you choices here. I *will* have Pocahontas, one way or the other. You decide." He smiled and shrugged his shoulders. "I am not going to hurt the girl, for goodness sake. All I am going to do is take her for a few days, and offer her back to Powhatan in exchange for our men that he has as hostages. Because she is so precious to Powhatan, he is bound to release our men very quickly, and we can have Pocahontas back with her beloved Kocoum in under a week. There will be no bloodshed, we will get our men back and relations between us can get back on a more friendly footing. I can really see no problem. I am not a violent man. You can trust me."

Japasaw looked into the fire with his eyes tightly shut.

COPPER KETTLE: 22 April, 1613

J apasaw and his wife Winanuske stood watching the large ship. They both looked splendid in their full ceremonial dress. Winanuske smiled as she watched the men washing down the decks and cleaning the wood. In her mind, this was a job for women. How fascinating that Longcoat men performed these tasks. "She is a very big ship" she said to her husband. He grunted in response.

"Come aboard, my Lady" shouted Argall smiling. He was ready either to set sail with Pocahontas peacefully, or to direct his men to raise the guns and take her by force, but his face did not portray the schemes that lay behind his twinkling eyes.

"Should I go?" she said to her husband. "I would really like to see what it is like on an English ship. He is one of your trusted friends, so it should be safe."

He looked down at her. His heart was sick. He didn't want his wife to go onboard, but Argall had promised that he would not harm her if she did. He was going to have to willingly allow Argall to take Pocahontas.

She was such a lovely girl, her husband, a worthy warrior, and their little boy just starting out in life. He was going to actively hand her over to the enemy. It was her life for the lives of hundreds in his tribe that would be killed if he did not comply. He really had no choice. He just hoped that Powhatan could meet the demands and get his daughter back as soon as possible. He knew Powhatan would be furious with him for handing over Pocahontas so easily - but he was a warrior and he would be no stranger to such a dilemma. Chiefs must protect the lives of their people. One sacrifice for the saviour of so many. It had to be done. If Powhatan gave in to the demands, Pocahontas would be returned unharmed - Argall had promised. What harm could there be? He looked down at his dainty little wife - she wanted to go on the ship, he knew she would. She was a woman with boundless curiosity. He knew he had to carry out the plan and entrust her to the care of Argyll - the alternative was too dreadful to think about.

He nodded his head slowly. "You must take someone with you" he said.

She looked up at him. She saw him deep in thought, his eyes staring as if looking for something in the far distance. In his blank face she detected hidden fear, but she dismissed the thought as she was so excited at the prospect of boarding this magnificent vessel. Japasaw would never let her safety be put in jeopardy after all.

"Who should go with me?"

She had walked right into his trap. Sadly, he knew that she would, and he hated himself for what he was doing. What could he do? This was like a large boulder that had been pushed down a hill and was rolling uncontrollably forward. There was no stopping it, and he had been forced to push the boulder. It was he who would be to blame if anything was destroyed because of it. He hung his head in shame.

Pocahontas huddled in the corner of the Yehakin cuddling Ko-kee and Kocoum. She knew what was coming. She had 'Seen' it. Today she was

149

going to have to leave the safety of the life that she had known for the past year and head into the unknown, she just needed a few more moments with her boys.

She heard a scuffle outside and a knock on the door. "Come in," she shouted.

Winanuske stood before her looking excited. "Pocahontas... would you like to come with me to explore the Longcoats' ship? They have invited me, and Japasaw would like you to come with me as chaperone" she said breathless with excitement.

Pocahontas was unmoved. She knew that this was a ploy, but poor Winanuske had no idea. "Hurry Pocahontas, they are all waiting for us - they have a meal prepared in our honour." She looked so innocent and happy, Pocahontas thought.

Kocoum stood up in front of Pocahontas and looked at Winanuske. "Thank you for the offer, but Pocahontas wants to stay with her baby, she does not want to go on the ship of the Longcoats." His mouth was stern, and his eyes staring with aggression. Winanuske pulled back. "You don't understand Kocoum. She will be in no danger. Japasaw has said that his friend Argall will take good care of us and we will be back by this evening. Don't you trust your own brother?"

"I know the ways of the Longcoats - and they are never to be trusted." Kocoum was raising his voice now, fear seeping into his eyes.

Pocahontas stood up, picking up Ko-kee and walking over to Kocoum, passing the baby tenderly to her young husband.

"We have talked about this day Kocoum. You know that I must go, I have no choice. It is my duty to my people." She looked at him from under long sweeping eyelashes, her eyes pleading with him.

"You know that you may never return to us?" he said, his face a mask of pain.

"No, I will be back soon - probably by this evening as Winanuske says" she tried to smile. Her eyes were watering. She was trying to convince herself as much as Kocoum. She lingered, looking around her, looking at her lovely baby and her handsome husband. Trying to hold on to the image, trying to make the time with them last longer.

"I don't understand" said Winanuske. "We are only going for a short visit, don't make it sound so tragic…"

"You go, Winanuske" said Pocahontas. "I just need a few minutes to say goodbye and I will follow you." Winanuske nodded, turned, and walked out shaking her head.

Pocahontas drew closer to Kocoum. "Please Kocoum. Do not try and stop me, and do not try to come after me. I have seen in my Dreams that today is the day. Thomas warned us of Argall, and until now we have not known how he would take me. Now it is clear.

I don't want you to be hurt. You must stay here and look after Ko-kee, I am sure that I will be fine, but I cannot risk your being hurt. Please tell me you will stay. Please tell me that you won't try and stop me. You must promise me this" she said, eyes begging, glistening rivulets of tears streaming silently down her face.

Kocoum said nothing. He stooped, wiped her tears away and kissed her wet mouth deeply and lovingly. "I will always love you Pocahontas. Please come back to me, no matter what."

She held him tightly. "I am yours for eternity. I promise that I will come back to you."

Kocoum and I walk hand in hand… but the world is covered with blood… as my heart is pulled from my body. Kocoum … he is fading further and further away 'til I am all alone, my tears splashing on the shiny copper kettle. My darkness begins.

It had all been so civilized, Pocahontas thought with a sinking heart. They had seemed so kind, showing them around the ship, giving them lovely food to eat and talking to them with the greatest of respect. What a clever deception. Even now, she wasn't sure whose deception it had actually been. Japasaw had obviously been in on it, and Captain Samuel Argall had been the instigator of the plan. He looked very smug and pleased with himself now.

Here she was - sailing down the river with Longcoats. To be fair, she knew it was going to turn out like this, but she did not realise how easy it would be for them. Japasaw had made it that much easier. She wondered if Kocoum knew the depths of deceit that his brother had gone to.

At first, she had thought that Japasaw was innocent in the ploy, but as Winanuske started to leave the ship, the soldiers suddenly pulled Pocahontas back, barring her exit. She had seen Captain Argall try to give Winanuske the biggest and brightest copper kettle that she had ever seen. Winanuske had looked startled and angry, and at first refused the kettle, reaching out to her friend, refusing to leave without her. But Japasaw with a stern face, signalled to his wife to leave. Her face confused, she accepted the copper kettle and disembarked from the ship, looking behind her with sorrow, every step heavy with the pain of leaving her friend.

Was a copper kettle really payment to Japasaw for luring her to her captivity? Is that all I am worth to them - a copper kettle? She shook her head. No - it must have been more complicated than that. She thought back to Japasaw. He did not look triumphant. He did not look pleased. His face had held agony. She had never seen him look so wretched. Winanuske certainly had been innocent as she ran crying hysterically to her husband beating his chest with anger, pleading with him to rescue Pocahontas. He stood mute, rigidly holding his emotions in check.

There had been two gunshots after Winanuske had left the ship. Pocahontas froze with fear. She was terrified that there would be violence and that her family would be murdered. She watched Japasaw on the riverbank turning and running to see what was happening, he had the same thought as she did. Who had died with the two shots? She started to shake.

the world is covered with blood...I feel a sharp pain in my heart as Kocoum fades into the trees... he is going further and further...I am all alone.

She knew. Her legs went from under her, she collapsed. Her world had ended, the love of her life had gone - she had *"Seen"* it... new images came fast and furious... no.... no...

He watched from the trees as the Longcoats handed over the copper kettle - he ran, his bow at the ready, his face contorted with pain shouting...Ko-kee stood with the Squaws on the side-lines and watched as the fire-stick blew a massive crimson hole in his father's chest where his heart had been. He saw his father lying on the ground twitching and he did not understand. Ko-kee ran screaming as fast as his little legs would carry him and threw himself on his father's body. He reached up and tried to look into his father's eyes - but Kocoum was gone. Ko-kee lay over Kocoum's body, covered with blood until one of the squaws tried to remove him. He kicked and screamed, legs and arms thrashing in the air.

Pocahontas came to and wailed with pure agony, a blood curdling sound that carried for miles, having seen in her mind the death of her beloved. She knew that her vision was true and the pain was so intense that she vomited, trying to block it out. In a haze of utter torment, she watched the last of the soldiers boarding the ship, releasing the ropes that tied the ship to the shore. She screamed and kicked and had to be physically restrained. Her arms flailing and tears cascading down her face, she started to feel the movement of the ship as it pulled away and fought like a wild bear, until exhausted. Limp with exhaustion and distress, she watched the village getting smaller and smaller, the puffs of smoke from the burning fires disappearing until she could see the village no more. Through her tears, she saw the small white figure of Waki and the black figure of Kitchi standing on the riverbank, looking into the distance, trying to see where she had gone.

Badger crouched next to her, but she wanted to die.

"Captain Argall, Captain Argall - there are two Indian warriors on the bank gesturing us stop. They have a white flag Sir. Maybe they have come from Powhatan." The first officer was pointing to the shore where two painted Indians stood.

Argall looked across. He had not given Powhatan much time to respond to his message before setting off for Jamestown. A purposeful move designed to provoke. It would be interesting to find out what the old man was thinking. "Drop Anchor" he shouted. "Lower the skiff."

Argall was sweating as he was rowed to the riverbank. This whole episode could be a massive feather in his cap - something that could get him the recognition he deserved, if only he handled it properly.

As they landed, the two Powhatans walked towards them, white flag flying. They nodded in acknowledgment of Argall and signalled to him to sit with them.

Argall was tense and turned towards his men. "Keep your guns pointed at all times. We must assume that this is some kind of trick. They may have many warriors behind the hill, so keep your eyes peeled and your guns at alert."

He walked over to the Indians and sat down with them. They passed him a pipe of tobacco as a gesture of peace. He took it, and as the fragrant smoke entered his lungs, he started to relax. So far, it looked as if this was a genuine offer of negotiation.

"Captain Argall, our paramount Chief Powhatan sends you his deepest wishes that we may come to an amicable arrangement about his daughter Pocahontas. He desires strong friendship and peace - it has always been his hope. He apologises for the indiscretion of some of his men, and the fact that on occasion they may have behaved badly, stealing, and capturing Longcoat men. These acts were not sanctioned by the Great Powhatan. He wishes to make amends in whatever way that he can, by returning your men and tools and giving you much corn.

In return he hopes that you will treat his daughter with great respect, returning her unharmed to him as soon as possible. He sincerely hopes that from this incident greater peace will come between our peoples, and that we can start anew, living alongside one another as equals." The warriors bowed their heads and placed their hands in prayer position. "Wahunsenacwh, The Great Powhatan now awaits you at Werowocomoco, where the exchange can take place. He also invites you to a feast and celebration to cement our relationship."

Argall puffed on the pipe; his face blank as he thought about the way Powhatan was dealing with the situation.

He looked at the two men, returning the pipe and smiling. "I would like you to thank Wahunsenacwh, The Great Powhatan for his kind invitation, and tell him that we would be delighted to accept his terms. We will be heading towards Werowocomoco directly to carry out the exchange." He got up and walked towards the skiff.

Arriving back on board his ship Argall shouted the command to restart the journey.

"Set sail for Jamestown!" He smiled to himself, he wasn't going to make it that easy.

LEAVING HOME

He entered the gun cabin where she was held captive, and took her hand, bowing to kiss her fingers. "My dear Princess Pocahontas. It is my pleasure to have you aboard my ship. If there is anything at all that you need, please make it known, and I will make sure that it is provided." He smiled at her.

She snatched her hand away, wiping it thoroughly on her suede tunic. He was dirty and he smelt of the musky smell of the unwashed, as did all the Longcoats. How could he approach her like this, when he had just murdered the love of her life? She hated him like she had hated no one else before him.

She glared at him and stepped away from him. How dare he touch her. He was behaving as if she were an honoured guest, when they both knew this was not the case.

Argall had sent word to her father that she had been held captive but had deliberately left Japasaw's village before her father had had a chance to respond. So far, there had been no word from her father. What was going on? Why did they not stay and wait for him to respond? It all seemed suspicious.

"Captain, my only need is to know how long you are going to keep me?" Her voice was stern. Her face emotionless. Underneath her heart was still breaking having been wrenched from the arms of her family, and it was this man who was responsible. She was sad and terrified, but more than anything, she was furious.

Yes, she had come easily onto this horrible ship, but she had assumed that they would ask her father for ransom, no one would be hurt and her father would comply, giving back the English soldiers together with some corn and the guns that had been stolen, and she would be returned. Everything should have been simple. This had not happened - what was going on? Had she walked into a lion's den?

He shrugged his shoulders nonchalantly and grinned at her. "Your length of stay with us depends entirely upon your father. We have not heard back from him, so we are taking you to Jamestown for safe keeping until he decides what he wants to do."

She stood tall and looked him straight in the eye. "My father will do what is best for his people" she said abruptly. Did he seriously think all of this was her father's choice? Her father had morals. Her father respected women, mothers, and especially Beloved Women. He would be outraged at what had happened.

"Let us pray then that your release coincides with what Powhatan thinks is in the best interests of his people" he said, again smirking. "In the meantime, I am ensuring that you are looked after in the manner of a Princess. Your journey to Jamestown is a journey of peace. Peace between our peoples. Remember that once before, when you were a child, you were able to make peace between the English and the Powhatan. This is another chance for you to work miracles Pocahontas. You must realise my dear, that it is an honourable thing that you and I are doing. I am a man of peace."

She had to bite her tongue outraged at his distorted view of the situation. "Don't patronize me Sir, a man of peace does not kill innocent men" she spat. "This is not about peace; this is about control. Control of a sixteen-year-old wife and mother, whose husband you have brutally murdered." She threw back her head. "I hope you are proud of yourself, oh 'Great Warrior', using me as a pawn for your own advancement. This is not about peace at all. I am not stupid."

He eased himself up to leave, sighing, impatience on his gnarled face. "Please try to remember, Princess... you are my honoured guest, and I was hoping you would behave accordingly. If I were you, I would accept our hospitality graciously as you have no idea what we are capable of. You can be a friend, or you can be an enemy. I hope it is the former." He bowed, reaching for her hand to kiss it again, but she pulled it away roughly, feeling his perfectly trimmed beard brush her skin. She shuddered at his touch and looked at him with disgust in her eyes. He nodded in acknowledgment of the message that she was so clearly giving him, and turned abruptly on his heels. He shut the door roughly and she could hear the bolt being slid home. 'Clunk'. She was left alone, looking around the sparse part of the gunroom that had been converted into her bedroom.

She sank on to the cot and sighed deeply. Her body shook gently as she cried silently. The feelings of fear and anger that permeated every cell in her body were screaming for release.

Her mind wandered to her beautiful Ko-kee. Her poor little baby had been traumatized seeing the death of his father and he would be broken-hearted at her apparent desertion of him.

Ko-kee lay over Kocoum's body,
  covered with blood until one of the squaws tried to remove him.
  He kicked and screamed, legs and arms thrashing in the air.

His world had collapsed, and he had been betrayed in the cruellest of ways. Her whole body trembled thinking about his distress. She forced her mind to eradicate the tortuous image and thought of better days. She thought of his large brown eyes framed with long eyelashes as they looked up at her. His giggle and his abortive attempts to walk. Had she been a bad mother leaving one so young? How would he manage without her? He did not even have his father - he was an orphan. She knew he wouldn't understand. He would think that she had abandoned him, and her heart ached. Her crying became more violent as her mind wandered to the images she had seen of Kocoum. She had to bite her hand to stop the sounds from being heard.

- he ran, his bow at the ready, his face contorted with pain shouting...
   Ko-kee stood with the Squaws on the side-lines
   and watched as the fire-stick blew a massive
   crimson hole in his father's chest where his heart had been.

Kocoum. She breathed deeply and closed her eyes. Her beautiful lover lying in a pool of blood. He was senselessly killed for her. She had naively thought that by meekly boarding the ship, there would have been no bloodshed.

Maybe she had given in too easily, but it was written in the wind that something like this was going to happen. It was not progressing as she thought it would, but often that was the way of Manito Aki and it was arrogant to question the Divine Wisdom. Arrogant, but impossible not to when the wave of despair overwhelmed her.

She closed her eyes, exhaustion taking over her small sixteen-year-old body which still shook as she held in the sounds of her emotions. Her face was wet with tears. She felt the up and down movement of the ship and the splashing noise as it ploughed through the water. Men shouting orders above as they manoeuvred downstream, running up and down the deck as they took her further and further away. The scent of dusty wood from the enclosed gun deck permeated her senses and slivers of light shone through the gaps in the side of the ship. She was so alone. She pulled herself into herself away from thoughts, feeling every breath, letting the universe take her as she sank... Now she was floating. Consciousness leaving her, Manito Aki taking her away to ease the suffering. She surrendered.

He is holding my hand. I hear him. "I am here Pocahontas, I am here... I will always be here" he whispers. I feel his hand as on the night of my Huskanasquua... there is nothing but his hand. It is joy. I hold onto the feeling as the image starts to fade, taken from me. I struggle. I want the image of his strength, his love...

Manito Aki is kind and the feeling of his presence remains... Even as the wind carries me away - another image - the fort - it is the fort that I used to play in when I was Little Mischief doing handstands across the courtyard - but it is not the same, this is dark, evil.

The feeling is fear, the colours are grey. Even the buildings are different, shrouded in blood... I search for his hand - and I feel it, I know it will always be there as I enter the darkness of what is to come...

JAMESTOWN REVISITED

⚜

She felt a shudder and shook herself back into consciousness. She was overcome by the heaviness in her body and the muzziness in her head after the restless dream-filled sleep. She had no idea of where she was. She could no longer hear the splashing of the water - maybe they had docked somewhere, but where? Perhaps they had sailed to meet with her father. Maybe at last she would be released, her heart leapt at the thought. She crouched down and tried to see through the cracks between the planks of wood on the side of the ship, but all she could see was movement and the sounds of the sailors shouting orders at one another. What was going to happen to her now? She heard someone approaching the gun deck and moved as far away from the door as she could.

"Well Princess. Welcome to Jamestown - a place you know very well, I understand." Argall entered followed by a young sailor. "Nathan, could you tie Pocahontas's hands behind her back please? We don't want our little prize trying to run away."

The young man walked towards Pocahontas. She crouched down, making herself as small as she could, holding her arms out of reach and trying to make it difficult for him to restrain her. Nathan bent down and tried to grab one of her arms. She lashed out violently and scratched him on the face, causing a red wheal down his cheek. "Don't touch me." She screeched, her voice menacing like an animal under attack.

"Savage Bitch!" Nathan shouted and jumped away holding his injured face. "You fucking Heathen - I will get you for that… "He started walking toward her again, the rope in his hand, a purposeful look on his face, teeth gritted. He was a lot bigger than Pocahontas, and he overpowered her, pulling at her arms and raising her roughly from the ground. She screamed and tried to lash out at him again, but he held her hands fast and was able to wrap the rope tightly around them so she couldn't move her arms.

With his attention taken with binding her hands, she saw her chance and raised her knee sharply upwards. She felt a sense of grim satisfaction when she made direct contact with his groin. He doubled over in pain. His face was red with rage and his eyes squeezed shut. He groaned, holding himself and breathing deeply.

As he regained his composure and stood straight, pausing for a moment, he walked over to her and smacked her face with the back of his hand with such force that she was knocked backwards. She landed, a dead weight on the floor unable to save herself because of her tied hands. Her mouth and nose spurted with blood. She went limp. There was nothing she could do to defend herself. She crouched, making herself as small as possible.

Argall, the spectator, came out of the shadows. "Come, come, Pocahontas. We don't have to make this difficult. You and I are friends. We talked before about both of us making peace between our peoples. We don't want to hurt you; you know we don't. I don't want to upset your father, after all… " Argall walked towards her and put his hand out to help her off the floor.

She looked up at him with hatred in her eyes and ignored his outstretched hand, spitting bloody mucus at him. He jumped backwards protecting his immaculate attire.

Slowly, but with dignity, she rose to standing. She stood erect looking Argall in the eye.

"I am the daughter of Powhatan and should be treated with respect." Her face showed no sign of the throbbing pain she was feeling as it started to swell. She ignored the gentle trickle of blood running from her mouth and nose and continued to glare at him, inside shaking, wishing him dead.

Argall bowed to her. "Of course, My Lady. I shall free your hands, but it is understood that you will not try to escape or Nathan will be forced to subdue you in any way that he thinks fit, and I am sure you don't want that do you?" He bowed and signalled for the scowling Nathan to release her.

"We have docked at Jamestown, and when we reach your new cabin, you can get yourself cleaned up to meet Sir Thomas Dale."

"What about news of my father." She tried to hold her voice steady, she tried not to show her desperation.

"Don't worry Pocahontas, there is plenty of time to discuss these matters. All will be well, I am sure. Your father will be looking forward to your release, as are we looking forward to the release of our captured men. Come now Princess, let us disembark for the next part of your journey." His smile was self-satisfied rather than friendly, impatience starting to show on his perfectly groomed face. She was more of a handful than he had expected.

She moved slowly towards the door, standing tall and trying to maintain the dignity of a daughter of Powhatan. She felt like a little girl, and wanted more than anything to see her father, and feel his strong arms around her. Maybe he would be there waiting for her, rescuing her? Maybe he had come as soon as he heard that she was captured? He must know by now that she was headed for Jamestown. She walked down the gangplank and was faced with the large wooden gates. It had been well fortified since the days when she used to come as a child, and as she walked through the gates she was surprised at the sturdy buildings that had replaced the originals of John Smith's days. It was still a triangular settlement, and as she walked through, she could see that there were well built houses, a church and a large meeting room. It was dry and dusty underfoot. She stopped to look around her and felt a rough push from behind which made her stumble and almost fall. She looked behind and saw the grinning face of Nathan. "Princess eh?" he mocked.

A large curious crowd had gathered. "Look it is the Indian Squaw!"

"What's wrong with her face?"

"Doesn't look like a Princess to me!"

"She does look Heathen though - bet she is a good lay!"

Jibes came from all directions as she was pushed again and again roughly by Nathan. Pocahontas saw several native women, all looking cowed and submissive standing amongst the men. She guessed what *their roles* were in this community of mainly men and shuddered to think what might happen to her if her father did not rescue her soon. She felt so alone.

The smell of the Colony started to permeate her senses. A mixture of smoke from bonfires mixed with the odour of faeces. The strong stink of the overflowing latrines hung over the settlement like a blanket. Added to this, the distinctive smell of unwashed bodies, sweaty as they crowded around jeering at her. Nathan tried to push them away, but some managed to get near to her and touch her. She tried in vain to dodge their filthy hands and bad breath.

The English were so dirty. Who do they think they are calling *me* a Heathen when they can't even keep themselves clean? She thought. Everything was so claustrophobic to her, not just because she was a prisoner. Here, as in every tract of land the English took over, it was barren, dusty and stripped of life. No trees, no wildlife, just a wooden fence enclosing a huddle of houses and a few hundred stinking men mostly with rotten teeth. Jamestown had changed unrecognisably in just a few years. She could see no one that she knew, only jeering angry faces with no compassion.

She stumbled onward following Argall until they came to one of the bigger houses. Argall opened the door.

"This is one of our best houses, my lady" he said. "I hope that you will be comfortable here. I will see that someone brings you something to eat, and you must let me know if there is anything else that you need." False respect oozed from his hypocritical smile.

Pocahontas looked around her. It was not a bad little dwelling. The English had obviously taken advice from the Powhatan and lined the walls with tree bark for insulation. The floor was rough earth, and there was a cot of straw in the corner.

Her face was sullen. She was tired, and thoughts were darting through her mind like wayward arrows. She was not sure how to get what she needed, or what she was facing. At sixteen years old, she had always been given everything without having to ask. She sighed, fixing her gaze on Argall.

"As I have said to you, Captain Argall… all I need is to know whether my father's response to the ransom order has been received, so that I can be released to go back to my family." Her face was throbbing with pain, her eyes were starting to droop and hunger pains were pinching her stomach. She felt wretched. Where were her people? Why had she heard nothing? Were they going to leave her to rot just for the sake of returning some men and some bushels of corn?

"Do not worry my Princess" said Argall. "You get some rest, and in the morning you can meet with Sir Thomas Dale. I am sure he will be more than happy to tell you how the negotiations are going and when you can expect to be returned to your family."

She shook her head and looked at the ground. She did not believe a word. Something was going on, and she did not have a good feeling about it. She could feel the anxiety of her powerlessness welling up inside, turning her stomach. Argall was not going to give her any more information, and she was just too tired to argue with him. She turned her back on him. "Please leave" she said starkly, as if to a disobedient servant.

Once the door was shut, she collapsed in a heap on the straw cot wracked with anger and fear, shaking as her silent tears fell uncontrollably. "Kocoum…where are you? I need you." she whispered.

Badger looked silently on.

SIR THOMAS DALE

Pocahontas felt her body start to awaken from a deep and restless sleep. The sounds of men shouting, wood being chopped, and pots and pans clanging permeated her half consciousness. At first, she thought she was dreaming, but through half shut eyes her surroundings started to take shape. Her heart sank when she remembered the events of the previous day. She touched her face and felt the stickiness of the blood that had dried on her mouth and nose, and as she rose, she noticed the bruises on her legs, inflicted by Nathan. Her beautiful suede apron was spattered with blood and her tiny bead encrusted moccasins were filthy from dirt and sea water. She sank back down on the cot and looked at the ceiling, her body aching and her stomach screaming for the food and water that she had so far been deprived of. She longed to wash her body of the dirt accumulated in her confinement. If only she could swim in the river and cleanse herself of the dirt from these filthy Tassantassas[1] and take a long cold drink of water. Her mouth was parched, and dehydration was setting in.

She heard someone walking towards her room, and sat up, bracing herself for who knows what. Nathan, the bully, appeared around the door holding a plate of food and a mug of water. He smiled the toothless smile of one who holds all the power.

"Good morning, Princess." His face was smug with enjoyment seeing her in captivity, but he kept his distance all the same, still aware of a throbbing in his groin from the day before.

She did not answer, and looked in the opposite direction, head in the air.

"I will not eat or drink until you tell me the response from my father" she said.

"If that is how you want to play it you Heathen bitch, so be it." He threw the mug of water at her, so that there was none left for her to drink, and started eating the food on the plate himself, chewing loudly and slobbering down his chin.

"I will come back later *m'lady*. If at that time you care to show me some manners, then I might allow you some food and drink." He walked out and slammed the door.

She turned around and looked at the closed door, shivering as the cold water soaked her body. What was she going to do? She could die of dehydration. Her mouth was dry and furry, and her throat parched. She was starting to feel a little faint. She walked over to the cot and lay down, her mind floating, searching for Manito Aki to tell her what to do, to rescue her from this hell hole. A nightmare of Visions assaulted her mind, darting in and out making little sense as the dehydration started to take hold and her throat constricted further.

The feeling is fear, the colours are grey. Even the buildings are different, shrouded in blood... I search for his hand - and I feel it, I know it will always be there as I enter the darkness of what is to come...

After what seemed like hours, she heard the door opening once again. She did not open her eyes, but lay like a corpse waiting for her enemy's next move.

"Wake up Bitch!" It was Nathan's booming voice screaming at her. Her eyes flickered, but she did not move. Her body felt too heavy, and unless he had water or an answer from her father, she was not interested. She waited.

"I said, wake up!" She could hear him stomping towards her and her body tensed, waiting for a blow from his fist.

It did not come. Instead she could hear him throwing something on the floor. "Sir Thomas Dale has ordered that you dress in these clothes. He does not meet with Savages in Indian clothing. He will be along shortly, so I suggest you get your lazy Heathen body off the cot and get dressed to meet your Master." She did not move. She had no 'Masters'.

Nathan stood over her wanting to punish her, but slightly wary of her seemingly feral tendencies. He bent over and grabbed her arm pulling her from the cot onto the rough earth floor of the hut. "Get up you whore" he screamed as he pulled and pulled dragging her until she was in the centre of the room.

Suddenly, the door burst open and another man entered the room. He was smartly dressed and had the air of authority surrounding him. Pocahontas could feel the room get colder and darker at his entrance. With her Shamanic powers, she knew that evil had entered, and she shrank back.

Nathan looked up and threw Pocahontas roughly away from him. "Sir Thomas" he said and stood to attention. "I was just trying to get her to change into these clothes, as per your instructions." Nathan's eyes were wide, and he was trembling. The other man stood stock still, hands on his waist, his face red.

"Do not touch that girl" Thomas Dale barked, his eyes steely and hard. "She is the Princess Pocahontas. Have you lost your wits? Get out of here you stupid boy, and do not let me see you again today, or I will have you flogged until you are unconscious."

The boy fled, leaving Sir Thomas Dale, hands on hips glaring at the young girl, dusty and blood-stained sprawling on the dirt floor before him. He sighed shaking his head and offered her his perfectly manicured hand to help her up.

She crouched even lower, turning away, feeling the negative energy in the room. This man would only bring her sorrow. Violent pictures flashed through her mind and she trembled, shrinking back further.

It very is dark and I am in a small room.
  I am crouched down on the floor... darkness...
  humiliation... searing pain...

"Now, now young Pocahontas. You have nothing to fear from me. I am here to make sure that you are looked after. Would you like a drink perhaps?" He smiled at her, his pale blue eyes as emotionless as a stone, his voice gentle like an axe going through butter.

She did not say anything, but she got up from the ground and nodded her head. She knew that if she did not drink, she would die. She told herself that she was not giving in - she just needed to drink.

Thomas Dale shouted for food and water to be brought. When the jug of water arrived, he very slowly poured it into a mug for her. Her eyes were focused as the silver liquid splashed into the cup, and as she stared, the stream of water became the waterfall that she used to play in as a child. She imagined the cool nectar hitting her swollen and parched mouth. She salivated, anticipating the feel of the icy water running down her throat. He moved the cup towards her. As she reached to take it from him, her face pleading. He pulled it out of her reach, leaving her empty handed, and he smiled. She cried out involuntarily.

"Not so fast Pocahontas. If I am going to be nice to you, you must also be nice to me - that is how it is going to work around here from now on. Do you understand?" She did not want to comply with this evil man, she knew what he was doing, but her thirst was too great to refuse. She nodded her head again and looked at the ground, in her mind praying to the Gods for forgiveness.

"As I am going to be looking after you from now on, and taking care of your every needs, I want you to bow to me, and tell me that I am your Master and you will obey me in all things." He smiled again. She saw his smile as a serpent spitting poison, and hesitated. What was she to do? If she did not do this thing, she would die of thirst. Manito Aki was testing her. She nodded her head and put her hand out to receive the water. She had failed. A tear slid down her cheek.

"No Pocahontas" he shook his head. "You must do as I say *before* I give you the water" he said, as if to a child.

She bowed her head slowly. "You are my Master and I will obey you" she whispered.

"Louder" he screamed, delight showing on his face. "... and look at me when you talk to me."

"You are my Master and I will obey you" she spat.

"You forgot so say 'in all things', my dear." Thomas Dale was clearly enjoying her torture.

She looked at him hatred shining out of every pore. Her eyes were focused and piercing, seeing his form as a devil-like creature. "You are my Master and I will obey you in all things." She spoke the words slowly and evenly with no emphasis. She was so thirsty and so weary, her mind swimming with unintelligible thoughts that at that point, this devil *was* her Master, and she *was* powerless.

He smirked, acknowledging her submission. "Here you are, my beautiful Princess" he said as he passed her the cup of water. "You see, if you are polite to me, I will look after you."

Her hand shook as she grasped the cup, raising it to her lips. She wet her lips and the cool sweetness overcame her as she gulped down the rest, spluttering as she felt her throat responding to the liquid that it had for so long been deprived of.

Thomas Dale then passed her a plate of fish. She looked at it, her stomach was almost past the stage of wanting food, it had been so long. She looked up at him. "Take it, my Princess you will need your strength if you want to become the Peacemaker between our Peoples."

She took the dish, and once the first bite passed her lips, she ate hungrily with her fingers, making sure that he did not take it away from her before she had finished every last scrap. He passed her another cup of water, which she downed. She stared at the ground.

"Now, I have been very kind to you, have I not?"

She stared at him. What was he going to do next? He had not been kind, he had only given her what one would give a starving dog. He held the power over her, but he would never have the power over her mind and her thoughts. She could play him. He was an evil thug and thugs are stupid. She nodded at him, playing his game.

"Now, as you are a Princess, I would like you to dress like a Princess, not like a filthy Heathen. Nathan has brought you some proper clothes to wear. Is that not kind? I want you to take off your clothes and put on these new ones for me." He pointed to a pile of rags in the corner. "I shall leave you to get dressed, and when I come back, we can have a conversation about the way forward." He marched over to the door, nodded at her, and left.

Alone, she looked at the clothes that were in a heap. He wanted her identity. He did not want her to be a Powhatan. What he didn't realize was that she would always be a Powhatan in her heart, and clothes would not make any difference to her. She was not going to make it easy for him though. She picked up the garments. A linen shift, a hard boned garment, stockings, ruffles of petticoats and a cotton gown. Shoes of leather were underneath the pile. The clothes reeked, as they had obviously belonged to someone else, and the grime around the hem was hard and ingrained. Under the arms was yellow and stank of musty body odour. She shuddered. Her beautiful and simple deerskin dress and apron were all she needed. She kicked the pile of clothes up in the air and they landed on the dirt floor in a heap. She was not going to put these filthy garments on.

I cannot get out. Why am I here? It is cold and grey. Evil abounds.

She heard someone coming towards her room.

Thomas Dale entered and stood looking at her, glancing at the clothes that were splayed all over the room. "What have you done Princess?" His face was stern. "I cannot have you disobeying me. You promised that I was your Master and you would obey me in all things. It looks like you are defying me. We cannot have that now, can we? After all, I have given you food, water and clothing. How can you repay me this way?"

He walked slowly up and down the room, his finger on his chin, seemingly deep in thought. "I am going to ask you once more, nicely, my Princess. If you do not do as I ask, I will have to dress you myself - or maybe I will ask Nathan to do it. Yes, that is a clever thought. He is quite good at getting things done. You do not want the indignity of that do you? He is a little primitive and clumsy, as you already know. I am not sure, however, that I can get him to resist your womanly curves if they are exposed, if you understand my meaning?" He walked over to the door and shouted. "Nathan, can you come here please, I need some assistance."

Nathan entered the room. He stood shaking, unsure what was going to be required of him.

Pocahontas was frozen to the spot. She prayed to Manito Aki. Surely the Gods were not going to subject her to such depravity. What could she do?

"Well, my Princess. Are you going to put these lovely Western garments on for us? They are a beautiful present from me to you. I am being nice again, Princess. Are you going to be nice as well?"

Pocahontas looked at the floor, unmoving. She was resolved to make things as difficult for him as she could, even if it meant the unthinkable.

"Oh dear Nathan. It looks like the Princess will need some help in getting dressed. I am sure your balls are still aching from your last encounter with her, perhaps you can give her a taste of her own medicine as you help her to get undressed." He beckoned Nathan with his finger. "Strip her" he shouted.

Pocahontas saw Thomas Dale's face red, his teeth bared and his whole body tense with anger. Nathan started walking toward her, and she braced herself, forcing her mind to think about her family, her father, the love, and respect that she had always commanded as an Indian Princess. She felt his hands on the neck of her dress. As he pulled, she felt the deerskin material start to rip exposing her breasts. Nathan was frenzied at the sight of her body, tearing at her clothing, scratching her skin, panting, sweat breaking out on his face, eyes bulging, until at last she stood naked. From somewhere she received the strength to stand upright and proud, staring into the eyes

172

of Thomas Dale with defiance. These are Heathens, she thought. They command no respect and therefore I have no shame in being exposed. I am a Princess.

Nathan started to put his hand between her legs.

Thomas Dale laughed an evil laugh. "Enough boy" he shouted. Nathan looked crestfallen as he stood back from her. He was inflamed with lust and it was difficult to pull himself away. He looked at her exquisite brown body longingly, and scowled at the abrupt end to his pleasure and muttered under his breath. "Heathen whore…"

"Leave us boy!" Dale screamed. Nathan scuttled out of the room, furious, his body pulsing with unrequited lust.

Pocahontas stood staring at Dale. The stinking clothes were still lying on the ground.

"Put some clothes on Princess. It is not seemly to be standing here naked in front of me."

Pocahontas reached for her torn deerskin dress.

"No!" he shouted. "Not those you Heathen. I want you to be a fine lady, in fine clothes."

She shook her head.

Dale's face was tortured with fury. "You WILL dress in these clothes, my lady or I will finish what Nathan started. Do you understand?"

She stood unmoved.

He looked at her, walking around her, taking in every curve of her body. He ran his finger down her spine, and she shivered with disgust at his touch. She could see desire in his eyes and his body and she looked away. She could feel his fingers running all over her body, getting closer and closer to his prize, and she closed her eyes willing Manito Aki to take her away. If he was going to violate her, she needed her mind to be somewhere else.

Her prayers were answered.

There are clouds and there is softness. The wind is blowing through my hair, and my beloved Kocoum is holding my hand. I am safe. We are walking along the shore of the river, laughing and he lowers me to the mossy ground, kissing me as my body responds to his hunger with the love that I feel for him. I feel nothing but him.

[1] English

LEARNED HELPLESSNESS

I t seemed like a lifetime since that first meeting with Dale. Her body ached. Her heart ached. Where was her father? Had she been forgotten? Dale had told her many many times that she was deserted, and her father no longer wanted her, but she refused to believe him.

She heard Dale's footsteps approaching once again, and braced herself. With the energy from Manito Aki, for weeks she had fought him like a wild cat, digging her nails into his face, kicking, and screaming. He was much bigger and stronger, and he always left with a smile on his face, pulling up his trousers and spitting at her. It became harder and harder to hold on to the sense of who she was and what her purpose was. Again, and again he forced himself on her until all feeling was gone as she slipped into a permanent numb depression, feeling neither pain nor joy.

"Good morning, my Princess" he said as he came in smiling and shut the door behind him.

She nodded, looking at the floor. "Is there word from my father?" She whispered in a monotone.

"I wish you would stop asking that question every time we meet, it is pointless. It has been almost three months now. You know the answer. Your father has forgotten you. Your father thinks you have betrayed your people. He knows that you are just a worthless slut. He has not sent the ransom that we asked for, and that makes it very clear, does it not?" He walked towards her and moved to touch her - she pulled back from his touch, his words like an arrow to her heart. He sighed, shaking his head.

"I am all you have Pocahontas, you really ought to be more grateful. You are a worthless Heathen, but I am spending time with you. I will educate you, dress you, and make sure that every ounce of the Heathen in you is removed. With my help, you will prove that Powhatans do not *have* to be savages." He motioned for her to sit, and she did so like a scolded dog.

"Do you understand what I am saying Pocahontas?"

She nodded looking at the floor. "I am the first Powhatan lady, an example to all. You are helping me transform into someone who is far superior to the lowly squaw that I was when you captured me." She looked around her. Dirty feet, sweat stained cloths, hair lank and greasy. The stinking bowl where she had been forced to urinate and deficate was placed in one corner, and her discarded little suede Powhatan shift was in another, she looked from one to the other. She had regressed a long way from her previous life. Powhatan's favourite daughter to a forgotten whore.

He sat next to her. He started running his fingers through her silky dark hair, and traced the lines of her face. Her self-hatred surfaced as his touch sparked a dim and distant morsel of comfort. She hated him with every bone in her body, and yet within her soul, lack of affection and touch had created a primitive desert, that craved another human being.

The Gods had abandoned her, her father had abandoned her, and she had not brokered Peace. Who was she? What use was she in this world? She was like the stinking bowl in the corner.

She thought of that day when she rode high on the shoulders of the warriors, triumphant, pulling the people together. She knew her father wanted her to be a Peacemaker, and that day she had felt as if she could fly. Now, she had betrayed his pride in her. He was justified in turning his back on her. She wished that she could die.

She felt Dale undoing her dress and lay down motionless and numb once again - "Kocoum... Kocoum... " she whispered. Dale stopped for a moment and stared at her.

"Do not speak, whore" he shouted as he smacked her across the face.

She froze, her cheek red and starting to swell, and stared at a spot on the ceiling above Dale's head.

As her body was controlled, her mind refused to surrender the last private enclave that would belong to the love of her life.

Now as I feel the devil violate me, the truth is no longer hidden, I am depraved. I have to wait to feel your hand in mine in the afterlife - I pray that I will not have to wait too long, and that you forgive me. I am not the great Princess Pocahontas any more - I am a dirty squaw that gives herself to Longcoats. I cannot make peace between our peoples as I am not the same person that you used to know. You would not want to be with me, if you could see me now. I am ashamed of what I have become. I am no longer Powhatan - I wear the filthy dress of the English, eat their filthy food, and lie with their filthy men. I am filth. I want to escape to the next world, and I pray to the Manito Aki that he takes me soon...

She sensed that Dale had left the room as she lay like a rag doll on the bed, weeping silently.

Suddenly, through her pain she felt warmth permeate the room. His hand wiped the tears from her cheek as he kissed her forehead. She reached out, but he had gone as quickly as he came, like the wind, leaving her alone. She curled herself up in the foetal position and drifted off to a fitful sleep.

DECISIONS

Opechancanough approached the Quioccosan. His eyes had a haunted look. He was a strong warrior, used to being in control, this feeling was unfamiliar - it felt as if his hands were being tied behind his back. He thought of all the things that had happened since the Tassantassas had landed in his world. Everything had changed. It had always been a fight to survive, fighting the will of Nature and opposing tribes, but the biggest threat now, were these so called, filthy Longcoats who were grasping at land that had belonged to his family for generations. They had come and taken, giving nothing but death and destruction in return. In his mind, the line had finally been drawn when they had kidnapped his brother's daughter, Pocahontas… and he was being held back from carrying out reprisals.

The familiar scent of the apook hit his lungs as he entered, but he did not feel the release of tension that he usually felt. He saw his brother, Powhatan on his long reclining throne. The change in him was remarkable, and he went cold. Powhatan looked at least ten years older. Although he still had the trappings of a Great Warrior, the trappings belied the diminished man beneath the paint and great headdress. Opechancanough felt sadness as he remembered this great warrior in front of him, who had previously won many bloody battles fighting to expand the area of Tsenacommacah for his people. Opechancanough stopped in his tracks and bowed to his brother - the shock increasing his anger. How could Powhatan let this happen?

Powhatan was surrounded by the Quiakros assembled to discuss the situation. The Quiakros always had the final say in decisions regarding the tribe, as they received their instructions from the Gods. Opechancanough looked at them with hope in his eyes.

"My brother, welcome" Powhatan put his hands to his chest and bowed.

Opechancanough bowed in return, also acknowledging the group of Quiakros whom he had respected his whole life.

Opechancanough felt like an arrow waiting to be released but prevented from doing so by the solemnity of the atmosphere. Powhatan started speaking.

"My brothers, as you know, the Longcoats have captured my most precious possession. We are here today to try and decide what we must do."

Opechancanough at last had his chance. "We must fight to get her back, my brother. We have, for far too long, allowed the violence and hatred of these Longcoats who take from us, refusing our friendship, but taking our corn when it suits them. Now they have our Beloved Woman, Pocahontas. We cannot allow this to go on. You have won many great battles in your time, and you have never avoided conflict when it was needed." His heart was beating faster, and his eyes were wide with anticipation.

Powhatan nodded. "I know you have always felt this way, my brother, and in the beginning, I disagreed with you. I tried to forge peace by friendship alone for many months. Clearly this has not worked. I have moved our dwelling, so we are not as accessible as a food source for them. This has not worked. I started to allow our warriors to retaliate when Tassantassas strayed from the fort stealing and rampaging. This has not worked. Now I am faced with the possibility that if we react with violence to get Pocahontas back, they may kill her. We now know what they are capable of." His shoulders were hunched, and his cheeks were hollow and drawn with the strain.

Opechancanough shook his head. "These Longcoats have no morals - we have learned this to our cost. You even made John Smith a Werowance, and he betrayed you. He never intended on joining forces with us. He never intended for his people to come under our rule - no. He has died and those that are left are even worse. They brought you a crown from their King, a so called "honour" and asked you to stoop before them - a King does not kneel before another King unless he has been conquered... and although you hesitated, you chose to allow them to push you down to receive the crown on your head! Do you not see the significance of these things?" Powhatan remembered how Newport had brought him a crown at the same time he had brought the Greyhound - indeed he had bowed as they put a crown on his head, seeing it as a compliment. Now he saw the true meaning. It was the bowing, not the crown that was of significance.

"We must act before they overrun our people. It is not only about Pocahontas; it is about our whole existence. If they can do all of these things, *and* the ultimate insult - to take one of our most loved Beloved Women without any reprisals, they are getting the message from us that they can do anything to us, and we will kneel before them."

Powhatan looked as though he had been slapped. "I know that what you say is true, but now my heart is in their hands. Now my heart of heart languishes in captivity, depressed and crying out for me and there is nothing that we can do to save her."

"Yes, there is!" Opechancanough looked around at the Quiakros. "What do the Gods say? Why are you not telling us? You are the priests. Powhatan will listen to your words" he was breathless with frustration staring at them. Why was no one seeing the truth of what was happening?

The eldest of the Quiakros cleared his throat. "Great Powhatan, so far we have given in to the demands of the Tassantassas. We have returned their men that we had in captivity, and we have returned any stolen guns. We have kept our side of the bargain, and they have not returned Pocahontas. The Gods say that in the future we must take action." His words were quiet and hesitant. All the Quiakros looked at the fire, shrinking back from what had been said.

Opechancanough stood up "If the Gods are saying it, and the Quiakros are telling us that we have to do something - why are we not doing something?" He was sweating, walking backwards and forwards.

"I hear what you say. Still, I cannot risk a hair on her head being hurt, and if we attack them and try and rescue her, she *will* be hurt. If she perishes, I will perish. It is as simple as that."

"It is not as simple as that." Opechancanough threw his arms in the air. "Everyone loves Pocahontas. The Longcoats will not harm her, she is of no value to them dead and they do not want to risk a war with us. They want to keep her to ensure they have us where they want us - in other words powerless, day after day allowing them to take more land, bringing more ships of people to eat our corn and kill our people, always with the threat that they will kill Pocahontas if we try to defend ourselves.

You are sacrificing everything for her. She would not want you to do that. She would want us to listen to the Gods. She would want us to raise an army to rescue her and at the same time let the Tassantassas know that we are no longer their puppets. You go on about being a peace lover - but you have killed many warriors fighting the Tribal Nations in the past. There is blood on your hands, and you are proud of it. You have extended the Tsenacommacah and made our people victorious through death and destruction before - why not now?"

Powhatan looked at him. "I have no choice. I cannot do it."

"You *do* have a choice… and you are making the wrong one." He spat.

The elder of the Qiakros started to speak. "It is true that the Longcoats have proved themselves to be our enemy, despite our acts of friendship. The Gods say that in time we *will* assert ourselves to take our lands back, but not through aggression. Now, the safety of our Beloved Woman is what we need to ensure for the sake of our leader, Powhatan. The Gods say that Pocahontas will be remembered for generations for the work that she will do. That work is not finished. As mortals we do not know what that work is. We have to trust in Manito Aki to tell us when the time is right. We will overcome these enemies one day, our people with thrive, and theirs will perish, but Powhatan has proclaimed that day has not yet come - and we must listen to him as our Great Leader."

Opechancanough had had enough. The Quiakros believed what he was saying, he could see it in their eyes. They just didn't have the courage to defy Powhatan and instead chose a milder interpretation of what the Gods had told them to appease the great leader. He knew he was defeated.

"That day *has* come; you just refuse to see it. One day in the future, our children, and our children's children will all look back and realise that we should have dealt with the Tassantassas before their strength could grow uncontrollably." He paused, looking at each one in turn, shaking his head, his dark eyes full of fear. "By then, it will be too late, and you will be responsible." He stomped out of the Quioccosan.

Powhatan closed his eyes.

MATACHANNA: August, 1613

Matachanna had not seen her beloved sister since she departed with Kocoum and Ko-kee to the tribe of Japasaw in Passapatanzy. She had missed her lively banter, and had been sad to see her go taking her little one away to another tribe for safety. She had barely had a night's sleep worrying about her since Kocoum was killed and she was kidnapped.

It was a tragic situation. Powhatan had complied with many demands of the Longcoats in an effort to get her back. In return there had been nothing. For months there had been no word of her, nor any messages of her safety. She could have been dead for all that they knew.

Then had come the messenger. She wondered if they were bringing news of Pocahontas. What else could it be? There had been no trade with Jamestown for months, and relations had totally broken down between the two peoples.

Powhatan had summoned her, and her heart was filled with fear. Was Pocahontas dead? Was that the news that they were bringing? Why was it that she, Matachanna was being summoned? Maybe it was good news. Surely, if Pocahontas were dead, there would be a gathering of everyone to be told the news of their Beloved? She made herself as presentable as she could and walked towards the Quioccosan fearing the worst, but praying for the best, her stomach churning.

As she entered, she saw Powhatan reclining on his throne. This was a familiar sight. His wives sat at either end of his couch, and the large fire roared in the middle, from which the apook scented smoke billowed.

Before him stood a young Longcoat of slight build, in his late teens, downy stubble on his chin and shifty eyes that went back and forth from Powhatan to the fire. His discomfort was obvious to Matachanna, and in turn she felt the fluttering of her stomach as she tried to contain her fear of what was to come.

"Ah, Matachanna, my daughter. This young gentleman has come with word of our Beloved Pocahontas. He tells me that she is well and enjoying her life with the Tassantassas."

At first Matachanna relaxed at his words, but then sensed something strange. She looked at Powhatan's body language to gauge the real meaning of the message that had been brought. Was he trying to hide something from her? His face was a blank canvas. She looked at the boy who was squirming with the discomfort of the situation. What was actually going on? Her mind whirled in circles. Then it came to her. How could a sixteen-year-old girl, wrenched from the arms of her husband who was subsequently killed, and taken away from her child and family be enjoying her life in captivity? It did not make sense.

"My father, that is great news indeed - if it is true." She clenched her teeth. "No doubt the young gentleman will require corn for his trouble? Is that why he is here?" The boy fidgeted, looking at his hands. "Do we have to make more payments to ensure her continued safety?" Her eyes flashed with anger. How dare these Longcoats arrive dangling news of Pocahontas before their eyes, still refusing to return her, despite most of their demands being met. What game are they playing?

"What say you" she shouted at the boy.

The young lad shrank back. "I only bring the message that has been given to me, my lady."

"I am sure that is so. That doesn't mean that we have to believe it" she snarled.

Powhatan leant forward. "Be at peace, Matachanna " he said. "Pocahontas misses you so much that she has asked that you come to Jamestown to be with her, that is all."

Matachanna felt her stomach lurch, her instincts told her that this was more complex than he was letting on. Was this some kind of trap? She was of no importance, she was just a squaw, not even a Beloved Woman. She was of little value to anyone - except Pocahontas. The people at Jamestown would not have even known her name, if Pocahontas had not told them. She definitely would not have told them, if she felt that to do so would put her in danger, she was absolutely sure of that.

"But I have a husband and a life to lead here? I cannot leave my husband."

"It is requested that Uttamatamakin accompanies you to Jamestown" said Powhatan.

"Pocahontas wants me to go and put myself in danger with my husband, giving up my life here, just because she wants some company? That does not sound like Pocahontas to me."

Matachanna was confused. She looked at the state of Powhatan. His sunken face and his bloodshot eyes from nights of tossing and turning, worrying about Pocahontas had turned him into an old, old man, blank of emotion. He would die if Pocahontas did not return, of that she was certain.

"Why can they not just send Pocahontas back" Matachanna pleaded.

"We are all working towards that end. They will return her when we have a harvest. For now, you can ease her discomfort by going to her Matachanna. She is only asking this one thing of us, and for her to have asked, she must be desperate." His voice showed a hint of the emotion she knew he was hiding.

Matachanna could feel a slow unravelling of something more complex than at first presented to her. "So maybe she is not happy then?"

"Matachanna, we must do everything we can to ensure her wellbeing. If they allow you to go to her, they must have a reason. It is my belief that the Longcoats need to ensure that Pocahontas remains well - not out of humanity, oh no… that is not their style… but because they need her undamaged to bargain with us. I am frightened that she already may be unwell Matachanna, and they are panicking in case they are left with no bargaining incentive." Powhatan's stature, diminished as it was, seemed to sink even further.

Matachanna's eyes opened wide as she turned and looked at the Longcoat boy. He nodded his head slowly in confirmation.

"Why are we not rescuing her then?"

"They will kill her if we try - that is why" Powhatan said.

SISTERS

~~~~~~

Matachanna and Uttamatamakin approached the gates of Jamestown. Matachanna could feel the bile rising in her throat as she trembled, not only because she was entering the enclosure belonging to the enemies of her people and had no idea of what to expect, but because her imagination had run wild thinking about what these filthy Longcoats had done to her little sister.

She felt the presence of her husband by her side. He was a great warrior and Holy Man and his strength and support gave her some comfort. Despite Uttamatamakin's reputation in the field of battle, in this situation even he would have little power to protect her or himself. They had known it would be like this, but had decided to come anyway, half expecting never to return to Werowocomoco, doing it for the sake of Pocahontas, Powhatan and possibly the whole tribe.

The gates opened. The Longcoats were expecting them and the guards lowered their fire-sticks. One of them came forward and gestured for them to follow him. Matachanna nodded and looked before her at the dusty triangular settlement bustling with the activity of day to day life in the

Colony. She glanced at her strong husband and squeezed his hand, as they took their first steps inside.

It was the heavy solemnity in the atmosphere that hit her first. Whilst there were many people roaming the enclosure, no one spoke, and no one looked around. It was if they were in fear of their lives. This was not a happy place. Most of the population seemed to be men, apart from a few Indian squaws who looked haggard and drawn. Some glanced up briefly and nodded, but fearfully reverted their gaze almost instantly.

They were led towards one of the larger houses, which were of a more complex design than the Yehakins that Matachanna was used to. Through the house they went, until they came to a locked door. The guide unlocked the door and ushered them in.

It was dark and stuffy in the room, being a hot August day, there had been little breeze to take away the stagnant and putrefying air. As Matachanna's eyes became accustomed to the dim light, she saw a small form curled up in the corner, cowering like a whipped dog. Matachanna ran over and knelt, realising that this was her dear beautiful little sister, Pocahontas. She reached out and touched her face tenderly, brushing the hair away to see her large watery brown eyes, that were fixed and staring. Her face was caked with dirt, little rivulets running down her cheeks where the many tears that had been shed were now dry.

"My little darling" whispered Matachanna. "What have they done to you?" She pulled her towards her chest and held her. Pocahontas collapsed into the arms of her sister, sobbing.

When Pocahontas stopped crying, she pulled away and looked up at her sister, eyes wide with sorrow. "Where have you been?" she asked. "I thought no one wanted me any more… I thought that I was dirty and shamed, and no longer of any use…"

Pocahontas looked down at the floor, her face drawn.

Matachanna was shocked. She gently took Pocahontas by the shoulders, and looked straight into her eyes. "You must never think that you are not wanted my little one. We have all been so worried about you but not knowing how to get you back safely. Your father is wasting away with the worry about you, and has done all that he can to get you back. He did not want to attack the Longcoats in case they harmed you."

"They told me that Powhatan did not want to give back the guns that he had stolen and the Longcoats that he had captured. They told me my father was not prepared to exchange these things for me. They told me that I was worthless." Pocahontas shrugged Matachanna's hands off and turned away from her.

Matachanna reached over and pulled Pocahontas back. "They have lied to you Pocahontas. We know that they lie to get what they want, and that is what they have done."

Pocahontas put her head in her hands. "I thought I would never see you again Matachanna. I felt that I deserved this fate and so, refused to eat, in the hope that as my usefulness had ended, the Gods might take my life into the next world, as it no longer has a purpose in this one."

"The Gods have ways and means of carrying out their plans. Your desperation has meant that Uttamatamakin and I are now with you, and this must be a sign to you that your work is not yet finished."

Pocahontas suddenly felt a flutter, a message.

"I was not sure until this very moment Matachanna, but now I know." Her face became illuminated, her eyes bright with the realization, and she sat tall.

She placed Matachanna's hand on her stomach, "Here is the new life that has for the first time spoken to me. This, and your coming, is a message from the Gods that I must carry on. I still have work to do."

A BAD DEAL: September, 1613

❧

Pocahontas had been unwilling, at first, to divulge her pregnancy to anyone, but in the end Matachanna had made her realise that before too long her appearance alone would be the breaker of secrets. Matachanna had presented herself to Dale, and with the help of an interpreter, had broken the news to him.

Sir Thomas Dale sat back in his chair on his own, thinking. His elbows on the table, fingers touching, creating an arch…Pondering… His body was tense, and he stared at the floor, trying to find answers that seemed illusive. Damned Heathen bitch, nothing is simple with her, he thought. There was a knock at the door, and he looked up.

"Come in Gates" He rubbed his eyes and sighed, maybe Gates would think of something.

"I've heard the news on the grapevine" said Gates as he lowered himself down in the chair opposite Dale. "Who is the father of this child then? Do we know?"

Dale shrugged his shoulders. "It is hard to say" he said. "I suspect that little bastard Nathan has been sniffing about - but I don't know for certain. It may be that she was pregnant when we captured her. These Heathen squaws are renowned for being little sluts. Even if it was Nathan, I can't really blame him - he probably was just having a little sport with her. Understandable really" he said chuckling.

"But this is very serious Thomas" said Gates staring at Dale with disbelief in his eyes. "If Powhatan finds out that one of our men has defiled his little Princess, there will be all hell to pay. So far he has been very quiet about getting her back, but my guess is that this would change all that. The Powhatan tribe feel very strongly about rape, you know."

"Rape - how do you know it was rape. Little vixen probably enjoyed every minute of it" Dale scowled, an unbidden thought entering his mind that stirred him unexpectedly, and he shook himself.

Gates leant forward. "Even if it wasn't rape Thomas, it will be perceived as rape" he said, his eyes boring into Dale. He leant further forward, glaring. "Thomas, do you not understand that if this young girl in our care has now found herself pregnant, it could put the whole peace process in jeopardy? It can't have happened before she came to us as, from what I am told, her swollen belly suggests she is only three or four months gone - and she was with us long before that. We must keep this very quiet for all concerned."

"Ok, ok, I hear you Gates. What do you suggest?" he leant back in his chair. "Maybe we should just allow her to have a "little accident" and be done with it. She is really no good to us after all. We had hoped that she would give us some damned leverage with Powhatan, but so far that has not happened. She is just a drain; she and her sister have not been as useful as we had hoped." He smiled, having found a solution to his liking.

"Are you mad Dale? If we kill Pocahontas, not only would it cause a war with the Powhatans, but word will get back to England, and the self-righteous religious fanatics there would take a very dim view of it. How would it look? A teenage pregnant Princess raped in captivity and her and her sister subsequently murdered. No medals for us there, I would suggest."

Dale looked at his fingers, picking dirt from under his nails. "You do have a point, old boy, but we could always announce that she has become ill... " he said slowly. "But, as you are so clever - come up with another idea" he said with sarcasm infusing his voice.

"As she gets bigger, word will travel that she is pregnant. We should try and keep this as quiet as possible - it is already making the rounds of our soldiers, and we must contain it. Maybe we could send her up to Henrico. That is far more remote than here, and there will be less chance that the Powhatans will find out. When she has had the baby, we can start re-negotiating - try to get a bit more corn, stop them attacking our soldiers with the promise that we will return her to them."

Dale looked pensive. "We must ensure that we use the capture of Pocahontas to our best advantage. There must be more than just corn that we can get out of them - after all, it is their beloved Princess... How could we get things going and stop this being inflammatory...?" He stroked his beard, looking into space as if an answer would come out of nowhere.

The two men sat in silence, minds whirling.

Gates cleared his throat. "I think I have an idea. We could forget about using her as a hostage, and get a more subtle advantage" he said. "One of the main goals for establishing this Colony, was so that we could educate the native people, converting them away from their Heathen ways and showing them the way of the Lord. So far, we have not addressed this part of our mission. What if we were to use Pocahontas as the first native to be converted to Christianity?"

Dale smiled. "My dear boy, that is a very interesting idea. The Virginia Company would be thrilled to know that a Princess had become Christian, wouldn't they? What if she did not agree though? She is not what one would call, compliant, is she?"

"No, that is a particularly good point. It has been hard enough for us to get her to wear Western clothing, let alone decry her religion." Gates's face fell.

"Oh, but we are forgetting something..." Dale's eyes widened. "She is having a baby... Even the feisty Pocahontas would be compliant in the face of a threat to her child."

Gates nodded. "Ah... so, she may be prepared to denounce her religion and her people for the sake of her baby... and if she did not do as we asked of her, we could threaten to take her child away. No woman would allow this to happen - not even a Heathen. She would be trapped and forced into Christianity, and we would be heroes, having achieved one of the original aims of this whole mission."

Dale sat back with a self-satisfied look on his face. "Yes, this all sounds rather good Gates. There are one or two little details to iron out, but basically, I think, at last, we have found a way to get Pocahontas to give us what we want - I will make sure that in the end she is begging to be baptized."

"Right. I will start making the arrangements to move her to Henrico for her confinement. I can also ask the Reverend Whittaker to take on the job of instructing her in the Scriptures" said Gates.

Dale looked very thoughtful. "The sooner the better, Gates. It is interesting how things are turning out though isn't it? Whoever fathered this child has done us a massive favour." He smiled.

Pocahontas was summoned. She had not set eyes on Dale for several weeks and she felt an instinctive sense of trepidation. In his presence, surrendering herself had previously been her only option. The arrival of Matachanna had been a turning point and a sign to her that her father and the Gods were still relying on her, and her strong and defiant spirit and determination to serve her people had been reawakened. She was a Beloved Woman and a Princess, and she would do what she needed to do for her people. She pushed all her remaining fears behind her and knocked on the door.

"Enter!" His familiar voice boomed out.

She opened the door and stood before him, presenting an air of strength as she stared down at him with hatred in her eyes. He had almost broken her and as she looked at him sitting smugly sitting in his comfortable chair, the tobacco smoke swirling around his face as he sighed with pleasure, she felt disgust oozing from her body.

"Well my little Princess, I understand from your sister that congratulations are in order." He gave a condescending smile and she felt the anger intensifying and rising from the pit of her stomach. She took a breath, determined not to give in to her baser emotions.

"Congratulations are in order for you too, My Lord" she spat at him.

"If you are insinuating that I had anything to do with your current condition, you are out of your mind - it is well known that many of our soldiers have access to you, any number could be the father." He raised his eyebrows and pursed his lips, blowing out more smoke nonchalantly, the lie slipping off his tongue with no hesitation whatsoever.

Pocahontas could hardly contain the rage that she was feeling, but she knew he had all the power and she could do nothing. She clenched her fists, feeling her nails digging into the palms of her hands drawing blood in frustration, trying to remain calm.

"This is your child Sir Thomas" she said with conviction.

"Yes, yes, yes... whatever... You can never prove that of course." He waved his hand as though dismissing her. Then he stopped and looked more intently at her, a thought entering his head. "No one would ever believe your word over mine, and I suggest you do not mention even the *possibility* of my having fathered that bastard, or there will be consequences that you do not even dare to think about, you filthy Heathen squaw." His eyes held evil.

She looked at him as if he was dirt. They both knew the truth. How very satisfying would it be to disgrace this cruel disgusting man? But sadly, she knew he was right, no one would believe her word over his - but it was liberating to have just enough evidence to bait him, seeing his basic emotions erupt with the possibility of his ruination. How primitive he is, she thought with contempt.

"My dear Pocahontas, let me remind you that your life and the life of your baby are in my hands. You may not care about your own life, but now you have a child to think about. The paternity of the child at this point is unimportant - what is important is the fact that you will now be responsible for the safety of that child" he said glaring at her. "In other words, my dear, you will do exactly as I command from now on, or I cannot guarantee that this baby will live. Do you understand what I am saying?"

Pocahontas put her arms across her tiny swollen stomach. "If you harm me or my baby, my father will not stand for it" she snarled, her eyes wide.

"Your father doesn't have a great track record of standing up for you now does he Princess? In fact, my guess is that he will be pleased to be rid of you as you have disgraced your family by becoming pregnant by an English man… good job your husband is dead, isn't it? I know the Powhatans have quite a loose arrangement surrounding marriage - but no man would want a woman back in these circumstances, even a filthy Heathen." He sighed with the pleasure of his power, leisurely blowing out the smoke from his tobacco, watching it swirl in the air, relaxed and happy with the game that he was playing with her. Like a cat and mouse, he knew she had no escape from him.

Pocahontas's face fell. Was there no end to how low this man would stoop? Her mind went round and round searching for something to pull herself out of the sudden sinking despair that swept over her when she realised the truth of her predicament. Kocoum - she knew he was dead, needlessly shot on the cruel orders of this monster, but she also knew that even in the afterlife Kocoum would understand. The love that they had shared would never be blemished by what had happened to her. They would love each other forever. But would her father understand? She was, by being pregnant, an instrument of the Longcoats. Was this her destiny? She felt confused, devoid of any of the power that had fleetingly been hers when she entered the room. She had to trust in the Gods.

As she searched for an answer, she felt a warm glow of the Gods infiltrating her body and making her feel light. Despair was being washed from her body, cleansing her soul. She saw the room became illuminated as at the glow of sunrise. She felt the flutter of the new life in her stomach, like a butterfly caressing her very depths. She knew this to be the sign. Suddenly she realized that this was not the end for her, this was the beginning. She felt safe for the first time since her kidnap. She was being watched over. The Gods were not forsaking her. Badger stood in the corner, his eyes sparkling.

A fluttering, a warm glow...

The man before her, glaring with hatred, thought that she was in his control. Indeed, she had thought that too. Now her sixth sense with the help of the Gods was reminding her that her fate would be decided, not by the evil of Thomas Dale, but by the love of Ahone. She would play whatever game the Longcoats wanted her to play, if necessary, allowing them to feel they had the upper hand, but knowing deep down that it was all part of her mission. They could do whatever they wanted to her, but they could never take that away from her. She was a Beloved Woman and daughter of The Great Powhatan. This child had been sent as a blessing to help her mission, not thwart it. She would protect this child, and she would see that the first Anglo/Powhatan baby became a symbol of peace, not aggression.

"This child must live" she said her face betraying nothing of the secret internal transformation that had just taken place.

"In that case, it is your responsibility to do exactly as I say" he said with an air of pomposity.

She nodded, if only to appease his ego. The game begins, she thought to herself.

"This child is half English. It must, therefore, be brought up as a Christian, not a filthy Heathen. For that to happen, you must be instructed in the Scriptures. You must publicly renounce your religion and convert to Christianity." He waited to see her reaction, half expecting histrionics. So far it had been easier than he thought. At first, she had been feisty, but now, she seemed strangely compliant, uncharacteristically serene. But he had her weak spot. He smiled to himself, happy that at last he was going to make a name for himself. He was going to be the hero that converted the first Heathen to Christianity and all because of his own illegitimate child. He would have what he wanted - recognition and a place in history. A vision of King James congratulating him came into his mind and he smiled, preening himself as if he were at Court.

Pocahontas stood, almost forgotten by Dale as he reveled in his imagined glory. Her heart was beating. The baby fluttered in her belly. She felt

Kocoum standing next to her. She felt the warmth of his hand in hers. She would do this.

Badger smiled.

A NEW FRIEND

"I am not sure I understand you Reverend Whittaker. Your God seems remarkably similar in many ways to ours... so why am I considered a Heathen, looked down upon with contempt? Why is it so important for me to renounce my beliefs when they are so similar in many ways to yours? Why can't we accept one another's differences without seeing those differences as inferior?" She frowned with concentration as her large brown eyes earnestly looked at the young preacher.

"Whoa, whoa, whoa, Pocahontas... so many questions... " Reverend Whittaker had been taken aback by the intensity of the young Indian Squaw. He had been assigned the task of teaching her the Gospel. Sir Thomas Dale had made it very clear that a great many things depended on his achieving complete compliance from her. When given the brief, he had been convinced of an easy time, brainwashing a dull and slow-witted child. How wrong he had been! She was intelligent with an enquiring mind, that often left him speechless with her deep and well thought out questions.

As soon as he met her, he realised that this was not going to be an easy task - but he relished the challenge nonetheless. Her questions often made him ponder his own considerable knowledge, and several times he had had to consult the Scriptures, reacquainting himself with the minutiae of a subject that he had studied in depth at Cambridge, as had his father before him. As a younger man he had often listened well into the early hours, as his professors argued about the true nature of Protestantism as they composed the King James Bible. He felt himself to be at the cutting edge of the religion that could make a difference to the lives of Heathens, but her intellect matched that of those learned men. How could a young uneducated girl think in such a sophisticated manner?

He had come to Virginia having rejected the life of a parish priest in England in favour of satisfying his driving ambition to do good by delivering the Word of God to the poor unfortunates who were starved of the Protestantism that was so essential to their wellbeing. He was meant to deliver the Truth, not to have it challenged.

Reverend Whittaker picked up the beautiful leather-bound Bible that was sitting on the table between them. "This is the Bible, Pocahontas" he said. "Everything to do with Christianity is contained within these pages. You will find the answers here."

She looked at him blankly. "But Sir, I cannot read" she said. Her frustration showing as she sat back and folded her arms, barely masking her contempt.

He nodded. "I will guide you through the pages to start with. A man called John Rolfe will also be instructing you in reading and writing, as well as continuing some of your religious instruction. John Rolfe is a young gentleman of good breeding who has volunteered to tutor you in reading and writing the English language.

We want to open up the world for you Pocahontas - open your eyes to how your life can be changed when you worship a God such as ours."

She could see the sincerity in his blue eyes. He was trying to give her something that he believed in, hoping that once she was educated about it, she would embrace it with her own free will, and she respected him and liked him for that. He was very different to Dale who wanted to take something away from her, forcing her for his personal gain. She hoped that

John Rolfe was equally likable, or things could turn difficult.

Despite her respect for the Reverend, she was wedded to her own beliefs, beliefs that were not just a point of view, they were part of the fabric of her being as a Beloved Woman. However, she could not help but be curious about the alternative that was being offered to her. Her mind was open to learning about their religion, as she was open to learning in general, and always had been.

She thought again about Dale. She would play his game, get an education, and protect her baby, but hold onto her own thoughts and beliefs. No one could see inside her head.

She sat forward and looked at the innocent and gullible Reverend. "Maybe we could talk about the similarities and differences of our beliefs? It may help me to understand more of what you are saying. For instance, the Powhatan have many Gods - some of our Gods are good, like Ahone, and some bring us accidents, ill wind, and illness, like Okee. We honour but fear Okee, we give him apook and worship him so that he does us no harm. Maybe Okee and Ahone are similar to your God and the Devil?"

The Reverend drew a breath. Where to start? He could not crush her enthusiasm, he had to listen to her. "I see what you are saying. There are some similarities, but there are also some very important differences. Our God is pure goodness. We worship and give thanks to Him for all that He has given us. All evil comes from the devil. We do not pray to the devil, as you give sacrifice to Okee, we pray to God to protect us and we shun the devil. Good Christians lead their lives being kind to others. Guidance from God, and following the rules of the Scriptures allow us to curb any desires and impulses sent from the devil."

"Powhatans are also kind to others" she retorted. "...and we also have guidance from the Gods." Her eyes were flashing defensively. "There seem to be more similarities than differences between our Gods. You have one God and the devil. We have many Gods, and the beneficent Ahone and the demanding Okee."

Reverend Whittaker could see that he had a very difficult task ahead of him. He understood now, that his days were going to be spent in discussion and debate rather than just lectures. Pocahontas was going to educate him as much as he was going to educate her. He looked at her beautiful face and his heart fluttered to the extent that he had to look away. Spending time with Pocahontas was going to be difficult in more ways than one.

HENRICO

I t was certainly better than Jamestown. In Henrico she had freedoms to move around and she could talk to people other than just Matachanna and Uttamatamakin. Despite this, she constantly daydreamed about Kocoum and Ko-kee, but had had to resign herself to the fact that there was nothing that she could do to change things. Every time she recalled the gunshot that she had heard that fateful day of her kidnap, a piece of her died inside. She knew - the intensity of the piercing pain that she had experienced, could only have signified the death of her soulmate.

I feel a sharp pain in my heart
  as Kocoum fades into the trees...
  he is going further and further...
  I am all alone.

She spent many hours meditating and praying to the Gods that one day she would be reunited with Kocoum if only in the next world. Her hope was that Ko-kee was safe. In return, she pledged to the Gods that she would continue her quest, her search for peace.

There was a knock at her door, she looked up with surprise as a face appeared at the door. "May I come in?" he said, his expression was tentative. "I am John Rolfe."

She looked at the man standing before her. Reverend Whittaker had mentioned John Rolfe. She paused. There was something in his rugged good looks that seemed familiar. Then she remembered. She had met him years ago in Jamestown. His face was more weatherbeaten, and he was slightly heavier set, but she was sure it was the same man with flopping golden hair, and hazel eyes, now in his late twenties. An image of the 'Starving Time' in Jamestown came to her and she shuddered as the horrors of it came back to her.

She thought back to when his ship had arrived to rescue the starving colonists during the famine. After John Smith's death, help from the Powhatans had not been enough. Most of the colonists were skin and bone, their large eyes staring out of sunken sockets, pleading for food and water with their last cries. Some had even turned to cannibalism in utter desperation, feeding on the flesh of their dead comrades. She recalled having seen John for the first time as he knelt to give water to a small child who was struggling to live. In her gut she had known that they would meet again, and she had never forgotten his compassion.

"I think we have met before, Sir" she said, her face softening. He looked at her, drinking in her beauty. He had thought of her many times since that awful day in Jamestown. He had hoped that one day they would meet again in better circumstances.

"I wondered if you would remember me" he said quietly, searching her face, hoping for a positive reaction from her.

She looked at him with sorrow in her eyes. "For many years I fought to bury thoughts of those terrible days" she said, "but the cries of children haunt me still." She looked at the floor.

There was silence between them as both, filled with the emotions of the horrors surrounding their first meeting, were lost for words. Pocahontas was surprised as she felt an invisible bond with this stranger. From where had this come? Perhaps sharing the horrors of that day had set them apart from others. Perhaps the bond arose out of having known him when she was a carefree teenager with her life ahead of her. Perhaps it was just the Gods showing her the way.

John broke the silence. "It is a long time since those days. Things are very different now. My heart is sad that the relationship between my people and yours seems to have taken a turn for the worse, and that you have been wrenched from your family and your people in such a way. But Sir Thomas Dale tells me that you want to learn about the Scriptures, and improve your English to strengthen the relationship between our people."

Pocahontas sighed. She looked closely at him. She hardly knew anything about him, but could feel his unexpected concern for her. Obviously, he did not know the reason she was learning about the Scriptures. He was looking at her, unable to hide the anticipation written on his face as he waited for her to respond to him.

"Yes, I am hoping to learn as much as I can so that I can understand your people. Often, it is not understanding the ways of others that prevents friendship. I would like to be an ambassador for my people - learning and bringing them knowledge that will help both our peoples to unite in peace." What she said was true. What she did not divulge was that she would never authentically renounce her identity as a Powhatan.

_____

She now had a routine of sorts as she was shaped into the mould designed by Dale and carried out by the naive Reverend Whittaker - to make her a compliant Powhatan Christian. The physical cruelty had stopped, and she used her years of Powhatan training to protect herself against the hours of brainwashing.

She saw John Rolfe every week, and their friendship had grown. She looked forward to seeing him. Her first impressions of him were correct. They were easy together, friends who seemed to have known each other for years. They talked for hours about nothing in particular, laughing together at the mistakes she made with learning English. It made her think of her first English friend, John Smith, and how they too had shared a love of learning each other's languages. John Smith was long gone, and she thought wistfully of how different things might have been if he had lived to help cement the relationship between their peoples.

Reverend Whittaker took a service weekly at Dale's plantation which was only a few miles away from Rock Hall where she was living. The Reverend insisted that she accompany him as part of her education. Dale all but ignored her. He had used her for his own purposes and had handed 'the goods' over to Whittaker and John Rolfe for finishing off. So be it.

She thought with a shiver of how events could have taken a different turn when Dale found out about the baby. She imagined herself at the gallows holding her newly born baby, should Dale have decided she was no longer needed. Or worse, Dale taking the baby from her and bringing it up as his own. She could not imagine her child being brought up by a a man with no heart.

She was still unclear as to what was going to happen to her. She had been in captivity a long time now, and although since Matachanna's arrival she believed that her father wanted her back, would this ever happen? What would Dale expect her father to give him in return for her release? She knew Dale well enough to know that he would not expend so much effort on her for nothing. Maybe John would know? She decided to broach the subject at their meeting today. John must know about her pregnancy; she saw the look of surprise on his face when they had first met. He was such a gentleman; he had not mentioned it though. John had alluded to the fact that Dale had spoken to him about her on several occasions, but she could tell that John had little respect for the man.

She decided that she had to confide in John. He was the only one she spoke to who had regular with contact with Dale. He might know what the future held for her, or if not, he might be able to find out.

She heard the awaited knock on the door.

"Come in John" she said quietly.

John entered, smiling. "Are you ready for another lesson then?" he asked, his hazel eyes sparkling as he looked at her. His stomach was churning as he struggled to hide his unexpected, but growing infatuation with her. She was looking at the floor, unaware of his plight.

"I wanted to talk to you about something John" she said. He looked at her. Her face was intense.

"What is the matter Pocahontas? Is there something troubling you?"

"Yes, John. I have been here for six months now, and I do not know when I will ever see my people again. My heart aches every day as I replay in my head how they brutally killed my husband Kocoum. He was innocent of any crimes apart from loving me. And my baby is alone - looked after by the tribe. I am pregnant again, as you can see." She caressed her expanding tummy. "We have never spoken of this, as there seemed no need."

John looked down. "Yes, of course I knew, but I did not want to pry. Such a matter is private."

"I appreciate your sensitivity John, but now I need to be open with you. I don't know how much Dale has told you about me, and I want you to know the truth. I am hoping that as my only friend, apart from my sister, you will not judge me harshly." She sought eye contact with him, her eyebrows drawn together with concern.

John looked at her. "Thomas Dale and I speak only as colleagues. He certainly is not a friend of mine. He has told me that you want to convert to Christianity, that is about all."

Pocahontas nodded. "To start with, I think my kidnapping was a fairly simple affair. Argall kidnapped me with a view to exchanging me for corn, and guns that had been stolen and some of your captured men. Then things changed. Thomas Dale took a fancy to me." She drew a breath. "I have never told anyone what happened to me whilst I was in Jamestown." She looked at the floor. Her face held tragedy. John was starting to panic. He looked at her, his eyes wide and unblinking, pictures flashing through his mind.

"What happened Pocahontas?"

"He raped me many times, John" she whispered, her eyes closing, a tear falling down her cheek.

John gasped. "Thomas Dale raped you?" His face turned ashen.

"Yes" she whispered.

John could not speak. He was shaking with rage. Dale had raped an innocent sixteen year old girl in captivity for Christ's sake! He looked at her sadness, and his insides turned over.

She looked at him again, searching his face to see his reaction.

His face drained of colour. He put his head in his hands.

"I am carrying Sir Thomas Dale's child John" said Pocahontas.

He looked up and shock flooded his face. He took her hand and raised it to his lips. He was lost for words.

At his soft and gentle touch, Pocahontas crumpled with relief, the tears that had been waiting to fall for so long, now released. She sobbed and sobbed, unable to stop, thanking Manito Aki silently for sending John to her.

As she calmed and John pulled her to him resting her head on his shoulder, her crying subsided. "The reason that I am converting to Christianity is that Dale has threatened both my safety and the safety of my child if I do not."

John's face turned from compassion to rage. He did not say anything. He could not speak because of the emotions that were overwhelming him.

Pocahontas looked at him with pleading eyes. "John, I need to know what he is going to do with me. I need to know if I will ever see my little son and my family again, and whether this child will be allowed to live. What more does the monster want from me? Please will you find out?" she asked, looking up at him, her face wet with tears, her eyes wide like the child that she was.

JOHN'S PLAN: December, 1613

J ohn had left Pocahontas with a heavy heart. He was confused, his mind going around in circles trying to think of how he was going to protect her. His thoughts were interspersed with unwanted images of Dale abusing Pocahontas's small childlike body. He tried to blank it out, but the more he tried the more the images came, until he thought that he was going to go mad.

He lay in bed tossing and turning. He sat up, tired of the search for peaceful sleep and got up, pacing up and down. He smoked and smoked until he ran out of tobacco, turning then to some of the Powhatan tobacco he had acquired for experimentation. This only seemed to make it worse. After what seemed like hours, his mind became fuzzy and he lay down, allowing his dreams to take him away.

Throwing aside the cross, I rise and go to her, she takes my hand but does not look at me. My whole body is taken over with feelings of desire and love for her - I do not care that she looks away, it is enough that she takes my hand. Any morsel, her slightest touch is like a drop of water to a parched mouth. We go, we float - she takes me to a Powhatan village. She walks into one of the houses holding her baby. I walk behind her. She walks over to a tall strong handsome warrior who is holding the hand of a small child. "John, this is the only man I will ever truly love, and my child conceived through that love" she says as she goes to them and embraces them, leaving me standing alone. I cry - she can never be mine. She walks back to me and takes my hand. You brought me back John. I love you more than I love my own brother. Come sit and eat with us." I look at her and I cannot bear the feeling any more. I turn and I leave knowing that I saved her, but I could not have her."

John woke himself up sobbing. Where did that dream come from? Was it the tobacco? The Indian Apook was known to induce hallucinations. This had seemed so real to him. Was she bewitching him? Was she a witch as so many people said? Were her Gods invading him? He recalled the dream as if it was reality - this was not like any dream that he had had before. He felt like his mind was being taken over. It is true that he had never forgotten her and always wanted to see her again, but now, things had intensified to uncontrollable proportions. It was as if he was addicted to her. His body and his mind ached for her.

His body tingled as he allowed fantasy to take hold. He imagined her hand in his and he sighed. He was flooded with thoughts of her. He could not stop. She was overwhelming his mind. What was he going to do? Maybe things would be better tomorrow. He knew deep down that this was a vain hope. He was now so bewitched that he was powerless, but strangely craving the powerlessness. Maybe this was just true love? Was this how people felt when they described being in love?

He thought back to Sarah, his first wife. He had loved her - but it had been nothing like this. He had wanted to be near to her, wanted to make love to her, but he had not felt as if he would not survive if she was not there. Yes, he had grieved for her, and for little Bermudas, his baby girl, but when they tragically died, gradually his thoughts had turned to his day to day living and whilst he still thought of them, it was only when he wanted to.

With Pocahontas he was flooded with thoughts that were unbidden. It was as if the thoughts were being implanted in his mind - maybe she *was* a witch. But he wanted the thoughts, he hated being infiltrated unwillingly, but strangely he *wanted* to think about her, he did not want a minute to go by without a thought of her. It was like picking at a scab - delight in the pain. But he hated himself for it.

The dream told him that he would never have her. It was like a hunger that was never to be satisfied. Maybe the dream was wrong? Maybe she could be his? It was a forlorn hope that would be his downfall, he knew that.

John thought of Thomas Dale and he felt as if he would burst with anger. He knew Dale to be a bully and a sadist, and he had always detested him for it, but this was an unspeakable crime. Dale was powerful, John knew he had to be incredibly careful in the way that he managed him. He could not let his instinctive anger and desire for revenge get in the way. What he would have liked to do is to beat Dale to a pulp and watch him as he died slowly - like Dale had done to so many for minor crimes. But he had to be smarter than that, and use his mind rather than his fist.

In the dream he saw himself throwing aside the cross and going towards Pocahontas. In that moment he knew that he had to marry her, it was a message. That was the only answer. Even although the dream had told him he would never have her, he had to try. He could not survive without trying.

He had to throw aside religion. She was thought of as a Heathen, and this was going to be something so out of the ordinary that it would cause an uproar in Jamestown and in London. However, she was learning the Scriptures, and Dale wanted her to convert to Christianity - maybe then it would be allowed. After all, an alliance between Pocahontas and himself could be the first bridge towards peace. He could say her baby was his, conceived in a loving marriage, and all the threat of it being born out of wedlock would be taken away.

Would she agree to this? Her options were very few. There were bound to be dire consequences if the baby was born out of wedlock - and Dale was very unlikely to claim the baby and marry her himself. He had already cast her aside, and there had been many rumours that he was looking to marry her younger sister, even though he had a new young wife still in England.

He would have to write to Dale in the first instance, as he could not trust himself to talk to him face to face with civility. He brought Pocahontas's face into his mind, so that every word he wrote, would be instilled with the sincerity that he felt.

It was to be a letter admitting his own weaknesses and how these could be turned into advantage for the relationship between the Powhatan and English.

Dale would love to look down on him for his transgressions, maintaining his own identity as honourable. Hypocritical though this would be - John knew that the stakes were high and sacrifices had to be made. He had to sell his marriage to Pocahontas in a way that made sense to Dale. He would have to make sure that Dale's prize of making a name for himself in the peace talks were the main selling point. He knew that Dale had been very worried about the next step in the deliberations with Powhatan about Pocahontas. It was a make or break situation - John had to make sure that Dale understood what a hero he could be if all of this happened. The first marriage of a Powhatan to an Englishman - and she was converted. Then, when her pregnancy was was made public within the sanctity of wedlock, this would be something else that Dale could present to London as a success for the relations with the natives.

John started to write.

He wrote well into the night a letter[1] spelling out his feelings for Pocahontas, that he wanted to marry her and why it would benefit the Colony.

Honourable Sir and most worthy Governor,

When you are able to take the time to read these lines, I trust in God that you will understand. This matter is very important to me.

As this matter has taken hold of my heart with such intensity, I am putting myself in your hands as you are older and wiser and I pray that you will help me take the right path.

You have known me for many years, and I believe that you have respected me as an honourable and Godly person. I still act honorably and hope that as you have known me well, you will stand up for me against anyone that doubts my motives for wanting to marry Pocahontas.

Even although my heart and mind have been entangled with her for so long that I cannot release myself, my main motive is not carnal desire alone, it is to convert Pocahontas to Christianity.

But God, who never fails me, has opened the gate and led me by the hand to see a safe path (and now I know why).

To you, noble Sir, Patron and father of this Colony, I will reveal my affection for Pocahontas - something that I have examined over and over and have looked for a cure, as one looks for a cure for an ulcer. I never failed in my prayers to God for his assistance and know that I am but a frail man prone to evil and wicked thoughts. I am not ignorant of God's displeasure at the sons of Levi and Israel for their marriage to strange wives, and for the trouble this caused. I have searched my soul to understand what should make me fall in love with an uneducated, ill mannered Heathen whose differences to myself leave me in fear, but I have stopped these thoughts.

I have had many sleepless nights, days and hours worrying about my feelings. I have felt anxious and astonished at myself, refusing to neglect my duty as a Christian and asking myself 'why do I not make her a good Christian?' - maybe that is why I exist - to make the Heathen a Christian.

Maybe my feelings for her are not about passing pleasures, but more about working in God's vineyard, planting and sowing Christianity, as I am a husband of the Gospel. It is in the service of Jesus Christ that I do this. Adding to this, her appearance of love to me and her desire to be taught and instructed in the ways of the Lord is further evidence that this is God's Will.

What shall I do? Shall I refuse His Path? Shall I not give bread to the hungry? Shall I refuse my duties as a Christian? Shall I risk displeasing the world by not revealing the way of God? I hope to be guided by his heavenly grace to bring the word of God to many.

Talking to others and reading the Scriptures, I have received some encouragement that has cleared my conscience. I could set down all my sins for you, but this would be pointless. I submit my intentions are for God's honour, the good of the Country and the benefit of the plantation, and to convert a Heathen.

If anyone thinks badly of me, let them know it is not to quell my hunger or my desire that I ask this. Please God to dispose of me when I have completed my Holy Work I will pray daily to God to Bless me, mine and her eternal happiness.

I take my leave, beseeching Almightly God to rain down on you such a wealth of Heavenly Graces as your heart can wish and desire, and so I rest,

At your command most willing to be disposed of

John Rolfe *

[1] See Appendix A

A BUSINESS PROPOSAL

He had been summoned. Thomas Dale had read his letter, and he was now to face the jury of Thomas Dale, George Gates, and Reverend Whittaker. His future happiness depended on the success of this meeting. He realised that he was obsessed, to the point of madness. He had to make them see how his marriage to Pocahontas would benefit them and the Colony at large. His heart was pounding and there were beads of perspiration on his forehead. His romantic feelings could not be revealed as the only focus here. He had to pull his emotions back and talk rationally. It had to be a business case for the good of the Colony.

He walked along the river bank towards the meeting house. The air was cold against his clammy face. He looked up at the tall Bald Cypress trees reaching up to the sky, their large multi-faceted trunks reaching down into the water, their branches devoid of foliage at this time of year. They looked so strong. He shivered. He was so insignificant - but he had found a strength from within that he never knew that he had, driven by obsession. He was determined to make a stand like these beautiful trees and not be moved. These trees were urging him on, singing to him in the wind - surely it must be witchcraft? Was this really him, confronting Thomas Dale to ask to marry a Heathen? He would never have imagined such a scenario from a callow Norfolk country lad who had set sail for Jamestown with his wonderful wife Sarah.

He threw a stone into the water and watched the spirals of silver filter out from the central splash. He lent against the large tree trunk and lifted his slightly warm pipe into his mouth. He breathed in the small amount of smoke that was still left from his previous lighting. There was only a faint flavour of the tobacco left, just enough to make him relax. He had found over the months of using tobacco that he was smoking it more and more, even resorting to some of the Powhatan ceremonial tobacco for its ability to make him float above his worries. Tobacco was an addiction too, he thought as he smiled to himself - tobacco and Pocahontas, and perhaps they were connected in some strange way. Both had entered his life by chance. Pocahontas's people had been smoking apook for generations and it was a part of their heritage. In Virginia it was mystical, a tribute to the Gods, and unwittingly he had been drawn to it, ensnared.

His mind began to wander thinking about what he was doing in this foreign land. He only had his tobacco as a focus, a random bit of serendipity, given his beginnings on a farm in Norfolk. The plants were thriving well in Henrico - much better than they had at Jamestown, but he was not experienced, he did not know the soil or the plants well enough to get the best from them. He had cleared new seed beds in January, which had taken a great deal of time. He needed more land and he was short of labour, and the next steps in the process were going to be even more labour intensive. He had had problems with worms, and difficulties in knowing when the tobacco was ripe for picking. Curing also had been a bit of a hit and miss - he was guessing all the time.

A random thought came into his mind. What if he were able to marry Pocahontas, and she was to persuade her kinsmen to help him with the tobacco? They had many generations experience of growing and curing, albeit their own harsh apook. These milder seeds taken from Bermuda could probably be grown and cured in the same way that the Powhatan had

216

been doing for hundreds of years. Perhaps he might then get more success with tobacco as an export.

Could this be another selling point for the marriage alliance with Pocahontas. He threw another stone into the water and listened to the sound of the splash. He knew he could do this. He would be seen as the one to make the sacrifice of marrying an uncultured Heathen for the sake of the advancement of the Colony, but in fact, he would be marrying the love of his life. His dreams told him she still loved Kocoum, but he would be grateful just to have her in his life, even if it was just as a friend. Enough of this procrastinating – he had to get his thoughts together. He paused, taking a few deep breaths.

He walked towards Dale's door, his heart beating. He lifted his hand to knock on the door. Now or never, he thought, and beat the door with a loud and assured knock.

"Enter" Dale boomed.

John went into the room and saw the men sitting around a table in front of the fire. They were well ensconced in conversation, probably having been in discussion for some while. They looked up when he entered the room. Their faces were grave. His letter was on the table. It was as if he were walking into a den, naked, his vulnerabilities exposed to men who held the power of his future in their hands. One wrong word and they could take away his dreams.

John wondered how the discussion had gone before he arrived. He knew that Dale had been very worried about the Pocahontas situation. It had been months now since she had been taken captive. John looked at them one by one.

The very ambitious Dale, was sitting puffing tobacco as he watched John come in. He must be starting to get worried that maybe the old boy didn't care about his daughter, and this might result in Dale's ideas of personal advancement and congratulations from the King for his services progressing the peace in Jamestown, coming to nothing. That would be too much to bear for the ambition of the animal who had raped a 16 year old captive. John reminded himself that he must keep his head. There was so much at stake. His revenge at the defiling of Pocahontas would be satisfied only when he was able to make her and her baby safe.

He wondered about Reverend Alexander Whitaker. What was he thinking? The Reverend was an idealistic wealthy young man with a driving conscience at having been born privileged. His mother came from very wealthy London stock, and his father, Master of the College of St. John's and Regis Professor of Divinity at Cambridge University. John had heard that the Young Alexander, who was ordained in 1609, was caught up in the work of writing the new King James Bible. Whitaker believed that as there had been so many obstacles in forming a Colony - starvation, shipwrecks, disease, Indian attacks - and the Colony was still thriving, it must be God's will. John believed Alexander Whittaker was basically a decent man. Undoubtedly, he was somewhat obsessed with his mission, but he had been kind and respectful to Pocahontas as he brainwashed her with the word of God. John wondered what The Reverend would think about a Heathen/Christian marriage. Would he see this as a success in conversion? Or would he see it as an insult to Christianity? John knew that the Reverend could not tolerate the carnal lusts of the Englishmen who had taken Powhatan women as mistresses, but maybe he would see this union differently. It was unlikely with his background that he had any experience with matters of the heart. He watched the Reverend's pensive face, as he scratched his beard, deep in thought.

Lastly, Sir Thomas Gates. An old colleague of John's. He had arrived in Jamestown after being shipwrecked in Bermuda for ten months on the same expedition as John. They respected each other, and had worked side by side on the sinking 'Sea Venture' as it limped towards Bermuda before foundering on its reefs. They had shared dangerous times together, and John hoped, Sir Thomas would think favourably on his ideas. But he was a strong and opinionated man, who would not be swayed by mere friendship alone. He would have to be convinced that whatever happened was for the good of the Colony that he had fought so hard to maintain. His initial arrival in Jamestown had seen him prepared to be conciliatory with the Powhatans, hoping that a peaceful alliance could be made. However, he had soon changed his tune when one of his men was tortured and butchered for no reason by Natives. He had had a cynical view of the peace process from that time onward. He had sought cruel revenge and had retaliated by drawing some natives together, enticing them with music and dancing, only to massacre them.

John sat down waiting to see who was going to speak first.

"Well, John. I have to say that this has all taken me by surprise." Dale said "I can see the attraction in a small dalliance with the native women, but this is something quite different." He was shaking his head and looking at the words written before him with a quizzical look on his face.

Reverend Whitaker cleared his throat, his knee jiggling, eyebrows drawn together. "With the greatest of respect Sir Thomas, small dalliances with native women outside of wedlock are a sin *never* to be tolerated. I have spent most of my time in Henrico and Jamestown preaching against these carnal liaisons. If these unions are the way you have described, the whole Colony will be heading for depravity." He turned to look at John. "You are at pains to stress that this union is not just carnal. I know you to be a man of God as I have been working with you to bring Pocahontas into the fold of the Lord, but I also know the weaknesses of men who are far from home and without wives, who sink into debauchery. We have to be very careful of the example that we are setting. " He looked at John not unkindly, but with a cynical lift of his eyebrow.

Sir Thomas Gates leant forward in his chair, stroking his beard nonchalantly. He winked at John, and smiled a knowing smile between friends. "She is a pretty little wench, even though she is a Heathen, and I am not surprised that she and John have, shall we say, fallen for each other, as they have spent so much time together alone in religious instruction. But John, you are keen to point out that one of your reasons for the union would be to bring about peace between our peoples.

Personally, I feel there will never be peace between our peoples - we have tried, and we know now that they just don't want us here. It would be better if we massacred the lot, took their land and be done with it. There - I have said what everyone else is too scared to say. I know one of the goals from the very beginning of this project was to convert Heathens - indeed most of the investors' money was given based on this promise. But it seems a lost cause if you ask me. If we consent to this, I see it as a gesture to expectations - but I cannot believe it will bring peace." He threw his hands up and shrugged his shoulders.

John took a deep breath and fixed his gaze on each of the men before him in turn. He drew himself up to full height and thought of the large bald Cyprus trees, taking strength from the image.

"Gentlemen, I know that each of you have views on my proposal and I would like the opportunity to explain here in more detail the advantage of this union, not to me - because that is a personal matter - but more importantly to King and Country. I know it seems almost incredible that the union of just two people could achieve more than has been achieved here since 1587 when the settlers arrived in Roanoke, but I believe with all my heart that this is true." John stared at Sir Thomas Gates.

Dale smirked, putting his fingers together and leaning back in his chair. "It seems an exaggeration John, to think that a mere marriage would achieve what you are suggesting, but I will indulge you. Convince us." He laughed.

John took out his pipe and filled it with tobacco. "Will anyone else join me?" he asked.

Gates nodded and filled his pipe, lighting it from the coals of the fire.

The bright red embers caught and crackled, the grey smoke spiralling up into the room. John 'drank' in the pipe, slowly drawing in the hot fragrance, feeling it enter his lungs, at once releasing tension. Tobacco was going to aid his argument, so he had to make sure that the room contained it's wonderful scent, enticing them into the pleasures of it, relaxing them and opening their minds. Bewitching them, as he had been bewitched.

"Sirs" said John, his voice clear and confident. "This Colony has come through war, starvation, and disease. If the Will of God for us to be here was absent, I believe that Jamestown would be like Roanoke - deserted of Englishmen. But we are here with an opportunity.

To finance the project, we promised we would start expanding the Colonies of Great Britain. Everyone realizes that the Spanish are well ahead of us in this, and it is becoming humiliating. However, an even larger concern of potential investors was that we make sure that the ignorant Heathens have the opportunity to open their eyes to the One True God. Remember 'Nova Britannia'[1] gentlemen. Remember the promises that were made in that document to investors? In due course there will be expectations of proof of the delivery of those promises, and we must be ready.

We promised, not only a financial return, but more importantly, the thing that became of prime importance was to bring civilization in the way of religion to the Heathens - not to intrude on the natives, but to work with them, lifting them from base Heathenism, teaching them to believe in God and Jesus Christ and keeping them safe by defending them against their enemies. We were to be the benevolent friend.

We likened our invasion to Don Jan Daquita's invasion of Ireland. He raised the citizens out of bondage, bringing them to religion. We also likened ourselves to Julius Caesar and his Roman Legions, who invaded our lands and civilized us. This is what we promised the investors. Sir Thomas Dale has remembered these pledges, and to his credit, has used the kidnapping of Pocahontas as a first step in proving that we are starting to convert the Heathens to Christians - but what if we could take that even further?" He paused, drawing on his pipe, allowing his words to linger. He could see that he had their attention. Each man here had a goal, and none of them had been able to achieve it. He was going to offer them a way.

"How do we prove that we have been working toward the goals that we so publicly advertised? It must be something that is recognized not only by *our* King and Queen, but by Powhatan and his people. Friendship between our peoples based on Christian family values and marriage. An example set by a high-born Princess converting from Heathenism to Christianity and to prove it, she falls in love with and marries a Christian. A Princess who publicly declares her love of a Christian will send a strong message to her kinsmen, and we can start converting them on a grand scale. They will trust their Princess to know what is good. They will want to follow her lead.

The three men listening looked stunned. They were lost for words. John's argument seemed so logical.

John had not finished. He drew another long breath. "Not only is it God's Will that the Heathens are converted. It is God's will that affection grows to such an extent between The Powhatan and The English that they grow to love each other enough to marry and raise children." He stopped looking at the ground, gathering his thoughts for maximum impact, then he looked at them one by one.

"Don't you see? Pocahontas will set an example. If *she* can love an Englishman, then the English *must* be friends and allies. They will trust her. She is their Beloved Woman. Why would they want to fight us if their Beloved Woman and Princess loves and is married to one of us?"

Alexander Whitaker was staring at the floor, rubbing his thumb and index fingers together nervously. "Pocahontas is a bright, intelligent young woman" he said. "My question is whether Pocahontas really loves you John? I am very fond of her, and I feel uncomfortable about the possibility of exploiting her for our own ends."

Dale looked across at him giving him a conspiratorial and condescending smile. "Oh, I see Alexander... I am wondering how fond of her you actually are? Perhaps you are rushing in a bit too quickly to be so gallant to the lady? What do we read into that?"

The Reverend's face turned bright red, and he fidgeted more with his fingers looking at the floor.

Oh no, thought John, the poor lad has fallen for her too. It all made sense. The Reverend spent a lot of time with Pocahontas, and because of his position there was never any hint of anything but proper conduct, and never would be. However, he was a very young man, from an exceptionally traditional background. It would make perfect sense that the unobtainable exotic Indian maiden would have stirred up something previously quite unknown in the loins of the poor virgin priest. He was probably in as much of a bewitched state as John himself. John smiled to himself.

The Reverend looked up. "Gentlemen, I am a man of God, I would never let my feelings get in the way of God's Work."

Gates laughed. "Don't worry Alexander, we won't make an issue of this. All young men have crushes - we can't blame you for that. Let's stick to the point please gentlemen, amusing as it is to see a young man squirm." He smiled. "What are the implications for this marriage in terms of the good of the Colony. That is the most important issue. Is it realistic to think that this could foster better relations between us and the Powhatan? To be absolutely honest, I am not sure. How special is this girl to her people? You would think they would have made more of an effort to get her back if they were really worried."

John could see that he was now only really dealing with Dale and Gates. The Reverend had gone into himself, probably worried that he might divulge more of his feelings.

John sighed. "You might take Powhatan's silence as lack of care" he said. "I think they are so frightened that she is harmed, that they are playing it as safely as they can."

"It could be that is true" said Dale. "Trouble is we won't know until we start negotiating."

"Absolutely right" said John. "So, we must start the process as soon as possible, so that we can gauge the situation and then decide the next course of action. Forgive me Sirs, but we can't just sit here twiddling our thumbs for too much longer." He drew on his pipe, pausing again for them to think about what he had said. He felt he had not entirely won them over yet.

He lowered his pipe and looked at Gates, who he felt would be the most likely to give him a chance. "One of our promises was also to work with them on the land. We have been taking their land, but not giving them anything in return. What if we were able to plant the new tobacco seeds that I brought from Bermuda, and they could help cure it through their years of knowledge?

We could have a crop between us - something shared, that would also improve relations between us. I admit that I do not have the expertise, but I do have the seeds."

Gates drew on his pipe letting the smoke sigh out of his lungs as he considered what John had said. "You may have a point there John."

Dale's eyebrows drew together "So what you are saying is that we have to make over a lot of the land to tobacco and use the Savages as slaves John?"

"Well, no, not exactly Sir Thomas. It would not be as brutal as that. If I married Pocahontas, I would be in a position to negotiate on friendly terms with her tribe. I would propose that we have a partnership whereby I provide the seeds and they provide me with education on how to cure the leaves. I am sure that these seeds, if cured properly, will give us a crop that London will be frantic to receive. I think it will be better than the Spanish tobacco that everyone is so fond of. I believe these seeds were left in Bermuda by the Spanish, and if we can cure them with Powhatan methods, we will have a crop that will sell like gold dust."

Dale was still looking troubled. "I am concerned that you will take up all the land that we need to grow crops to feed ourselves. We cannot eat tobacco. This is what happened before - people didn't plant crops because they were so keen to find gold. You are saying this is the new 'gold'."

John could see Dale being the obstacle to his plans. Bastard, he thought to himself.

"No" he said brusquely. "This would be done slowly and in a controlled way. We would acquire extra land over and *above* that used for crops, to plant the tobacco. We could also enlist the help of the Powhatans for labour, so that our own labour could still be used to provide vital food. If it didn't work - we would have lost nothing but a bit of Powhatan labour, and the land that we had cultivated for the tobacco could be re-used for crops."

Dale nodded his head. John could see that he was starting to see the benefits of his idea. He really is a cold and calculating person, thought John. Gates too nodded. "I can see some merit in this John."

Reverend Whitaker bit his lower lip and sighed. "For me, the most important thing is that we do not take advantage of Pocahontas. She is a vulnerable girl, away from her family. There must be no suggestion of forcing her into marriage, as there would be uproar not only from London, but I dread to think what the consequences might be from her father.

We *must* be convinced that she is marrying you out of love and her own free will - not just as a cynical political convenience. I must also be assured that she has completed her religious instruction, that she takes a Christian name and she revokes all belief in the spirit Gods of the Powhatan. I would add that she will also have to convince her own people of these things if they are to follow her lead."

John nodded enthusiastically. He was giving the performance of his lifetime. "Believe me when I say that we are a couple in love" he said convincingly, knowing that this was the biggest lie he had ever told.

John saved his piece de resistance until last.

"There is one other thing… Pocahontas is pregnant. I know that people have been speculating, but we must keep the truth a secret. We can announce her pregnancy after the wedding to convey that her baby was conceived in a loving marriage. The baby could be promoted as the first Anglo/Powhatan baby ever to be born. We do not know who the father of this baby is – and we don't have to. If this is handled correctly, I can claim parentage after we are wed and this baby can be seen as a symbol of peace between our peoples. If handled badly, it can be seen as rape of a Powhatan child by an unknown Englishman, a symbol of dominant violence of the Powhatans by the English - which would The Virginia Company prefer?"

[1] See Appendix B

IMPERFECT SOLUTION

❧

P ocahontas knew that John was meeting with Dale, Gates, and Reverend Whittaker, to try and find out what he could about what the future held for her. She sat, looking around the small house that had been her home for the past few months. Her belly was quite large now. It was not long before she was due to give birth, so she felt heavy and uncomfortable. The baby's movements had slowed down as there was very little room. She touched her taught belly. What does the future hold for us, little one? Will you survive? A tear slid down her cheek. She had no power to protect this baby, and her father did not even know that he would soon have a new grandchild. Will you be a boy or a girl? What will you look like? Will you have fair hair like your father, or will you look like me? Where will you live when you grow up? There were so many questions.

John knocked and came into the room. She tried to get a sense of his mood. He looked sombre. Perhaps the news was not good. He looked at her as if something tragic had happened. Her heart fell. John had been such a good friend to her, but even *he* was powerless in the face of the evil of Dale. John could only do his best for her, and she hoped it would be enough.

John sighed. "Dale will spare your life as long as you embrace Christianity and renounce your Heathen faith... but there is something else... "

Her body tensed, what else did he want? "Just tell me John. Tell me what I have to do and when I will be able to go home again."

John spoke softly and slowly, he was shaking, partly with guilt, partly with anticipation. It had been his idea, even if he had done it to save her, it had given her few choices, "When you have had this baby, you will be allowed to visit your family... "

"What do you mean visit? I must go home to my child and my father... " She had at first been relieved, but now she was starting to panic. Was this more demands on her from the Gods, or was it just the evilness of Dale?

John took a deep breath. "Dale wants you to visit your father to tell him that you are Christian, that your name is no longer Pocahontas, but it is now Rebecca. He wants you to tell your family that you have embraced Christianity and you believe that it is the one true religion and that you urge them to convert as well. You are also to tell your father that you have fallen in love and you want to marry an Englishman and have English children to forge the peace between our peoples."

Pocahontas looked at him with wide eyes full of fear. "Marry? Who am I to marry... not Dale?" she whispered, her face white with fear.

He reached for her hands and gently held them. "Me" he said, looking into her eyes, pausing, holding his breath, waiting for a response.

At first, her face was a blank canvas. She was trying to assimilate what he had said. "I am... to... marry... you?" She faltered. She shook her head. "John, we are friends, but I cannot marry you. I will always belong to Kocoum. You cannot spend your life with someone who does not love you, and whom you do not love, just for Thomas Dale. No, it would not be fair on you to have to do such a thing."

John was still holding her hands. "I do love you Pocahontas" he said. She looked into his eyes. There were no lies there.

Her heart lurched. He had laid bare his feelings, and he looked vulnerable, like a child wanting his heart's desire, but fearing it was going to be denied. She did not want to crush him, but neither could she lie to him. She owed him that.

"John, I love you as a friend, and respect you as such. I could never give you the kind of love that you deserve from a wife. You are a young man, you need to find a wife that will give you the close bond that is between husband and wife."

His eyes were moist, his eyebrows drawn. "I love you so much that if you would be prepared to marry me, I will accept whatever terms you dictate. I will never take anything from you that you do not give freely. I will never touch you intimately unless you desire me to do so. Not all Englishmen are like Thomas Dale" he said with melancholy in his voice.

Pocahontas shook her head again. "It would be unfair of me to accept."

"Pocahontas, I have given this hours of thought. I am absolutely sure that this is the only solution for both of us. I am mad with love for you, and you are in danger. What will you do if you do not marry me?"

She was lost for words, thinking about the trap she was in. She would not trust any other Longcoat.

"I trust that you would never abuse me John. If I *were* forcibly married to anyone else, I would have to take my own life as I would be faced with a future of rape and servitude."

He felt a deep hurt at her words, as it became clear that she saw him only as an escape from an unacceptable alternative. He would have to learn to accept the reality.

He sat next to her and gently put a brotherly arm around her shoulders. Feeling the warmth of her small body made his heart beat faster, but he would have to learn to put these feelings side. "Allow me to look after you and your baby. You have a life ahead of you, and I would like to be a small part of it."

"I believe the Gods must have sent you to me John."

A fluttering, a warm glow... a friend...

THOMAS: February, 1614

John sat next to her as the pains came infrequently. Soon, he would have to leave her as the baby started to come. She brushed his cheek. "I do love you in my own way, John" she said as she smiled at him. He bent towards her and kissed her cheek.

"I love you more than I have ever loved anyone before" he said. "… and when the baby has arrived, and we get married, I never want us to be parted."

Her heart lurched for him. She knew his infatuation was painful, but he was willing to take what little she could offer of herself. The situation was not perfect, but it was the best that they could do for one another.

"Oh, John… I think the baby is coming now. You should go outside and Matachanna will call you when it is over." She doubled up with pain as she squeezed his hand.

As the baby made it's way into the world, Pocahontas bore the pain stoically. Her mind went back to her first pregnancy and birth. How different her life had been then. Pictures of the tiny black haired little Ko-kee, with his black eyes and little perfect ears came into her mind. One lasting memory was of him toddling towards Kocoum, giggling, and falling over as Kocoum threw him into the air, peals of laughter coming from both father and son. She would never forget.

What memories would be made with this little one? John was not the real father, and she did not love him like she did Kocoum - what would that be like? Would John be able to love this child knowing who the father was and how it had been conceived? What would be the reaction from Thomas Dale when he saw his offspring?

Another pain came. "The baby is nearly here Pocahontas" said Matachanna. Pocahontas gave one last push, and heard the wonderful sound of the cry of a healthy baby. "It is a little boy Pocahontas" shouted Matachanna.

Pocahontas sat up as Matachanna put the baby in her arms.

She looked down at the little crumpled face and smiled. "Welcome, my little peacemaker. You are a very special little boy." She marvelled at his pale skin and sandy coloured hair - so different to his big brother, but so beautiful. "Matachanna, please let John come and see this little one."

John came in, peering at Pocahontas and her baby. He too had memories of his first little baby. She was called Bermudas. She had been so small and weak that she had sadly died after only two weeks of life. He remembered her little tiny coffin, and his agony as he saw her being put in the ground in Bermuda. His heart had been hardened by his overwhelming feelings of loss, until he had met Pocahontas. Now this little boy was healthy and hearty, screaming his lungs out to let the world know that he had arrived. Thank God. Maybe he had another chance to be a father.

Pocahontas watched John - what would his reaction be? She need not have worried. John beamed with happiness as he bent down and kissed her on the cheek and the baby on the top of his head.

"Are you well, Pocahontas?" he asked. She looked tired, but happy.

She smiled at him. "This little one has arrived safe and sound. It was pain, but nothing compared to the joy at holding him now." She drew him to her breast, and he started to suckle. She felt the wonderful flow of her milk and watched as his little head bobbed up and down, sucking in the nourishment, little sighs showing his contentment with his new world. Just like Ko-kee, she thought, as a pang of grief wedged its way into her happiness.

"What is his name to be Pocahontas?" asked John startling her back to the present.

This was the one thing that Pocahontas had been worried about. Should the baby have a Powhatan name? Should he take John's name as he was going to be his father?

The decision had been taken out of her hands in a final act of cruelty.

"Thomas" she said, looking John straight in the eye.

John pulled back and took a deep breath. Pocahontas could see disappointment written all over his face, and she looked away, devastated to have hurt him.

Thomas Dale had made one further demand that John was not aware of. He wanted them both to remember his power over them. He wanted them always to remember whose child it was.

She took John's hand and squeezed it.

LAST JOURNEY: March, 1614

❧

It was a long journey from Jamestown to Werowocomoco. Thomas Dale was determined to stamp his authority on Powhatan. He did not want peace, no - he wanted complete dominance, and he needed to ensure that the Heathens understood this. He needed to overpower these people and convert them to Christianity. It would also be useful to use the land that they had already cultivated - perhaps the Heathens, once converted and tamed, could even be used as slaves to till the land, bringing the Colony to its full potential. He had already made a good start, but what they really needed was more land - land that the Powhatans already had.

He paid lip service to all this nonsense about Pocahontas. Yes, yes, he knew he had to be seen to do things by the book. Pocahontas was going to be an example of how the Indians could be tamed to fulfil the obligations that had been made to the investors. Yes, conversion to Christianity was important, but even more important was making money - he was going show those in London who financed the Colony, that there was great financial potential in these lands and these people. Great potential for expanding the Empire and taking over their resources. Exploitation - such an ugly word really.

No one liked to utter it, but everyone who benefited from it (as long as it was not *seen* to be exploitation) was quite prepared in the end to turn a blind eye. Yes, he could make a name for himself. John Smith had had the same idea, but he never carried it out. Who knows why? At least he could take up the mantle and control this land once and for all.

He thought of Pocahontas. He had been in his element. She was a challenge at times, but he liked that about her. She had spirit. He had grown weary of her though. John Rolfe's plan seemed to be an elegant solution. John could marry the filthy bitch and take on the bastard as his son - and Dale could take credit for a job well done in integrating the Heathens into Christian society. Simple. If Pocahontas even breathed a hint that Dale was the father of the child, he had a neat little accident planned for her. It was an added knife in Pocahontas's back to insist on naming the bastard child, Thomas. He smiled to himself.

His mind wandered as ever, to his own physical needs. He had heard that Pocahontas had a younger sister. Maybe he could have her as a replacement. He could replicate those first few months with Pocahontas, but with a younger version. He could even marry her sister. That would not only be extremely satisfying, but would be further argument that he was doing his bit for integration. That said, there was no doubt in his mind that there was something exciting about Indian Squaws. Much more interesting than the pale and boring wife that he had married only a year previously in England.

The ship ploughed through the water, and Dale could see that some Powhatan Warriors were shadowing the ship on the riverbank. He thought with satisfaction of how he had landed further down the river and already burned several houses and killed a few savages - just getting the message understood of course. Dale knew that Powhatan would soon learn of his evil deeds - a deliberate message to the old boy that they meant business.

A message had also been sent to Powhatan to let him know that Pocahontas would be returned if he gave up the rest of the hostages that he had taken, supplied corn and returned the guns that his men had stolen - but Dale knew this was actually not going to happen - Pocahontas would never go back to her people.

He smiled to himself. It was a good plan, of that there was no doubt. He had shown his strength to the Savages, and he had primed Pocahontas. She knew what her options were. He had always meant to return her, hadn't he? It was her own love of Christianity and of John Rolfe that had been the deciding factor. Nothing whatsoever to do with him.

He banked on Pocahontas giving the performance of her lifetime - If she slipped up - even a tiny amount, he would not only kill the tiny suckling halfbreed that she had just given birth to, but he would annihilate her tribe, making sure to find her other child as well, and he would kill him while she watched. He had told her that he would pull the child limb from limb and cut his heart out to present to her. Although she was a Savage, she certainly was not stupid, and she knew what he was capable of.

At last she was heading back to Werowocomoco. She had not seen her home or her family since she had fled to the protection of Japasaw. She had reluctantly left the tiny little scrawling bundle that was Thomas, with Matachanna. There was another nursing mother that would feed him while she was away. She could feel the agony of being without him as her breasts hardened with milk, painful without his little mouth sucking to relieve it. They needed each other. This prompted her to think back to her first little one. Her little Powhatan baby. How she loved him. How she ached for him as well.

Ko-kee - she wondered how much he would have grown in the year since she had last seen him. He had been toddling then, but by now he must be running around and talking... she sighed. She had missed so much of his growing up. Maybe she would see him when she went ashore? Excitement raced through her body at the thought.

She was looking forward to seeing Werowocomoco, her home, but it would not be the same without Kocoum. He would not be there with his arms open wide to embrace her, holding Ko-kee's hand. Her heart lurched. Nothing would ever be the same without him. He had been the love of her life, and he still was. His spirit gave her strength when she needed it. His image appeared regularly - he would never forsake her, but her loss of him was raw.

Dale had told her what she must do when she saw her family. She would do it - not just because *he* wanted her to do it, but because she believed it was a way to forge peace. She doubted very much if she would see her father. He would know that if he was kidnapped the way that she had been, that it would be the end of the tribe, and he would never risk that - even to see her.

She stood on the deck smelling the earthy forest that surrounded them. She saw the warriors lined up on the bank, spears at the ready, waiting to either welcome or defend, as they gauged the mood of the approaching Longcoats. She saw her Uncle Opechancanough standing in the middle, his face stern, as he watched the ship coming nearer to the edge of the river and her two brothers Pochins and Parahunt standing next to him.

This was to be a moment of political importance, and it could be that the goal of peace would finally be achieved. But for a young seventeen year old girl, it was the moment she was coming home, away from the foreign and unfamiliar life that had been imposed on her. She had dreamt of seeing these familiar trees, breathing in this familiar air, and being part of something so familiar that it was welded into her very soul. Home. Tears came to her eyes.

There was no sign of her father, as she knew there wouldn't be. Even although she had known he would not risk coming to this meeting, her heart sank with the disappointment. She longed to see her father and to feel his huge arms circling her. She wondered if she would ever see him again? If she would ever feel like a small child, - helpless but empowered, the way she felt with Powhatan when she nestled into his large chest.

She watched as Dale disembarked with one of his aides, Ralph Hamor and John followed, accompanied by many soldiers pointing their guns at the Powhatan warriors. The atmosphere was solemn and tense. One wrong move on the part of either side, and there would be bloodshed.

Dale was speaking to Opechanough, and she could see their heads nodding as if at last they may be coming to an agreement. Opechancanough was pointing to the trees - maybe indicating the absence of Powhatan. Dale nodded and spoke to John who started to make his way over to her.

He signalled to her to disembark. He held her hand as she walked over towards Opechancanough, Pochins and Parahunt. They were looking intently at her approaching in her Western clothes. The hem of her dress dragged in the mud, and the shoes became soggy and wet. How she longed for her shift and her moccasins... She walked slowly at first, making sure that she had her footing, then she threw off John's hand, and started running, abandoned, throwing herself into the arms of her brothers and her uncle. She sobbed and sobbed, full of the emotions that had been pent up for the last year. She pulled back from her brothers, and breathed in the air, looking up at the sky and opening her arms to embrace it. She could feel the spiritualism of her home, something that was lacking in all the lands taken over by the Tassantassas. This was life; Jamestown was duty.

For one brief moment, she could feel the joys of just being a Powhatan squaw, before she had to sacrifice it forever. She hoped her sacrifice could save this native world, save this way of life for her children and her children's children. Where was Ko-Kee? Where was her little Ko-Kee? Could she bear to see him and not stay? Her lovely little Biibiins...

She took a deep breath to ground herself. A large circle had surrounded her. She looked at them one by one, her eyes darting frantically until she came to a squaw who held a young child by the hand. As Pocahontas looked at the child, he broke away from the girl that was holding him and came running to Pocahontas.

"Djoodjoo, Djoodjoo" he cried, his little legs running as fast as he could. She opened her arms. Her heart soared. "Ko-kee, my little Biibiins". She was trembling as he threw himself into her arms. She enveloped him, snuggling him. The tears were streaming down her face, and it was as if there was no one in the world but her and Ko-kee. She held him for what seemed like only a few seconds, just breathing him in, his little body melted into hers. She thought of all the things that she had missed, and her tears fell. She clung to him.

Dale signalled for the squaw to take him away. She struggled to hold onto him, and he screamed and screamed, "Djoodjoo – please take me with you. Please Djoodjoo… " His large brown eyes looked at her streaming with tears through his torment and he was forcibly pulled from her arms. He continued to scream, reaching his arms out to her, wanting her to come to him. She held her arms out to him, but was pulled backwards, her life force draining from her. Why had she been chosen to do this? Maybe she would just refuse to leave – but she knew this was not possible. These people, these lands might be saved from war by her sacrifice.

She forced herself to look at the ground trying to empty her heart of pain. She could not bear the torment, this was the worst moment in her life - she had to let him go. Her heart was breaking. She looked up at Dale. One wrong move, and he would kill Ko-kee. She had no choice but to let him go.

She frantically looked to see him again, but his little form had disappeared through the crowd. She could still hear him crying "Djoodjoo… Djoodjoo… please do not leave me again…" but the plaintive cry was getting quieter and quieter as he was taken further and further away from her. She whispered to herself "Biibiins, I will love you forever… " She looked to the sky and said "please Ahone, make him understand… please look after him and let him know I will always love him. I will never ask for anything of you again." She bowed her head and focused her eyes back on the crowd, but everything was blurred. To stop the pain, she had to stop feeling. She had to calm herself and perform, she had to do this for Ko-kee. Maybe one day he would understand and not hate her for leaving him. She had to make them all believe that she was happy with the English, that she wanted to forsake her Powhatan life and religion and become Rebecca, the wife of an Englishman. Remember, she thought to herself, this is not just for Dale's satisfaction, it is to save my people, to save Ko-kee, to save these trees, to save this land from utter destruction and war. She looked up and Badger was watching, encouraging.

As she spoke, she felt like she was someone else - she could hear her own voice and see herself standing in front of her people, but she did not feel that the words coming out of her mouth were hers. She was frightened - what if it wasn't good enough? What if Dale decided to kill them all anyway? But as her speech went on, she could see that they were all nodding and smiling. They believed her - even although her heart was breaking to think that she was now a different person, a Christian who would marry an Englishman, with only one baby, not two. As she finished speaking, Opechancanough and her two brothers came over to her and hugged her. This was goodbye.

John came and took her hand protectively. Dale was smiling. It had all gone so well that he and Opechancanough were now the best of friends, laughing and smiling and patting each other on the back. There was even the promise of regular shipments of corn to seal the deal.

Rebecca stood looking around her for the last time at the place that she had known as home for so long, trying to brand the image into her mind, so that she could recall these beloved faces in the dark moments of the future when they were lost to her. Everyone seemed to be happy except her. For her, there were so many memories, so much joy that had gone in an instant. So much loss. Blowing bubbles into her baby's neck, her father's musky embrace, the meaty smell of the venison crackling over the fire, the wide blue sky, the trees whispering, the pungent apook... Kocoum...

She was compelled to look away. There he was, by a tree... he smiled and nodded, his eyes sad, but resigned. Her silent tears fell, unnoticed by the celebrating crowd around her. Why did everything have to be this way? Why had she been chosen?

UNION: April 5, 1614

Her wedding day arrived. How different things were today from the day she married Kocoum. That had been one of the happiest days of her life. Today, there was no joy, she was trapped. She was Powhatan's daughter, this marriage would bring peace.

Personally? She felt sad, but determined she was going to make the best of it. Dale had instructed everyone that her name was now Rebecca. She was still unused to it, hating the name as it had not been given to her by her father. It would take time to come to terms with this new life. There were so *many* new things, apart from being married to someone she hardly knew, and giving up her beautiful Ko-kee. Since her last meeting with him, his weeping brown eyes, and his little voice begging her not to leave him, haunted her. She had had to accept that she would never see him again. She whispered to herself; "Biibiins ... I will never forget you..."

She heard a knock on the door and startled, looked up. It was John.

"Poc... Sorry...Rebecca - I wanted to come and see you before the ceremony. How are you? Are you happy?" His eyes were pleading and hopeful, as he walked towards her and sat down.

"I am grateful" was all she could say. This strong and handsome man looked so hopeful, so wanting to please her, when inside she wanted to run away from him, turn back the clock, be sitting by the fire with Kocoum and Ko-kee. She felt for him, but not in the way he wanted.

"I just wanted you to know that this marriage will be what you want it to be. I have no expectations of being physically close to you, if that is not what you want. I will never touch you in that way, unless it is something that you desire." His face was earnest and sincere.

She looked at the floor. "I am sorry that I cannot give you what you deserve John. I will always love you as a friend. My heart belongs to another and there is nothing that I can do about that." She looked up at him.

"You have always been honest with me about that Rebecca. We can make this marriage work because we have love and respect for one another." His eyes held sorrow, and she knew that he wanted so much more from her. The fact that he was willing to sacrifice his physical needs to be with her, made her heart ache for him.

She got up and walked over to him and taking both of his hands, pulled him out of his chair. She looked up at him as he towered above her and put her arms around his waist, resting her head on his chest. "Thank you John" she whispered.

He stood stiff, unable to move. He wanted her so badly it hurt. Just to feel her arms, just to smell her scent - enticed him almost to the edge. He kissed the top of her head, unwrapped her arms and took her hands in his. "There is no need to thank me ever again. This morning we will be married, and by marrying me, you will make me the happiest man on earth. I want nothing more than for us to live together as friends, and to bring up little Thomas together. You and your family can help me with the planting of the tobacco, and life will be good Rebecca. We will stop the wars and make this land bountiful again."

She smiled at him. He was such a good man. He had no idea how her heart was breaking, and she was determined to keep that from him to repay for what he was doing for her.

Kocoum would always be the third person in this marriage. She would never be able to put him out of her mind, and she knew these feelings would always prevent her from getting closer to John.

Her father had given his blessing to this marriage. He was not coming to the wedding, because it was too dangerous, but he had sent her Uncle Opachisco to stand in for him, and her two brothers had also come to the ceremony.

"I think it is time for us to go now John. You must go ahead, and I will come with Matachanna when I am ready. Opachisco will bring me to you at the altar."

As he left, Matachanna helped her change into her beautiful dress. It was of the palest yellow lace, cinched in at the waist with embroidered daisies. She had little white pumps made of satin, and her glossy hair hung down her back. She had a crown of wildflowers in her hair and she carried a bouquet of fragrant flowers, the scent of which was intoxicating.

Just as she was about to leave, Pochins knocked on the door.

"Pocahontas" he said. "I have a present from your father. He asked me to give you these, so that you could wear them at your wedding to remind you of him."

He opened a pouch of the softest deerskin and she peered inside. She held her breath as she pulled out a string of the most beautiful and delicate string of pearls that she had ever seen. Their sheen caught the light and made them glow.

"Oh my goodness" she whispered. "Pochins, please will you tell my father of my gratitude to him. I will always carry these pearls with me, so that I feel he is closer to me." Her face was beaming. Maybe the only thing today to bring her happiness.

"Please Matachanna, can you fasten these pearls around my neck, so that I can wear them for the ceremony."

These pearls would remind her that she still belonged to Kocoum and her father, she was still Powhatan, and that everything else was a bad lie told for a good reason. She allowed herself to smile. She would never take these pearls off, they were symbolic of who she was.

She walked down the aisle with Opachisco. As she walked, she looked around at the assembled group. There was a familiar face. Thomas Savage. She had not seen him for a long time, and for a moment she faltered, remembering past times when she and Thomas were different people hugging in a circle with Kocoum. He smiled and nodded at her, and she felt her stomach doing a somersault. Was she doing the right thing marrying a man that she did not love? She looked ahead of her and saw Reverend Whittaker at the end with John next to him. John's face was full of anticipation. His eyes sparkled, and he could not stop smiling at her. She knew she looked beautiful, and she smiled back at him, only glad that she was making him happy. She glanced back at Thomas Savage - there were regrets, but it was too late to consider them. She gave him a smile that spoke volumes.

Thomas Dale stood on the side-lines glaring at her. Dale was powerless to do anything to her now. She was his peace envoy - his ticket to fame - a mere commodity. It would have been so nice to spit in his face, but she had to curtail her hatred to see this through.

His son, Thomas started to cry at the back. Dale looked around straining to see him. Was that concern on his face? He shook himself. "Remove that child" he bellowed, the voice of cruel authority once more.

Reverend Whittaker proceeded with the ceremony.

Finally:

"Rebecca, daughter of Powhatan formerly known as Pocahontas, and John Rolfe of Norfolk, England, I now pronounce you man and wife."

She looked up and there was Kocoum. He smiled warmly at her and bowed his head.

Kocoum understood and was giving her his blessing. She smiled at him. In the moment that she should have been sharing her heart with John, she was sharing it with Kocoum.

She looked at John with tears in her eyes. He took her hand and squeezed it.

"I will be here for you forever" he said.

She nodded, but could not return the words.
She felt her pearls as Badger looked on.

A NEW LIFE: 1614

Her new home at Varina Farm Plantation, which was just across the James River from Henrico, was very different from what she was used to. But, as she looked around her, she felt content. Her heart still ached for all that she had lost, but for now, she had managed to achieve a start to the peace that she had been working towards.

Uncle Opechancanough had kept his promise, and regular supplies of corn arrived from Powhatan, to the delight of Thomas Dale. No doubt Dale felt smug and pleased with himself that things so far had gone so well. He had used her to his best advantage. She shook her head in disbelief at the way things had turned out.

Her relationship with John was good. They were best friends, and as promised, he had never tried to be intimate with her. They loved each other in their own ways, and whilst she knew that this would never be enough for John, he was prepared to sacrifice his desires for her sake. Maybe in another time and place they could have been lovers, but that was just not possible, and John had been as good as his word in treating her with respect.

She had not realised the extent of the work that her new husband had done with the tobacco seeds that he had brought from Bermuda. Since they were married, he had spent many hours talking to her about it, his eyes sparkling with excitement, about the new "Gold" that he wanted to cultivate as a valuable commodity to send back to England. The Virginia Company were getting angry that the Colony had not supplied the returns that had at first been promised. It was thought that gold could be found in Virginia - but it had turned out to be 'fools gold', sparkling minerals with no value, and investors were starting to think the whole project a waste of time.

With the tobacco crop, John was starting to turn things around. He had named the Apook 'Orinoco' - he told her this was after an explorer called Sir Walter Raleigh who had traveled up a River called 'Orinoco' when he was searching for the City of Gold. John felt this crop to be even better than gold. He had already spent several years testing and trying it out on friends striving for a mild and delicious strain that would appeal to Londoners. She smiled, thinking of his childlike enthusiasm for the "new" crop that had been the backbone of her culture for generations.

John needed land, men, and expertise to make this apook grow into a valuable commodity. He had already exported some back to England, and it had received positive feedback, but he was convinced that he could do so much better. He put his heart and soul into finding the best recipe for exporting to London. He spent his days in the fields working to achieve his ambition. Sometimes, when she could, she also helped him.

Pocahontas knew her people were experts on the cultivation of tobacco - and she had seen another opportunity to push for peace. If she could engineer a way for the two cultures to work towards a common goal - surely she had to try? She had succeeded.

Now she watched as her kinsfolk worked alongside her husband and his workers, clearing vast acres of land to sow the apook seeds. She smiled to herself. Maybe things were going to work out after all?

A few months ago, no one would have thought that the two cultures could work so well together - and she knew that it would not have happened without her. They were even calling this the "New Peace" which made her heart swell with pride.

Thomas was thriving. In private, they called him, 'BaBa' a rebellious gesture to Thomas Dale. He was three months old now, and no one had mentioned the date of his birth and who his father actually had been. He had fair skin and hair confirming his English heritage, but the deep black eyes of the Powhatans. John so far had been a wonderful father to the little boy. He loved him dearly. Men generally seemed a little awkward with tiny babies, but John had picked him up with confidence the first time he saw him and had continued since then as if he was his father. She knew John had been very disappointed when she had not named Thomas after him. He did not argue with her, he had accepted it, apart from never actually registering the baby in the Jamestown register... maybe he had just forgotten?

As she stood in front of the house that John had built, she heard little Thomas start to cry. She had only stepped out for a moment to bring in the dry washing. She turned around and rushed inside to see what the baby needed.

She could hardly believe her eyes.

"Ah Pocahontas... how lovely to see you again my dear."

Dale was holding Thomas. She went to take the child from him, but he moved away, holding the baby in the air. Thomas's little face was red, and his eyes were staring with panic. Dale was looking at the baby with an expression on his face that Pocahontas had never seen before. Could it be affection?

"The child has the same opinion of me as his mother, I see" he said.

Pocahontas was trembling. She rushed forward, eyes pleading. "Please leave him alone" she whimpered.

Dale laughed. "I only wanted to see him and get to know him. I love children. They are so innocent and pliable - and of course, there is the added benefit of this one being mine. You can hardly deny me access to my own flesh and blood. " he said, cradling the baby in his arms.

She bristled. "I can certainly deny you that. You are frightening him. Give him back to me at once" she commanded. Externally she appeared as a

246

lioness protecting her cub, internally she was falling down a deep crevasse into the unknown. Surely he did not want him back?

"So, you haven't lost any of your aggressiveness then? For Goodness Sake, stop him crying, that is what mothers are for isn't it?" He spat as he thrust the screaming tear stained baby towards her.

She grabbed the baby, soothing him and rubbing his back, pulling him as far away as she could get, scowling at Dale. "It is alright BaBa" she whispered into his ear.

"What do you really want? Why have you come here after all this time?"

She looked at Thomas, focussing on his beautiful features, breathing slowly stopping the arrows of panic that were piercing her chest. Surely having married John, she would now be protected against this monster? He would not dare touch her or take Thomas - but then again, it was Thomas Dale - he was capable of anything.

He smiled. The smile that told of menace rather than amusement. His thin lips stretched wide to reveal yellow teeth. His perfectly manicured beard shaped to a point, matching his straight and pointed nose. Her stomach turned, her memories started to flood in - his hands like snakes invading her body. The bile rose in her throat and she shook herself back to the present.

Dale saw her stricken face. "Oh, I can see that I have caught you off guard, Princess" he laughed. "Please don't worry. I have come with the most wonderful news."

The crevasse was getting deeper. Dale never brought good news.

"I am going to marry your sister"

Pocahontas looked as if he had slapped her. This could not be happening. Which sister" she asked, eyes wide.

"Why your little one - Kanti" he said.

"But she is only 13 years old, you cannot marry her."

"I can do what I like, Princess... I have appointed Ralph Hamor, a man very familiar with your people, to deputize for me in the negotiations with your father. He is setting out tomorrow on my behalf to the Powhatan village to ask Powhatan to give me your sister's hand in marriage. If he agrees, I will meet him to finalize the deal before we have a lavish wedding.

I wanted you to be the first to know after all we have been through together. I was so keen to see your face when you heard the good news. You have set such a good example marrying John, that I thought I would marry a Powhatan squaw to reinforce the peace between our peoples the way you and John have done. That is what you want isn't it?" He looked at her grinning, his eyebrows raised in amusement.

"But you have a new wife in England" she stammered.

"Powhatan women are so much more interesting than English women, from my considerable experience. My English wife is of no consequence when I am in Virginia. Shame for her - but what can I do?" He shrugged his shoulders. "I hope you will be an honoured guest at the wedding of Kanti and myself. Opechancanough has become a very good friend, and I am sure he will put in a word for me with Powhatan - you never know, we may even get the old man to come to the wedding. Now that would really make headlines in London... You could be my sister in law... "

Thomas started to cry again.

Dale walked towards her, looking at his child. Pocahontas turned trying to get away from him.

She placed Thomas in his cradle, tucking him in and kissing his forehead. When she turned back, Dale had gone leaving nothing but a cold breeze.

Pocahontas sat looking at the closed door. She could not let this happen. She could not allow her beautiful little sister to suffer a lifetime of abuse at the hands of Dale. It was true that Opechancanough, who had always been sceptical about the merits of making peace with the Longcoats seemed to have changed his mind, based on her convincing act. No one realized that her baby's life had been at stake when she defected to the English.

If Powhatan agreed to Dale marrying Kanti, it would be because he had an unreal view of what the English were like, because of her. It was her fault. She had convinced them that she was happy and that the Longcoats were to be trusted. She never imagined forced marriages to be part of the peace. Maybe she had been naive. She was frantic. What could she do? She must get to Powhatan before this 'Ralph Hamor' secured a marriage contract for Dale.

Thomas was now fast asleep in his little cot. She would have to leave him with Matachanna as the journey was too difficult to contemplate carrying a baby. Thomas was not heavy, but it was such a long way to Matchcot and she didn't feel it would be safe to take him with her.

She went running outside to find Matachanna.

She saw her working hard as usual, picking tobacco leaves.

"Matachanna… Matachanna… come quickly, I need you" Pocahontas said. Her chest was rising and falling, and her eyes were flashing as she tried to contain her panic. "Quick Matachanna, I have no time to waste."

Matachanna looked up from what she had been doing, and immediately realised that there was something wrong.

"What is it Pocahontas?"

"I have to go to Matchcot NOW."

Pocahontas explained the dilemma that was facing her and when Matachanna heard the seriousness of the situation, she went inside to look after the sleeping baby without a word of protest.

"Please tell John where I have gone, and that I will be back as soon as I can. He must try and keep my absence a secret, and under no circumstances must he follow me. If Dale finds out what I am going to do, he will try and stop me, and that could mean my life." Her words were rushed, but Matachanna knew Dale, and knew that Pocahontas was not exaggerating. She kissed Pocahontas on the cheek.

"Good luck my little sister. The Gods are with you and the wind will carry you."

———————

Pocahontas changed out of her fussy English clothes. She knew the terrain that she was traveling on was not conducive to petticoats and delicate slippers. Putting on her old clothes that she had refused to throw away, gave her a certain comfort. She would never be anything but Powhatan, no matter what they did to her. These clothes only reinforced that.

At first she felt frightened all alone wandering through the forest. Gradually her true self re-appeared. She began to connect with Nature again, the wind howling through the trees became her friend rather than her foe. At times she ran, at times she walked. Occasionally she glimpsed Badger - how she had missed the life with Nature. She breathed in the sweet scent of the pine and the earthy smell of the detritus under foot. She savoured the moment of being alone. Something that she had not been allowed for a long time.

For hours and hours, she plodded on, tiredness eventually taking its toll. Her breasts were getting uncomfortably full of milk, but she would just have to ignore the throbbing in her chest.

She relaxed as the forest became familiar. Darkness was falling, and she needed to get there while she could still see. She was forced to stop though, even *her* young legs were not capable of continuing without rest. It would only take a few moments to catch her breath.

She sat down in a soft pile of leaves, putting her hands out to support herself. It was only a few more miles, she thought. Suddenly she felt a sharp pain in her hand. She looked down and saw the tell tale sign of two puncture wounds with spots of blood. As a Powhatan, snakes had never been a problem to her. It just meant putting the snake powder on the wound, and all would be well. Now though she looked with horror. She no longer carried snake powder - now she had nothing to deal with it. Her hand was starting to swell and turn blue. She had to try and make it to the tribe as quickly as possible. If she did not get the powder, she may die.

She rose from the sitting position, catching a glimpse of the brown and white slithering snake as it dove beneath a pile of leaves, rustling as it went. She had been tired before, but now she could feel herself weakening as the venom started to take hold of her body. The swelling was getting worse, and the throbbing, searing pain was almost unbearable. The venom was moving up her arm, and she was powerless. She was staggering, breathless and dizzy.

Why did this have to happen? How much longer could she go on? Half an hour passed, and she had not made much headway. Her light-headedness was getting worse, and now it was becoming difficult to breathe. She had to get the snake powder. She felt herself falling. The ground came up to hit her with no effort. She lay looking up at the darkness of the trees that no longer gave her comfort. "I must get to Matchcot" she whispered to herself.

She tried to pull herself up but could only raise her shoulders. Her head felt like the weight of ten men. She began crawling along the ground. She had to try, she could not give in. She could hear herself groaning. The pain infiltrated her world - throbbing, red and angry it invaded her whole consciousness.

The darkness was descending upon her - was this night or was this death? The realization hit her that she was not going to make it. This was it. Pocahontas was dying. There was so much to do though. She started to accept the reality and sink into the soft blackness of unconsciousness. Ko-kee... BaBa... Kocoum... where are you?

Badger curled up next to her.

A CHILD AGAIN: May, 1614

*K*o-kee... BaBa...Kocoum... *drifting on a cloud...*

Kocoum takes my hand, and I look at him. We have been apart for so long, and I have missed him so much. He is so strong, and I feel so weak and small. He smiles and pulls me to him. "Have you come to me Pocahontas?"

I want to say 'yes'. I want to go to him and be with him forever.

The smell of the apook fills my nostrils, and the sounds of chanting filter through the haze, Kocoum fades... "Come back" I cry. "Come back Kocoum, I want to go with you... it is time... "

Pocahontas started to feel sensations as the dream faded. She was lying on something soft, covered by a warm furry deerskin. She was warm, and the comforting smell of apook took her back to when she was a child. The feeling of being safe, safe with Powhatan, Matachanna and Kocoum. Nothing worried her. The smell of the smoke and the venison cooking made her mouth water, and the sounds of the Quiakros chanting was pleasant and satisfying. She belonged. She never wanted to leave this feeling or this place. Home. She did not want to open her eyes.

When she did open her eyes, she smiled. It was as if she had been transported back in time. Nothing had changed. There was Powhatan sitting beside her, and Waki came over and licked her face. "Oh Waki, where have you been? I have missed you so much". Waki's large brown eyes were soft and soulful. Pocahontas was surprised to see them filling up with moisture as if she were crying with joy to see her mistress again.

Powhatan stood up and tenderly pushed the hair away from Pocahontas's face, bending down to kiss her lightly on the forehead. Pocahontas thought he looked very old and tired, the wrinkles around his eyes had deepened, and his eyes drooped with the burdens that had faced him since the arrival of the Longcoats. He was not the same as when she had last seen him. When *had* she last seen him? Her mind started to whirl as things started to come back to her. Had Kocoum died? Where was Ko-kee? Flashes of another child filtered through her mind. Fair hair and dark eyes – Thomas…BaBa? In her mind he clung to her, his legs wrapped around her body as if he was a part of her… and his father… Had she really been married and had a Longcoat child? It was all fuzzy with flashes of one thing and then another - nothing making any sense. Surely it was a dream.

Her face fell as she took in the scene before her. As her eyes wandered, she realised that this was the stark reality. She was not a child. Her stomach began to contract with anxiety. A vision of abuse appeared in her mind. She was not safe, even although her father was here, and yes, she would have to leave this place very soon. She looked up into the face of her father and a tear ran down her cheek, the vision of Thomas Dale and Kanti overwhelming her as she remembered.

"How long have I been here father" she asked at last, grabbing for his hand, her eyes piercing him with their intensity as she tried in vain to sit up.

"My child, you have been here many hours. We found you last night. The snake bite was very bad, and when we brought you back the Sunsquaa gave you snake powder. We were not sure if the Gods would take your soul. It took a long time to work. You have been lying there for many hours. Outside the Medewin[1] has been danced throughout the night. The whole tribe have been dancing and praying to the Gods for your recovery. I believe the Gods saved you - most people would have died. You are saved because you are a Beloved Woman." He bowed his head with his hands at his heart.

He looked up, raising her fingers to kiss them. "What brings you to us, my child? Were you not happy with your husband and the Longcoats? To come alone like this, your mission must have been pressing." His face was long, and his eyebrows furrowed, increasing the deep lines around his weather-beaten brown face.

She took a deep breath. "Father, Sir Thomas Dale - The Chief of the Longcoats wants to marry Kanti. You must not allow it." The words shot out of her mouth like arrows. She had to get it out, she had to let him know her mission as soon as possible.

At that moment there was a commotion outside the Yehakin. Pocahontas could hear shouting and her heart stood still. What if it was Dale, and he found her here? His ruthlessness terrified her. To plot against Dale was not something one did lightly.

One of Powhatan's warriors came in and stood before them, breathless. He stopped and bowed.

"I beg forgiveness my Mamanantowick.[2] There are Longcoats outside. They say they come in peace. They want to speak to you urgently and have a message from Sir Thomas Dale." The warrior stood at attention staring straight ahead, his chest rising and falling with the exertion of his mission.

Pocahontas tried to lift her shoulders up from the cot, her hand still throbbing and painful. "Father, please don't let them know that I am here. You must make them wait while I tell you why I have come. If they find me Sir Thomas Dale will be very angry."

Powhatan looked from the warrior to Pocahontas and back to the warrior and nodded. "Tell them that they must wait. The Great Powhatan is in prayer and cannot be disturbed." He nodded his head to dismiss the warrior.

————————

Dale had taken one daughter, there was no way he was going to be allowed take another. Powhatan could not remember a time when he had seen Pocahontas so anxious to get her message across. Her eyes had been wide with the fear of Kanti being taken and married to Thomas Dale. Powhatan knew there were things that she was not telling him, things she could not tell him. He could read it in her eyes. Had Dale been cruel to Pocahontas? Why was she so determined that Kanti should go nowhere near him? It could have furthered the peace process if two Indian women were married to Longcoats - but his instincts and the Gods were telling him to listen to his daughter. Listen to the words of a Beloved Woman. He knew Pocahontas would never jeopardize the peace process and he must trust her without question.

He approached the Yehakin where the Longcoats were waiting for him. As he entered, the visitors stood up and he looked around to see who was before him. The friendly face of Thomas Savage was amongst them, and Thomas stepped forward bowing his head, placing his hands to his chest in greeting.

"Great Powhatan, it is so good to see you again after such a long time." His blue eyes smiled with genuine warmth at seeing the old man again.

"Thomas, I had not expected to see you - it is a pleasure to see a familiar face. Please introduce me to your traveling companions."

"May I present Ralph Hamor to you. He has come with a message from Sir Thomas Dale. I will translate for you."

Powhatan looked at the man that Thomas was referring to. He was short and stocky with an engaging smile. Powhatan walked towards Hamor, looking quizzically and intently at his neck. Hamor walked backwards, putting his hands up in front of himself defensively, unsure of what the old man was going to do.

Powhatan stopped and looked at Thomas. "Thomas, I do not see a chain of pearls around Mr. Hamor's neck. I would like you to tell Mr. Hamor that at the last meeting I had with Sir Thomas Dale, he promised that should he send an emissary to me with a message, he would give the emissary a chain of pearls which he would have around his neck. I do not see the chain of pearls. Sir Thomas said that if there were no pearls that I should send the emissary back without speaking to him. What am I to think? How do I know that this man is who he says he is?"

Thomas looked at Ralph Hamor with his eyebrows raised in surprise as he relayed the words.

Ralph Hamor's smile faded; he could see that the tone of the meeting was being set. "I know nothing of this Thomas. Try and persuade him of my credentials. I cannot go back empty handed just because I haven't got a bloody necklace!" His bonhomie turned to irritation.

Powhatan smiled to himself. This was indeed a pact that he had made with Dale, but it had obviously been forgotten. No mind, he would just play this out for a while baiting him and extending the time before he refused Dale's offer of marriage to Kanti.

Thomas Savage looked at Powhatan. "Great Powhatan, you know me. I have never betrayed you or let you down. I vouch for this man. He is indeed the Secretary of the Colony and he brings a request from Sir Thomas Dale. The ritual that you mention, must have been forgotten, but please hear what Sir Ralph has to say."

Powhatan looked at Ralph Hamor and then at Thomas Savage. "I will hear what Sir Ralph has to say - but only because I trust *you* Thomas. You have been like a son to me." Powhatan's face showed no emotion. His mind flashed back to Pocahontas and her desperation. He was tired of the games that these people played, but for now, he had to continue with the meeting. "Let us sit and enjoy the apook while we talk." Powhatan walked over to his mat and sat down, picking up the pipe with apook and lighting it. He gestured to Thomas and Ralph Hamor to sit opposite him. The fire raged in the centre of the room and the smoke from the apook rose into the air creating a fragrant and warm atmosphere.

"I trust the health of Sir Thomas Dale is good?" he said as he breathed in the smoke, handing the pipe to Ralph Hamor to take his fill.

"Yes, Sir Thomas is very well, I am pleased to say." Hamor partook of the apook while Thomas translated for him. "Sir Thomas Dale extends his compliments and best wishes to you. He holds you in the greatest of esteem. Your daughter, Pocahontas, now known as Rebecca is also well and happy, so happy that she does not wish to come back to her tribe."

Powhatan smiled at the dig but bowed his head in acknowledgment, knowing full well that Pocahontas, far from well, was in the Yehakin not far from where they were sitting. "So, Mr. Hamor... Why have you come here, apart from to tell me that my daughter no longer wishes to see me?" said Powhatan.

"Sir Thomas Dale would like to cement the good relationship between our respective peoples. He would like to do this by asking your consent for him to marry Pocahontas's sister, Kanti. Pocahontas also would very much like her sister to marry Sir Thomas and be near to her." Lying came easily to the Longcoats.

Powhatan shook his head staring at the ground. There was silence. Powhatan started to watch the fire and breathed in from the pipe full of apook, his face stern, showing displeasure by the stance of his body.

"No. I cannot agree to this marriage. I have already agreed Kanti's marriage to a respected Werowance. She has already left three days since."

When Hamor heard this, his face dropped. "You are a great man with many powers Powhatan. You can recall your daughter, and Sir Thomas will pay you much much more than the Werowance for her hand in marriage."

Powhatan's ire was rising. "Kanti is one of my favourite daughters, as dear to me as life itself. I need to know that she is married and in proximity, I have already lost my beloved Pocahontas, and I am not prepared for the same thing to happen to Kanti. It is not a brotherly thing that Thomas Dale does, asking me to give another of my daughters. He is no friend." Powhatan looked intently at Hamor. "I would also like you to tell Thomas Dale that if there are any repercussions from my refusal, I will move my tribe further into the forest, and you will never find me - there will be no further corn and no further help from my people. This is the final word of Powhatan."

Powhatan got up from his mat, his face like thunder looking straight ahead as he walked out of the Yehakin.

Powhatan saw Pocahontas sitting on the edge of the cot nursing her sore arm. She looked up; anticipation etched on her face.

"It is done" he said. "I have sent them away. Kanti is safe. Your old friend Thomas Savage was interpreting for them. How is your arm feeling now?"

"It is still very sore, my father. But I will have to face the journey back to Varina very soon. I don't want anyone to know that I have come here."

"We will dress your arm again for you, and you will be accompanied by my warriors until you are near Varina. You can always say that the snake bit you when you were looking for firewood." Powhatan sat down next to his daughter and put his arm around her, drawing her close to him. "Tell me, my little one, how have things been? Are you happy as they say you are?"

Pocahontas snuggled into his large body, breathing in the musky smell of apook that permeated his clothes. How she wished she could just stay here and never face the perils of Varina...

"I am happy enough father. I am not as happy as I would be living here with you - but I chose to make that sacrifice for peace. My heart aches for Ko-kee and I am saddened to the core of my being that Kocoum lost his life.

What keeps me going is the thought that I will do everything in my power to protect my people. Kocoum sacrificed his life, and I have sacrificed the life that I crave and my beautiful baby Ko-kee, and I will not let those things be for nothing. Every day I am learning about the Longcoats. I am learning their customs, and what their intentions are.

My husband, John Rolfe is a good man. He treats me well, and we are friends." She looked at him, her eyes full of sorrow. "But I will never love a man as much as I love Kocoum, and no man will ever have my soul the way Kocoum had my soul. John is kind, and he treats me with gentleness, as if I was a precious and fragile dove, and I have my beautiful BaBa.

Never believe when you hear that I have betrayed my people - I would never do that. I am forever a Beloved Woman of the Powhatan. They think that I have converted to their ways, but that is only at a very superficial level, and because it is useful to our cause for them to think that. At heart I will always be Powhatan in mind and body, no matter what they dress me in or what they make me say." Powhatan held her closer, his brown lined face seemed to droop with the sadness of what he was hearing. She looked up at him and raised her undamaged hand to his face, touching his rough bristles tenderly and smiling at him. "Don't be sad for me father. I have had sadness in my life, but I have also had joy. I am a mother of two beautiful healthy babies, I have loved the best man in the world, and I have had the honour of being tasked with the goal of creating peace by firstly marrying John and then infiltrating his world in order to find out anything that I can that will help my people." She lowered her arm from his face and looked at the floor. "... but I do miss you and Ko-kee and I know, with the wisdom of a Beloved Woman that this will be the last time that I will be able to see you in this world." A tear ran down her cheek as she looked up at him.

"I know that you speak words of wisdom my child. With a heavy heart I will make provision for you leaving us… and you must see Ko-kee for the last time. Before you leave us forever, I swear on the honour of the Gods that Ko-kee will be looked after as befits the son of a Beloved Woman and Grandson of a Werowance. You can leave today with sadness as well as joy, knowing that Ko-kee will be a great warrior and will have all the care we can give him. We talk to him about you often so that he never forgets, and we will always make sure that you are remembered."

As he finished speaking, the flap of the Yehakin opened and little Ko-kee rushed in. Pocahontas burst into tears, unable to hold in her emotions as the toddler threw himself at her. She held his firm little body, ignoring the pain that still raged in her arm from the snake bite.

This moment would have to last her a lifetime, whatever a lifetime was for her.

[1] Medicine dance

[2] Spiritual person

MORE DEMANDS: May, 1614

She walked towards Varina with a heavy heart. For a few hours she had been with her real family again. Memories would never be enough, but she knew that she had to accept the inevitable. She had become a Tassantassa - she would never wear her beautiful suede tunic and moccasins again. She would never see her father, never see Ko-kee again, except in her dreams. Her fate had been sealed and she knew with the instinct of a Beloved Woman that there would never be any going back.

Now she must get her comfort and her sense of purpose from knowing that she was working towards the goal of peace. Peace for Ko-kee and for little BaBa. Maybe one day her babies would meet as equals and hopefully be proud of the mother that they shared. They would be the decision makers of the future on both sides of the divides who would carry on the work that she was starting... and John. What of John? She wished that she could love him as she had loved Kocoum, but she knew her love of Kocoum was a once in a lifetime thing. She could never replicate the feelings that she had had for him and even if she grew feelings for John, she was determined to push aside any chance of intimacy with him as it was the utmost betrayal. She could not allow herself such weakness. The vision of Kocoum had not visited her since her wedding day, but he was in her heart.

As she drew nearer to Varina, she saw a figure approaching her. It was John, and he was holding the swaddled baby Thomas, her BaBa. What a picture they made. He looked so strong against the vulnerability of the tiny baby in his arms. Her heart missed a beat. There was no doubting that he was a handsome man with his shiny hair flopping in front of his face. He was strong, and the outdoor work with the tobacco had given him a tanned complexion. He started to run towards her.

When he got nearer to her, he noticed her arm bandaged and supported with a sling. His face instantly changed from joy to concern. "What has happened? Are you alright? He held the baby in one arm as he reached to touch her cheek. "I am fine now John. A snake bit me, but the Sunsquaa treated me. I am healing nicely now."

John looked at his beautiful little wife. Her suede tunic and small moccasins made her look both exotic and vulnerable. On impulse he gently embraced her avoiding her injured arm, burying his face in her neck. She felt his warm breath on her and melted at his touch. For an instant she allowed herself to feel his hard muscular body, clinging to him allowing herself to be enveloped in his affection. The baby cried as he was sandwiched between them, wanting the milk that he so desperately needed. His mewling little cry pulled her back to reality and she put her hand on John's chest gently pushing to create distance between them. She had found comfort in John for a split second. Surely that was only because she was now missing her family. Wasn't it?

She took Thomas out of John's arms and focused on his need for milk. She fussed around the baby, unable to meet John's loving but hurt gaze. She felt a stab of guilt like a knife to her heart. He had done nothing to deserve such forceful rejection.

John stammered as if to say something and then stopped and looked from her face to the ground. He had tried so hard to keep his feelings to himself, but his fear over her safety and the realization that she was injured forced his emotions to reveal themselves uncontrollably. "I am so sorry Rebecca, Matachanna told me where you had gone, and I was very worried about you. I know that Ralph Hamor went to Matchcot and I was frightened that he would find you there and you would come to harm. I was counting the minutes until you returned safely."

Pocahontas had placed Thomas at her breast and she could feel him tugging as he sucked hungrily, eyes closed, pleased to have his mother's milk rather than the goats milk that Matachanna had been giving him while she had been away. She continued to look down at the baby as a way to avoid looking at John. Trying to block out the last few minutes when she had initially succumbed to her feelings and then cruelly pushed him away. Her thoughts were running away with themselves. How could she be so cruel to such a good man? She was angry with him for loving her, and angry with herself - what was she angry with herself for? She did not know what was going on. Surely it was all clear cut? She had married John as it suited both of them, and she was his friend.

In contrast, she had married Kocoum and she still loved Kocoum - she could not love two men - that was impossible. If only Kocoum's spirit would appear to her again, if only she could connect with him, then she would remember her vows to him and it would be easy. A tear ran down her face. She turned and walked away from John. She could not face him, could not face the fact that she had enjoyed his embrace, the feel of him, the scent of him, more than she was admitting to herself. The only solution was to keep her distance from him. She would renew her resolve and focus on Thomas and the peace cause.

He caught up with her and they walked slowly back to the house together, but apart, each lost in thought.

Suddenly Matachanna came running towards them.

"Pocahontas, come quickly - Sir Thomas Dale is coming" she shouted, fear in her eyes.

Pocahontas looked at John hugging Thomas protectively to her chest. "What does he want now? I must hurry back and change out of these clothes."

263

"Quick - give the baby to Matachanna, and I will go and meet him to stall him" said John. She passed Thomas to Matachanna and he immediately started screaming. "Try and keep him quiet Matachanna. If Dale hears him he might come to find out what the problem is.

Matachanna cuddled the baby into her chest whispering softly to him until his cries became muted.

Pocahontas darted towards the back of the house her heart beating, so that she could slip in without being seen. Why wouldn't that demon Dale just leave her alone? What could he want? He would never waste his time coming all the way to Varina for no reason. Maybe he knew about her visit to her father? Surely she had not been betrayed?

John walked on towards the front of the house, and saw Thomas Dale approaching on a large black horse. He pulled up beside John. John patted the flank of the shiny beast - so rare in Virginia - a status symbol of only the high ranking.

"Good afternoon Sir Thomas. To what do we owe the pleasure of your company?"

"Ah John, the newly wed! How are things going with your Powhatan bride? Hope she is behaving herself... or not!" he said smiling viciously.

John ignored his insult. "We are fine Sir. It is kind of you to enquire." His answer was formal. Dale was no friend of his, but he had power, and John could not risk upsetting him.

"The real reason I have come to this God forsaken plantation is to discuss your progress, or otherwise, with the tobacco." He dismounted his horse and tied it up, rubbing it's black velvety nose with affection. The horse snorted and pawed the ground in acknowledgment.

John and Dale walked towards the house as Pocahontas appeared at the front door.

Dale looked in her direction smiling his old contemptuous smile. He stopped when he saw her bandaged arm. "Oh my goodness Rebecca, I see you have hurt your arm. I hope it is not serious. What happened?" No sincerity graced his question.

"A snake bite" she said quietly, rubbing her arm, not making eye contact with him.

"A snake bite is nothing to a savage I hear. You have magic powers to make it better, so I am surprised you have been so badly infected. Funny that it is bound with Powhatan materials… " he raised one eyebrow.

"I always keep Powhatan medicines in the house in case we need them." She was not going to fall into the trap. "Unless you want to see me Sir Thomas, I must go and attend to the baby." He did not respond, so she turned brusquely and walked away, relieved that no mentioned was made of Kanti.

John beckoned Dale to come into the house. "Please sit down, Sir Thomas. Can I get you a drink?"

"No John. I am here because I have a serious problem that I have to discuss with you. The Virginia Company investors are getting very worried about the lack of money that we are making from crops. Since I have taken over and made sure that everyone is working, things have improved. However, we are still not out of the woods. If we are not careful, our funding will be withdrawn. When you started this project with tobacco, you promised that you could make a good return from it. I need to know how things are going."

John was taken by surprise at the sudden interest. "Things are going relatively well, Sir Thomas. However, I have only been working with Pocahontas… I mean Rebecca's people for little over a month. They have helped not only with the manpower needed to clear the land and plant, but also with the techniques. My first attempt was good - but I know that I can make it better.

Dale sighed. "The trouble is, I need proof. I need to be able to tell the 'powers that be' that we can not only create a superior tobacco, but that we can produce it in quantities enough to make a lot of money."

He leant forwards placing his elbows on his thighs and fixing John with his gaze. "We had two main aims for this project - one was to convert the Indians to Christianity, and the other was to use the resources of the country to make money - a lot of money. Gold deposits don't exist, so now our only hope is your tobacco. The success of the Colony rests with you my man. I agreed to your marrying the Squaw, so now I want you to repay me by producing the tobacco that we need. Things will be difficult if you don't - if you know what I mean?" His eyebrows were drawn and his eyes stared.

John felt a churning in the pit of his stomach. This man had so much power over him. He could do what he liked - he could take Pocahontas back, he could take the baby, he was paralyzed thinking of the things that Dale could do to him. "Sir Thomas, I am doing the best that I can. We do have some tobacco ready now - but not large quantities as yet."

"I need to have some ready to go. Samuel Argall and Ralph Hamor are sailing back to England at the end of June. I need to know that we can send at least samples back to the Virginia Company."

"I will do what I can Sir Thomas, a lot depends on the weather" said John. He could feel the pressure building, and the sweat was beading on his forehead at the six week deadline. "I have learned a lot from the Powhatans. We are now hanging individual leaves on a rack instead of just covering them with grass and letting them dry in the sun. We are also piling up earth around the base of the plants, removing the top seed head. This has all been much more successful, but as you can imagine, such techniques, though resulting in a superior product, is very labour intensive and take time." John knew he was rambling, trying to convince Dale that work was being done.

Dale did not look impressed and his eyes started to glaze over. He grunted. "Time is something I do not have John. I need to know that you will have some ready or I will replace you and get someone else in charge of this project. This cosy little arrangement with you and your Squaw will not be allowed to continue unless I have what I want. Do you understand me John?" Dale had the talent for looking cruel, but it went further than that. Everyone knew that he was a sadist, and he never made threats, he always took delight in carrying out the worst. John knew that he meant what he said, he was not interested in the process of growing tobacco and he had no understanding of issues with the weather or of processing. He expected John to do what he asked, regardless of the realities of the challenges ahead. John and Pocahontas's lives depended on him getting this tobacco ready

266

for the end of June of that he was sure.

He nodded reluctantly. No words were necessary.

Dale got back on his horse, saluted John with a nod, and rode away. John cursed.

"Damned that pig of a man" John said as he savagely kicked a stone out of his way.

————————

Pocahontas lay next to John. They had shared a bed since being married just over a month ago. John understood that Pocahontas did not want intimacy with him, and he had never crossed that line. They had agreed that sharing a bed was something that was expected of them, but they were going to do it as close friends, not lovers. He kissed her on the cheek each night before they went to sleep, and that had been enough - at least for her.

Now she could hear him breathing and was acutely aware of his closeness. Was he asleep? Her feelings when she saw him after her few days absence had taken her by surprise. And now… there was still a yearning to touch him, to feel him, to let his hands wander over her body. She stiffened, determined to control it. Why was this happening? She was a Beloved Woman, she had special powers, and yet it seemed that underneath she was just a young nineteen-year-old girl out of control of her emotions. Her mind wandered….

… no rules, no obligations, no thoughts - only the feather-like feel of his touch as he roams my body with his large hands. In my dream he is gentle and loving, kissing my neck, and moving slowly, so that I can savour every sensation that he creates. He knows exactly what my body is craving, and pleasure is overwhelming me as his touch becomes like a feather teasing me. I am floating and he moves slower - a slowness that increases my desire for him. I need him to be gentle, but I also feel urgency and need more. I feel so small against his strong hard body and surrender to his every movement

till at last the sun, the moon and the stars collide. Everything is pure and right. I lie quietly and at last I look into the depth of his eyes, his soul. When I awaken, my heart stops... It is not Kocoum...

John, I love you. I kiss him as he sleeps... just this once...

Morning finally arrives, and Pocahontas hears BaBa crying and gets out of bed. She looks over at John. John stirs and sits up smiling at her as usual.

"John" she says, her face drawn with the tragedy of what she is about to say. "I think it is better if I sleep in BaBa's room from now on - he needs me." Her heart is breaking at the look on his face and that her dream will never come true.

FURTHER EXPLOITATION: 1615

Dale was restless. He had only volunteered to come to Virginia for three years and already he had been there for much longer than that. He had had neither the success nor the glory that he had been hoping for, and he could not see it getting any better any time soon. Perhaps it was time for him to leave? It was almost a year since he had reached a dead end with his request to marry Powhatan's daughter. How dare Powhatan turn him down? He was only asking for his mangy daughter. Not that much to ask surely? It would have been quite a coup if he had managed to pull that one off. He would have gone down in history as having married one of Powhatan's daughters. It would send a message of peace and goodwill, but it would also mean that he would have legal rights to her body, all thirteen years of it - he remembered Pocahontas and smiled. That had been fun. He wondered if John Rolfe was reaping the same benefits as he had. There had been no further pregnancies, so maybe Pocahontas was not as close to John as he had professed in his letter.

Last time he had seen Pocahontas he had thought she still looked good.

About 19 - not over the hill yet. It had made him keener to get at her sister. He sighed remembering the shocked look in Pocahontas's eyes when he told her he was going to marry Kanti. She had tried to compose herself, but he knew her too well - he had hit a nerve with her. And when he had picked up the baby, that had been even better. It had been worth the journey to see her squirm. It was a gift to see he still had power over her. She knew he was capable of untold cruelty, she believed that he wouldn't hesitate to squeeze the neck of that tiny squalling brat – funnily enough, children were his soft spot, but he would never let anyone know that. He hadn't seen her since that day almost a year ago. Now he was going to meet with John again.

He had another plan for Pocahontas - another way that he could exploit her for his own gain. He would never let her win. He just had to speak to Argall and set things in motion. One last challenge, squeezing the last bit of advantage he had, before his interest in Pocahontas came to an end.

He could hear John's footsteps as he approached.

"Ah John, my man. Come in and sit down. Let me pour you a glass of ale, and join me in smoking some of your wonderful tobacco." John sat down as Dale passed him a tankard of ale and started to light up a pipe full of tobacco. Dale inhaled the tobacco sighing with pleasure and exhaling the smoke slowly as he passed it to John. "There is no doubt, John, you have done a fine job with this tobacco. It must be said that you have worked very hard." He smiled at John, reaching to take the pipe again. "Managing to get a shipment ready last year was well worth the effort. It had rave reviews in London."

"Thank you, Sir Thomas. It has been a challenge, but I think we have now got a good process going, and we are managing to produce a lot of tobacco for export." John was suspicious - was this the only thing Dale had asked him to come all this way for? A year ago when he had managed to process enough tobacco to send back to England Dale had not carried out the threats that he made, instead he had rewarded John and made him First Secretary and Recorder of the Colony, treating him with respect for once. Dale knew he needed John. He had to keep him sweet, or there would be no more tobacco. Since then John had kept his head down hoping that Dale would leave them alone. But what now?

Dale's eyebrows drew together, and he stroked his beard deep in thought. "John, I have some worrying news" he said. "The Virginia Company is in quite a bit of trouble. Some of the investors are getting very twitchy that we have not worked harder to make them money. A couple of them are even taking law suits against the Virginia Company. I am getting a lot of grumblings from London and the mood is not good. However, I have come up with an idea that might go some way to mollifying the dissenters."

John could see by the look on Dale's face that the 'idea' must involve something unpleasant. He nodded and waited to hear the worst.

"The investors wanted to make money out of this venture, obviously. They also wanted to believe that they were doing something honourable in the eyes of God - and hence one of the main goals was to introduce the Heathen Native population to Christianity. There had been so many false starts getting this Colony up and running as you know, but despite these setbacks, we kept on rising above it. This gave us the credibility that the investors needed. Your marrying Rebecca, and her conversion to Christianity was a huge boost to the cause, and of course your son" he stopped and coughed. "... is proof of the merging of our cultures in a civilized and respectable manner. Some investors are starting to believe that the success of this Colony is ordained by God and we must make sure that the rest of them see it this way too.

Now, I was thinking of how all these ideas could be accentuated in a way that the investors could really understand. They need to see it as exciting, compelling, and morally justified." Dales eyes sparkled with the enthusiasm of what he was saying. "To this end, I propose that we undertake a huge publicity drive and take Rebecca to London. She can be presented to the King and Queen (as she is royalty herself) and London Society could get to know her as a great Princess. We will dress her in beautiful silks and the newest fashion, and parade her around London. She will have huge novelty value as no one will have ever seen someone like her before. The fact that she is the first Christian Powhatan will be incredible. We also have the advantage that she can speak English. They will love her!" Dale sat back in his chair looking up at the ceiling basking in thoughts of success, taking in another puff of tobacco, a self-satisfied look on his face. "So what do you think John?"

John was speechless for several moments. He was trying to take in the idea of taking such a young girl with such a small baby across the ocean. He remembered the dire conditions that he and his first wife, Sarah had faced on their journey to Jamestown. His mind went back to that time, and he started to shake as the harrowing images flashed back to the cruel mountainous sea and the fight for survival as the ship crashed onto the rocks.

Dale was oblivious, smoking his pipe and revelling in his genius. He suddenly realised that John had not responded to his amazing idea. "So, what say you John?" he boomed at him.

"It will be a very expensive project…" stammered John.

"Oh, don't worry about the cost John. The Virginia Company have said they will pay for Rebecca and her entourage. You, my man will have to fend for yourself though I am afraid, but you should manage that with some of the tobacco money. Of course, you will accompany her, but you will not receive an income."

John was frantic. "It is a long journey for someone so young. She has never been on a ship across the ocean before - and the baby is so tiny. I am just not sure they will survive."

"Nonsense John! We will not leave until next year, and she will have had enough time to get used to the idea and the baby will have grown bigger by then. I will hear no more whining. Go home and tell her the plan. We need lots of tobacco and your wife and son to be ready to set sail in eleven months' time on Argall's ship, the 'Treasurer'."

Dale had listened to John's protestations and he could see the dangers that might lie ahead for the young woman and her baby. He imagined Rebecca dying - if she died, undoubtedly it would cause a sensation, but it would be no bad thing. He shook his head. Either way, he would get the publicity he needed out of her and that was the most important thing.

ON THE OPEN SEAS: May, 1616

She stood next to John looking up at the 'Treasurer'. This ship had been the start of her new life. It was this ship that Samuel Argall had used to kidnap her. She clung onto to BaBa, who was wriggling and trying to get down to explore. John watched her, and it was as if he could read her mind.

"I know Pocahontas. This ship has so much meaning for you. Let's just pray that this journey brings the peace that you are striving for."

She smiled at him. "Peace is all I have ever wanted John. If this journey is successful, maybe our Peoples can live together without any more killing. I need to see what England is like, and I need to know more about the English people. That way Powhatan will know what he is dealing with, so we can forge better bonds."

John looked at her innocent face. Was she being naive? He would give anything for her to create a world where people lived together on equal terms. But, somehow, knowing the greed and immorality of white men, he could not see it happening. Christian? Heathen? John was very devout, but he was beginning to question the very spirit of the way his comrades interpreted the Scriptures. Even this trip was a sham and another attempt at exploiting an innocent young girl for financial gain.

She had been desperate to come though, and as much as he had tried to dissuade her, she had fought him with an idealism that he could not combat. She needed to know exactly what her people were up against, and for that he could not blame her. He just hoped that the truth did not destroy her.

As she climbed up the gangplank with John at her side holding BaBa, Pocahontas looked back at the land that she was leaving. The vista had changed immeasurably over the past few years. Jamestown was stark and much of the land surrounding it had become cleared of the beautiful trees of her childhood memories. If this amount of change could happen in just a few years, what would happen in the future years? Maybe going to England would give her a clue as to how these Longcoats really lived and what they wanted to do with her country. She stepped onto the deck and memories flooded back to the day she was kidnapped on this very ship... and there they were, her kidnapper and her gaoler - Samuel Argall and Thomas Dale, waiting to welcome her aboard yet again. Was it really a welcome, or was it to gloat at their power over her once again? This time she was not a prisoner, she was supposedly an honoured guest, but that was how it had started the last time, she thought wryly. Japasaw had given her up - but she knew that was the way of the Gods and bore him no ill will. This time she wanted to come. She looked at Dale and Argall and nodded, no emotion on her face.

John had warned her that the journey was going to be harsh. Seven weeks on a small ship, very little sanitary facilities, and no respite from the rolling angry sea. She knew he was sceptical of the motives of Thomas Dale.

He was concerned about her and little Thomas's safety. The last sea journey that he had taken, had ended in a shipwreck and he had lost his wife and baby daughter, and he was haunted by the thought that such a thing might happen again. But despite all these reasons to stay safe and sound in Varina, their home, she had come so far and sacrificed so much, she had to do all she could towards her cause and that meant continuing the journey to England.

Their relationship had remained unique and precious, even although they no longer slept in the same bed. She knew he still loved her by the way he looked at her. His eyes held hers as if he never wanted to stop looking at her and his gaze, even as he glanced at her in the most ordinary of situations, bore into her soul. She kept her distance from him as much as was possible, aware of the urge to touch him that she fought with on a daily basis. She was thankful that he was to be at her side for this foray into the unknown.

He had taken her down to the gun deck, where she, Matachanna and the other six Powhatan squaws were to sleep, to inspect the accommodation that was to be hers for the duration of the journey. It was cramped, and dingy, with the only light coming from the ports where guns had been situated. Straw pads had been put on the floor for each of the women and there were a few upturned wooden boxes to sit on. It was primitive but clean, and Pocahontas was relieved that the sailors had obviously given the accommodation for the womenfolk some thought. John and the sailors and the rest of the men were to sleep either on the top deck or on the lower deck beneath the gun deck in hammocks.

Having inspected her and BaBa's sleeping arrangements, they went back up the steep stairs into the open air. The scene that confronted her was one of frenetic activity, sailors running around shouting, Argall gesturing and booming out orders as they started to pull away from the dock, the large ship creaking and groaning with the movement.

As the ship pulled away from the dock, she knew - this was it. This was the point of no return. Pocahontas was excited but frightened in equal measure. Would she ever see her homeland again? It was something she dared not think about too much. She watched, as Jamestown got further and further away. BaBa was crying - wriggling and unsure of what was happening to him. It was going to be hard for him on a ship for seven weeks. At least she was still breastfeeding him so he would have nutrition and the continued comfort of the closeness of being at her breast. She balanced BaBa on her hip, and reached for John's hand as he looked out to the horizon. She looked up at him standing tall and strong next to her.

"As much as I know I must do this, I am frightened John. I am taking BaBa to the land of his forefathers, but I have no idea what we will find there. I know he will be looked after, because you are here, but I am not sure of what will happen to me.

I will be surrounded by the same people who have for so long looked down on my people, thinking them primitive. I am not sure that being Powhatan's daughter will make any difference to how they see me. I am prepared for some hard times ahead, and I just want you to know that I would not be able to do this without knowing that you will be at my side."

John held her hand tightly, his eyes starting to water as he pulled her towards him. "I am here for you Pocahontas" he said, his voice breaking. He was unable to say more.

––––––––––

That first day on board 'Treasurer' had given Pocahontas no true feeling of what the journey was going to be like. All the Powhatan men and women were unprepared for the relentless monotony, the cold, the wet and the tasteless food.

The ship was a microcosm of what two cultures living in proximity looked like. Men with dark skin and few clothes, long black plaits, and body paint, mixing with scruffy sailors from the slums of London. The sailors drank ale to ease their boredom, and the Powhatans chanted and banged drums seeking the protection of their Gods, each culture avoiding the other where possible.

Uttamatamakin, Matachanna's husband became the speaker and leader of the Powhatan people on board. He was a fearless warrior and was prepared to stand up for the honour of his people at all costs. Pocahontas knew that he felt it his duty to look after her on behalf of her father. She thought back to the first few days when Dale had tried to force everyone on board to come together in Christian prayer. She smiled to herself. Uttamtamakin, or Tomakin as he was named for ease, stood his ground. He had lined up all the Powhatan men together and they stood defiant staring unwaveringly at their English counterparts.

The Powhatan men had brought their spears, and standing painted with red pocheen and chanting, banging their spears on the deck, they looked and sounded, a formidable force. Added to this spectacle were the drums. The drummers banged a war beat that sent shivers down the spine of everyone that could hear it.

Tomakin walked forward and signalled quiet. The chanting and banging of spears and drums died down. Tomakin had a sprinkling of English as he had spent his time in the English settlements since he and Matachanna had joined Pocahontas in Jamestown, and he started to shout above the noise of the wind and the waves.

"We are Powhatan. We are proud men and women that worship Okee and Ahone. We speak to the wind and listen to the waves. We do not worship your God. We see how you live and we do not share or like your ways. Our way is the way of Peace and Ahone. We die before we change our way."

This mission was so important to Dale, he could not handle dissidence the way he usually did, by hangings. He had to placate. Pocahontas revelled in it - he had to be civil and succumb to men and women that he considered inferior. He put his hands together and bowed to Tomakin.

"Sir, I wish you no offence" Dale said. "Please worship as you will, and we shall do the same." At that he turned tail and walked to the bridge as quickly as he could. Pocahontas hid her face as she could not contain her amusement at Dale's discomfort.

One of the worst things was BaBa's plaintive crying. It was constant. His little face contorted and red, and his fists banging and crashing, trying to let her know that he needed something - and he didn't know what it was. Pocahontas felt sick, cold, and tired. She slept very little and ate hardly any of the salted beef and ships biscuit that were offered to her. She was disgusted by the lack of hygiene as no washing was allowed and toileting could only be done in pots that had to be emptied overboard. Rats ran around the gundeck looking for spare crumbs, squeaking in the night and spreading their faeces around the deck. Pocahontas had never felt such revulsion.

How could she have brought a child into this situation. The poor little boy was distraught despite the constant attention that he had from all the Powhatan women, who took it in turns to look after him. His toileting was the most problematic of all - Pocahontas was able to wash his rags when he soiled them, but drying them was another matter. It was fine when the weather was fine, but that was not very often. For the most part, it rained and rained continually and the ship heaved and dipped, rose and dipped, until she thought that she would go mad. Would they ever reach land? Would she ever be warm and nauseous free again? Would little BaBa ever stop crying?

Occasionally she took BaBa up on deck for a bit of fresh air. But it was so cold. There was no colour to the sea or the sky and nothing but seemingly miles and miles and miles of endless grey. The ship rose and dipped and the wind cut through anything in its path. Thomas clung to her and buried his face in her neck, to escape from the icy sea spray, and after only a few minutes they had to return below deck for shelter.

Days turned into weeks, and the sea turned from bad to worse, to bad again, over and over. The lightning flashed, and the rain came down like needles of ice. The noise of the wind in the sails howled like wolves on the prowl. The ships 'biskit', the only staple food left after all those weeks, had grown stale and maggoty. Water could only be drunk if diluted with ale to kill the dirt and bugs.

I toss on the sea...

The prayers from Christian and Powhatan alike, although directed to different Gods, asked for the same thing. Just to be safe and on dry land again.

At last the sight they had all been waiting for appeared through the mist.

Pocahontas pulled BaBa to her chest, silently weeping. "We are finally here, my little one" she whispered. Over the past few weeks his crying had decreased. His eyes stared ahead, and he was no longer inquisitive and naughty. The change in him frightened Pocahontas. She had found it unbearable to hear his constant crying, but this stunned silence was worse. It was as if the little boy had given up. Given up asking for the things that he needed, or even caring, because he had asked so many times and been denied. Her heart was breaking for him. It was her fault. If she had known what it was really going to be like, she would never have brought him. John had tried to tell her, but there was no way she could have imagined the horror of the journey that they had just endured. She stroked BaBa's forehead, and looked into his vacant blue eyes. "It is going to be alright now, little man" she said, her face sad and moist with silent tears.

PLYMOUTH: 22 June, 1616

"Sir Thomas Dale... arrived at Plimmouth in May or June 1616 to advance the good of the Plantation, Master Rolfe also with Rebecca his new convert and consort, and Uttamataakin (commonly called Tomocomo) one of Pohatans Counsellours came over at the same time."

Rev. Samuel Purchas

Pocahontas stood on the deck with Thomas and John as the 'Treasurer' moved towards the dock. She shivered in the cold and damp air and watched as the final conclusions to this fateful journey took place. She felt the shudder of the ship as it touched the dock, and the smell of fish, mingled with seawater as Captain Argall shouted his orders, and took control of the procedures necessary to land them safely. She saw on the quay a man in a smart uniform with lots of medals waiting to welcome them - she learned later that this was Sir Lewis Stukely, Vice Admiral of Devon.

Having docked the ship safely, Sir Thomas Dale and Captain Argall walked down the gangplank to meet Sir Lewis, and she saw them shaking hands as Dale pointed to her and John standing on the deck.

Her legs were shaky, and she knew that she smelled of all manner of unmentionable things as there had been no facilities for washing on board. Her hair was matted and dirty, and she had lost a lot of weight. Poor little Thomas was starting to struggle, which was a good sign, but she found it difficult to hold him in her weakened state. John reached over and took Thomas from her. She smiled gratefully at him. He always knew what she needed.

The time came for them to disembark from 'Treasurer' and she walked slowly down the gangplank, her legs wobbly and unsure from the lack of exercise during the past seven weeks. On solid ground at last, she stood for a moment, taking in the scene before her. It was dark, even although it was day time. There were multiple buildings surrounding the port, all made of wood and all drab and dilapidated. The thing that struck her most was that there were so many of them. She thought back to Jamestown, and had expected something similar - but here there were so many people and so many buildings crowding out the sky. There was hustle and bustle as people seemed to be scurrying everywhere. There were horses pulling boxes filled with people or goods and the noise was something that she had never experienced before.

Was all of England like this? So crowded, so dirty, so noisy?

She looked down at her dress. She could hardly criticize others in the state that she was in. Her long flowing dress was covered in dirt, and the hem was ingrained with at least three inches of filth. Her Powhatan friends fared slightly better than herself, as they had only skimpy native dress. However, they also were uncharacteristically dirty. They were used to bathing every day - and it was quite clear that the English bathed very little, even when they were on dry land. It was so cold, and as the grey sky began to release droplets of rain, Pocahontas sighed. What had she done?

Thomas Dale started walking towards her and John, an air of pomp surrounding him.

"Rebecca Rolfe... my most eminent lady" he said, his voice oozing false respect, "I would like you to meet Sir Lewis Stukely, who is the Vice Admiral of Devon." His voice boomed out as he bowed to her and ushered Lewis Stukely towards her." Pocahontas ignored Dale looking past him and focusing on Sir Lewis.

"Sir, I am pleased to meet you" she said, in perfect English.

He bowed to her and took her hand, bending to kiss her fingers.

"Welcome, Princess" he said smiling at her. "We have prepared accommodation for you in Plymouth so that you can refresh yourselves until the tide is favourable for the onward journey to London."

…onwards to London. What did he mean? The journey was not at and end? Her heart sank and her knees buckled at the thought of boarding the ship once again, and it was all she could do to stop herself from crying.

Pocahontas's main concern was BaBa. The poor little mite had been torn away from his routine and thrust into a cruel cold and dirty world that tossed and turned constantly, day and night. She had thought, when they reached land, things would calm down. In some ways they had, but there was so much that was new to him that poor Thomas was overwhelmed and he screamed and clung to her, fear etched on his tear stained red face.

They had taken a horse-drawn carriage to a small inn in Plymouth, and she was astounded by what she saw as they went through the small lanes that were edged with ramshackle houses that looked like they were going to fall down. It was June, and at home she would have expected the weather to start turning warmer, but here it was misty, cold and miserable, no glimmer of sunlight was to be seen and the grey on grey continued. She held Thomas tightly, but he was inconsolable until they reached the inn.

The inn itself was small, but reasonably comfortable. The one thing that gave Pocahontas a glimmer of hope was the large roaring fire. At this time of year in England they did not usually light fires, but John had requested that they do so today, as he knew that it would comfort her.

She sat in the dark room of the inn in front of the roaring fire. BaBa cuddled up to her and suckled at her breast, peaceful at last. John brought her over a large mug of hot liquid. She sipped it slowly, feeling the warmth permeate her body from the fire and from the strange new drink.

"What is this that you have given me to drink John? It tastes pleasant" she asked.

"It is something called cider. They heat it by putting the poker from the fire in it. I thought it might warm you up. You look so exhausted."

"I *am* tired, I think if I had a bed that did not move, warm blankets and a room with no rats running around it, I might sleep for days" she smiled at him, feeling all the aches and pains from the seven weeks on the ship.

"BaBa certainly seems more content on solid ground" he said. They both looked at the little boy, who having had his fill of milk had fallen into a very deep sleep at his mother's breast.

She drained the last bit of Cider from the mug. "Is London like this John?" she asked.

John laughed. "Well, it is a bit like this, but much, much bigger and much, much busier."

"I don't see how anywhere could be bigger or busier than this" her eyes were wide open trying to imagine.

John stood up and bending down picked up the sleeping child.

"Come on, Pocahontas, those are questions for another day. I will take you to your bedroom now so that you can rest. We will board the ship again in a few days' time, when the tides are right for Captain Argall to navigate the ship along the coast and up the river to London. It will not be a long journey though - maybe only about fourteen more days. The ship will have been cleaned and restocked with food and water though and we will be hugging the coast, so there will be lots for you to see, and hopefully the sea will be kinder to us than it was in the middle of the ocean."

"Could we not just walk to London from here John? I am not sure I can bear to take Thomas on that ship again."

John smiled. It brought it home to him how naive she was to the world outside of Virginia. It was going to be a huge shock to her when she experienced the realities of London.

LONDON

~~~~~~❦~~~~~~

Nothing could have prepared Pocahontas for what happened when she and her entourage finally landed on the banks of the Thames in London.

She had changed from her dirty sea salt and grime encrusted gown to a new clean, but functional ill fitting dress which had been hastily found for her. Her heart was beating fast as she felt the judder of the ship as it tied up at the dock. The Powhatans had all been briefed extensively by Sir Thomas Dale before landing, on how they were to behave, and Tomaco had all his warriors lined up painted, with spears at the ready to face this new world.

As Pocahontas looked at her fellow countrymen and women, she realised that their appearance in terms of physical features and apparel could not have been more different to that of their English hosts. Of course, this had always been the case, but here, the grey misty environment accentuated the discord. They were dressed for the simple Powhatan way of life, and they had landed in a seething mass of people and frenzied activity, so far removed from the forests of Virginia. In Werowocomoco, their bright colours and exotic looks blended with nature as they moved at one with the land. Here, in the damp grey mist, their wide-eyed shivering belied the dignified pose that they were attempting to maintain in the face of Tomoco's instruction. Pocahontas felt for them, as she mirrored their discomfort and started to question her own desire to be here.

As she disembarked from the ship her senses were assaulted from every angle.

The smell of sewage mingled with fish from the nearby fishing port. On top of that, any manner of unidentified obstacles floated in the water, from old boots to dead rats - everything with a stink of its own. The noise was deafening. She had never experienced noise like it. Merchants, set up along the quay, were shrieking to outdo one another over the already overwhelming sounds of horses and carts rumbling over cobblestones, and fights among drunken men falling into gutters. Ladies - whose faces were caked with makeup which almost hid their suppurating sores and pox marks, roamed the dock, swinging their hips and calling to the sailors as they passed. And mud. There was mud and horse dung everywhere. Poor little BaBa buried his face in her neck sobbing with sensory overload as they started to climb into horse drawn carriages.

Pocahontas peered out of the windows of the carriage, her body shaken as the carriage navigated the cobblestones, her eyes wide, her eyebrows furrowed with disbelief at the poverty and filth that she was witnessing. The streets were very narrow and dark, with dilapidated wooden houses framing the small lane on which their carriage manoeuvred. She could see even narrower and darker alleyways radiating outwards between three storey houses, the second floors of which stuck out over the lane. Detritus and people in rags, many shouting and swearing angrily at each other, crammed together creating a seething mass of activity. Fumes from the open fires of so many houses cramped together in such a small space, choked the air and mixed with the foggy atmosphere coating everything in an unpleasant grey mist.

What surprised her most of all were the small children running wild with dirty faces, scantily clad in what looked like sacking cloth. Toddlers, slightly older than BaBa were begging in the streets with wide eyes and tear stained faces. Her heart stood still, watching their misery as they struggled to survive in such a dark and cruel place, reaching up to passing strangers with arms outstretched, only to be battered down and left helplessly crying. She thought of the children of Werowocomoco and how they played in the forest and swam in the rivers, laughing and happy, fed and wrapped in the love of the tribe.

What had she come to? Was this the civilized society that she was to learn from? What was their God doing to help them, the God whose principles the Great and the Good had tried to indoctrinate in her - their God seemed to have forgotten these little people. Or was suffering part of his plan? How different this was. How Heathen. She smiled at the irony. Maybe her new religion did not have all the answers.

it is cold, it is filthy,
   there are no trees.

John sat next to her and squeezed her hand in encouragement, or was it in apology?

Finally, they arrived at the inn. John told her that it was called "La Belle Sauvage" a few yards off a famous street called Fleet Street.

Pocahontas jumped down from the carriage, shaken from the journey, but hoping that by some fluke, things might get better.

The courtyard of the inn stood on three sides of a square, three storeys high. Each layer of the building was framed with a wrought iron gallery. If it had not been for the filth in the courtyard below it, Pocahontas would have been encouraged by what she was seeing. She looked skywards to see the building towering above her. Even the largest Quioccosan that she had ever seen did not reach to the sky as this building did. However, the courtyard was muddy and strewn with rubbish, with vagrants lying about drunk and shouting. It looked like they could have been trying to act out a play. The whole courtyard was a mass of people shouting, laughing, punching, eating. It was chaos.

As everyone started to get out of the carriages a crowd started to gather.

"What is happening, John?" Pocahontas asked, holding BaBa close to her.

"It is nothing to worry about, the local people are just a little bit curious to see you and your people." He clutched her hand pulling her towards the door of the inn. As he did so, the crowd started to move forwards blocking their way. By this time Tomocomo and his warriors and the other Powhatan Squaws were also getting out of their carriages and seeing what they were confronted with, their bodies were poised for trouble.

"What 're these Heathen scum doing here then Guvn'r" a voice from the crowd boomed out.

"They don't hav look funny."

"Send 'em 'ome, I say!"

"Yeh, send 'em 'ome - we don't want no Heathen injuns round 'ere mate."

At that point Pocahontas saw one of the men lurch forward to try and touch one of the warriors. Tomocomo stood his ground, fury on his face, and all the warriors put their spears up defensively to protect the squaws that were behind them. Pocahontas could see that it would take one wrong movement for the situation to turn into a blood bath.

John ran forward in front of Tomocomo with his hands in front of him, trying to smile as if it was a joke.

"Lads, lads" he said. "There is no need for any trouble. These gentlemen have come as guests of the King, and I do not think that it would be wise to cause them any distress, now would it."

The ringleader looked at John. "They are guests of the King? The King entertains Heathens now does he? …not sure I am buying that, are you lads?"

John stood his ground. "My wife is the famous Princess Pocahontas, and she is a Christian lady." He pointed at Pocahontas. "I think that it would be unwise of you to cause trouble with Royalty as you could find yourselves in Newgate."

The ringleader stood back and looked at John then looked at Pocahontas cradling Thomas, considering his options.

"Mmm… I see, Govn'r. Didn't realise they was Roy'lty." He smiled sheepishly. "Don't want no trouble." He started to back away. "Come on lads" he gestured to his mates to retreat. "Apologies, Sir. We meant no 'arm, they just look funny and a bit scary, to be honest. Let's go and get some ale to toast the Princess, lads." He nodded at John and they all started to walk away.

John walked back to Pocahontas. "I am sorry about the welcoming committee" he said.

Pocahontas felt numb. It was so much to take in and she had not expected such hostility. "I can see that it is going to be difficult for people to accept us." She said. "There is a lot of work to be done if our people are ever going to live in peace." Her shoulders were hunched - partly from tiredness, but partly from the realization of how different the two cultures were. The task ahead at that moment, seemed impossible.

She looked around for Badger. He was crouched in the corner, watching her, giving her strength.

A LADY IN TRAINING

❦

Pocahontas watched Cecily as she played with Thomas and Martha. Thomas was putting wooden blocks one, on top of the other and knocking them over with peels of laughter. Cecily and two year old Martha, her youngest daughter, both clapped and laughed. It was so nice to see BaBa playing with children of his own age. He was bigger than his age of course, as his date of birth had been invented for convenience. Nevertheless, the two children were happy in each other's company, and Pocahontas could smile for a moment.

Cecily was the wife of Sir Thomas De La Warr, who was the largest investor in the Virginia Company. John had known Sir Thomas since 1610. Sir Thomas's ship had arrived up the James river just as the ship that John was on with Sir Thomas Gates and Sir George Somers was leaving Virginia. Conditions in the Colony were tragic, with many many people having died of starvation and it was decided that they could no longer survive without further supplies. Sir Thomas De La Warr had saved the day bringing those supplies - and prevented the Colony failing.

Cecily was about ten years older than Pocahontas, dressed in very elaborate attire, makeup and hair, the height of fashion as the De La Warrs mixed frequently with the King and Queen and all the upper echelons of Society. Cecily had taken Pocahontas under her wing and seemed determined that her protege was going to be the toast of London. This had meant hours of dress fittings, learning the different utensils used for eating and what was used for what, and understanding the different ranks of Society and how to address each one. There were so many details of how a Princess should behave when being paraded through London's Aristocracy, that Pocahontas's head was spinning. Did they really have a silver fork for fish and a completely different one for meat? It all seemed so excessive.

And the clothes! Pocahontas thought back to her lovely simple little deerskin shift. Now her dresses were so large that she could hardly sit down. A huge farthingdale made of wicker spanned out from her waist in circles keeping the extravagant silks wafting around her like a huge tepee sweeping down to the floor from her waist. Her small waist was made even tinier by a tight whalebone stay that meant she could hardly breathe. The sleeves were enormous, getting in the way of everything. Ribbons, lace, and silk, were brought to London from Italy. She had to admit that the colours of the fabrics were very beautiful, but oh how she wished she could sit down without a major effort to manage her attire. It was easier to stand. She had had to practice for hours simply walking, sitting, and eating. She was growing tired of all the pretence, but at the same time, she was learning about these strange people, and that was what she had really come here to do.

"Pocahontas… Pocahontas… " said John, breaking into her stream of thought.

She stopped watching little Thomas playing with Martha and turned towards John. "Sorry John" she said. She was in the offices of the Virginia Company in Philpot Lane at a meeting where she and John were discussing her London schedule with Sir Thomas De La Warr and his wife, Sir Edwin Sandys, one of the founders of the Virginia Company and Thomas Dale. Her mind had wandered as, it seemed to her, that she had no part in the discussion or any say in the decisions that were to be made. She was irritated but decided that the best thing to do was just to accept this for now. No doubt Thomas Dale would arrange something to punish her, he always did.

"… as I was saying…" said Thomas Dale, "We need maximum exposure of Rebecca if we are to get value for money. The Virginia Company is prepared to a pay a stipend of £4 a week for Rebecca, plus we will pay for all the clothes that have had to be made for her. This is a great deal of money, but we can't let it be seen that the Virginia Company are not treating her like the Princess that she is. John, unfortunately you are not part of the deal - you will have to pay for yourself as you are not the attraction here. You are no use to us, apart from your tobacco."

Pocahontas sighed. Why was Thomas Dale always so nasty.

John drew himself up to full height. "I see. What can I say Sir Thomas, let's hope my tobacco brings in enough to pay my expenses." John said pointedly.

Sir Edwin Sandys leant forward to speak. "To change the subject, a small detail that might make a difference to the success of this visit, is what we are to call this lady. She is a Princess; she is Rebecca and she is Pocahontas Matoaka. I note that you, John address her still as Pocahontas. What will take the imagination of the people? Do we want them to think of her as Christian Rebecca or maybe if we use Pocahontas, it will tell more of the story of her conversion? Her conversion is what the people are really keen to know about. Investors want to know that we are converting the Heathens as that is what the whole project is about. Pocahontas is clearly a Heathen name and it illustrates our success - a Heathen turned Christian."

Thomas Dale nodded. "I agree, I think that Pocahontas might be the best name. It is different and exotic, and will instil a certain mystique around her" Thomas Dale looked at Pocahontas and smiled. She did not return his smile.

"Lady De La Warr, how is the instruction and ordering of dresses going?" said Edwin Sandys.

Cecily looked up from playing with the children. "I have a delightful and able student. She is well equipped to meet the most dignified of persons and she will charm them all, of that I have no doubt." Cecily looked towards

Pocahontas. "My dear, do you have anything that you would like to add? I know that it has all been very strange for you, but I hope that your education has been of some amusement as well as hard work?"

Pocahontas just shook her head. What was the point? Cecily had been very kind to her and no doubt she meant well, but the whole thing had been extremely tedious.

"Well, it is gratifying to know that everything is set for Pocahontas's debut. What occasions have we lined up for her?" Sir Thomas De La Warr asked.

Edwin Sandys cleared his throat to speak. "We have some very eminent people that have requested an audience with our fair Princess and there are several dinners and lunches with investors. We have a special invitation from The Lord Bishop of London, Doctor King. He is very keen to meet her and has arranged a gala dinner at his palace. He looks forward to talking to her about her conversion to Christianity and the possibilities that more Heathens might emulate her. He has arranged for many colleagues to attend this dinner, and hopes to meet with her as well as her Indian comrades - he mentioned Uttamatamakin in particular, as he is such a vibrant figure and very representative of Powhatan culture."

"It looks as if our efforts are paying off then? It is a shame we have not yet received an invitation from the King. That might be because John is not in good favour with the King." Thomas Dale looked at John with his eyebrows drawn.

John's eyes were wide open. "What have I done that has put me out of favour with the King. I am unaware of any wrongdoings" he said.

"Well John. You did not seek permission from the King to marry a Princess. This was an insult. Also, the King does not approve of the smoking of tobacco - and we all know tobacco has been your success story."

John stuttered and his face became red. "...but I sought your permission as the agent of the King. It was your responsibility to communicate this to the King."

"Yes, I know. Sorry John, old boy. Let's just hope that he does not see fit to incarcerate you in the tower. It would be such a shame." Dale smiled, his eyes twinkling with mirth. "Well, I think we have just about covered everything we need to in this meeting, haven't we?" said Dale, cutting of any further questions from the clearly outraged John.

Pocahontas was tense. Would the King really arrest John, or was this just something Dale was saying to cause fear as usual? She went over to Thomas and picked him up off the floor. As she did so, with horror she saw Thomas Dale walking towards her.

"He's a fine strapping lad Pocahontas, your *Thomas*" He was genial, talking to her as if she was a close friend. "Is he the same age as Martha? He looks a lot older, doesn't he? Maybe he just has strength and size handed down to him from his father." He smirked at her.

She knew his meaning. He could not leave her alone. He could not just let her live her life with John and little BaBa, he always had to do something to cause her pain and distress. He knew this secret, and he was never going to let her forget that he knew.

John came towards her and took BaBa in his arms, looking at Pocahontas with a question mark in his eyes. She looked down at the floor, shaking her head.

"Dada" said little BaBa as he held out his arms to John.

John looked at Dale and his look spoke a thousand words.

AUDIENCE WITH THE KING AND QUEEN

There had been so many gatherings of people curious to see Pocahontas and her accompanying Powhatan squaws and warriors that she was struggling to remember who was who and what was what. Her head was spinning, and she longed for peace and quiet and time with John and little Thomas. This was not to be. The Virginia Company wanted their pound of flesh and she was marched around London with her entourage until she was almost at breaking point.

She had very quickly realised that she hated the City. London was filthy, crowded, full of disease and hatred. The Fleet Valley renowned for its stinking lanes was only a few yards from the Belle Sauvage. All the Powhatans struggled to breathe in the smoggy London air, and longed to scrub the grime from their skin. They were used to bathing daily, and this was not possible in London. The most they could do was rinse themselves in cold water with a rag each day.

The formality was exhausting. Pocahontas looked down at the dress that she was wearing. Some would have said that it was beautiful - and indeed it was very elaborate. The silks made her young skin glow and she smiled when she remembered the look on John's face, the first time he had seen her wearing it. It was so uncomfortable though - itchy, coarse and impossible to sit down in. She felt even more sorry for the other Powhatans though. Sir Thomas Dale had insisted that they attend each event dressed in traditional dress to gain maximum impact of their novelty. This was fine as they did not have to endure the indignities of wearing English clothes, but the climate was cold and damp, and he allowed them no protection from the elements. He insisted that they had to be seen by the public, for the Virginia Company to get their money's worth. Poor Uttamatamakin, the warriors, the squaws and Matachanna bore it reasonably well, but they too were growing tired of the constant need to put on a show, when no notice was taken of their discomfort, and the attention they received was not always friendly.

Today, Pocahontas had had to make a special effort with her appearance, for she was going to meet King James and his wife Queen Anne. Many times she had been told that it was a great honour to be presented to the King and Queen, and Lady De La Warr was fussing around her like a bee around honey, making the last minute alterations to her hair and dress.

"Now, my dear" she said. "Make sure that you curtsy as I have instructed you to do. You must not look at the King or Queen unless they speak to you, and you must only speak if you are spoken to. Do you understand Pocahontas?"

"Yes, I do understand. But I am Royalty myself, why do I have to bow before them?"

"Just do what I say Pocahontas. You would not even have had the honour of being seen by the King and Queen if you were not the daughter of a King. King James is curious to meet you, and you should be very grateful that they have granted you this audience. Uttamatamakin and Matchanna and some of the warriors and squaws will accompany you to create the spectacle that the King expects."

"I will do exactly as you say, Lady De La Warr" said Pocahontas. She was very curious to see this King of England. Would he be as impressive as her father? What could she find out that would be useful?

Pocahontas walked down the sweeping stairway and saw that Uttamata-makin, Matachanna and the others were waiting for her. John was also at the bottom of the stairs smiling at her. He took her hand and led her outside to a waiting carriage. She looked at him and immediately felt relief that he was going to accompany her. She felt so alone despite the constant hoards of people that surrounded her, but she knew he was on her side, no matter what, and that made it bearable.

As the carriage stopped, Pocahontas looked out of the window to see The Palace of Whitehall. She had never seen such a large and grand building in her life. John had told her that the palace had 1,500 rooms, and was one of the largest buildings in the whole of Europe. It was going to be difficult to explain to her father the vastness of the building that this King lived in.

As Pocahontas and her entourage walked towards the palace, they crossed through the Court Gate and walked up the stairs to the Great Guard Chamber. Pocahontas had an intake of breath when she saw the two hundred guards in their beautiful flame red uniforms guarding the inner sanctum. At the end they came to a large door with iron bolts that went right up to the ceiling. As they approached, they were stopped.

"Halt" said one of the guards.

Lord De La Warr bowed and signalled towards Pocahontas. "This is the Princess Pocahontas, her sister Matachanna and her brother in law Tomocomo. They have been invited to the palace to meet the King and Queen.

"I will fetch the Lord Chamberlain to announce them" replied the guard. "He is expecting them."

He duly did so, and he and three other guards began to open the huge wooden doors to reveal a room of utter extravagance, at the end of which were two elaborate thrones, upon which sat King James and Queen Anne.

The Lord Chamberlain walked into the room and bowed.

"Your Majesties. May I present to you Princess Pocahontas, also known as Matoaka, also known as Rebecca. The Princess is accompanied by members of her tribe of the Powhatan Nation." He bowed again and retreated.

"Come forward Princess Pocahontas and bring the members of your tribe with you" said the King.

Looking at the thrones, Pocahontas compared them to her father's throne. The principle was the same, but nothing could have prepared her for the splendour that she was witnessing. The King himself was unimposing. He was stocky, thickset with a high forehead and pock marked face. Pocahontas thought that underneath all the trappings of state, he in fact looked very effeminate - not what one would have imagined the Warrior King of the Longcoats to look like.

His Queen, although probably in her fortieth year, was still attractive. She had blond hair done up in the latest fashion and a tiny waist that was accentuated by a band of jewels. She had gems on her hands and in her hair, and her face was encrusted with makeup making her cheeks look pink, as in the first flush of youth. Pocahontas was surprised that the King seemed to be ignoring his Queen, more intent on watching one of the squires. Pocahontas watched them both, taking in every detail. Then she remembered and lowered her eyes. Lady De La Warr had told her not to look at them until she had permission to do so.

Pocahontas walked forward with Matachanna, Tomocomo and the other Powhatans behind her. She looked around to see where John was, but realised that he had fallen back from view, and was not accompanying her. She faltered slightly, but then remembered what Thomas Dale had said about the King not holding John in high regard. John had set her on her way, and then had disappeared into the shadows. She took a breath, and continued forwards.

When they reached the front of the room facing the King and Queen, they all curtsied and bowed as they had been taught.

The King pulled his attention away from the squire, his eyes wide with surprise. Uttamatamakin looked extraordinary with his feathers, paint and beautiful Powhatan sword. His appearance stood out, even in the colours and extravagance of the room in which they were situated.

"Welcome to London, Pocahontas and all your kinsmen and women.

We are very pleased to entertain a Princess, the daughter of The Great Powhatan." King James bowed his head and put his hands together at his chest. When the Queen saw what he was doing, she hurriedly copied him, looking extremely awkward.

"I am very pleased to be here Your Majesty, and I bring you best wishes from my father Powhatan and all the Powhatan people." She stood tall. Ambassador of her People. Caressing her father's pearls that were around her neck – a symbolic reminder.

"So…. you have made a great impression on many of the people in my court, young lady. Lord and Lady De La Warr are very impressed, and of course Sir Thomas Dale and his very good friend Sir Ralph Winwood, The Secretary of State, have also sung your praises. I hope you have enjoyed all the entertainment that has been put on in your honour. I have heard that the Bishop of London's reception was a great success." He smiled at her, staring at the incongruity of her Powhatan persona swamped with the embellishments of an English lady. "I am surprised that your English is so perfect, Princess. Who taught you the language? Whoever it was did a very good job."

"Your Majesty, John Smith, who held the position of President of the British Colony for a time in Virginia taught me."

The King looked thoughtful and scratched his chin. "Ah yes. I do remember now" he said turning towards his wife, who was staring into space, bored. "Smith wrote to you Anne did he not?"

The Queen started. "Oh, yes…. John Smith wrote me a glowing letter[1] about you Princess, telling me how you saved his life and what a help you have been to the Colonists. He recommended we invite you to the palace. I thought it would be good fun to meet with someone so exotic." She smiled, fixing a curl that had gone out of place, and rearranging her petticoats.

Pocahontas felt like an arrow had gone to her heart. "John Smith wrote to you, Your Majesty?" She felt a little unsteady, and fought to maintain composure.

"Why yes, my dear. He said that he felt I would be interested in meeting with you - and he was quite correct. I love to see exotic people, and you and your family are definitely very interesting. I received the letter from him last week. I believe he has been in Northern Virginia on his new project and only discovered you were in London when he arrived back."

Pocahontas went pale. He was alive! He had been in Virginia all this time. Why did he not contact her before? How could he have betrayed her this way? She was stunned and silent for a moment taking it in. The Queen was staring, eyebrows raised. Waiting.

Pocahontas had to say something. But what?

"I shall have to thank Mr. Smith for writing about me in such terms" she said hurriedly.

"Now," boomed the King. "How can we entertain such important guests Anne?"

"I think it would be rather fun if they all came to the court Masque. They would surely brighten it up. It is such a lovely occasion, and I do believe it is going to be one of the best this year. I am sure you could do with a bit of light entertainment Pocahontas, after all these stiff, formal dinners." The Queen's eyes lit up and she giggled. "Yes, I will have an invitation sent out to you straight away." The Queen looked like a child looking forward to a special treat as she smiled and clapped her hands.

The King rolled his eyes as he watched her and turned back to Pocahontas. "Yes, it is one of the most elaborate and expensive Productions in England" he said."So Please come and enjoy it with us." This was clearly not an invitation; it was an order.

"I am most grateful Your Majesties. I look forward to the honour of joining you for the Masque" Pocahontas replied.

"Now you may go, my dear" said the Queen, who was obviously starting to get bored and could think of nothing more to say to this rather strange Princess and her weirdly attired companions.

Pocahontas retreated, smiling to herself as she saw Badger peeping out from behind the King's throne.

[1] See Appendix C

THE MASQUE

The Masque took place in the great banqueting hall at the Palace of Whitehall.

As they entered, Pocahontas gasped to see gold and silver balls on top of glittering pyramids at intervals around the room. This was the 50th Anniversary of King James's reign of Scotland, and he was determined that this masque was going to be a masque that outshone any that had gone before.

King and Queen - a castle,
gold and silver balls on top of
glittering pyramids, painted faces, music

Thousands of candles flickered illuminating the fanciful decorations that were adorning every nook and cranny of the enormous 110 foot room. Tiers of benches lined each side of the room to serve as seating for the guests, many of whom had already taken their places. There were to be so many guests that the King had proclaimed a ban on the wearing of farthingdales, which meant, for once Pocahontas did not have to manoeuvre her attire to make sure the wicker frame sat where it looked elegant.

The three of them were led to the front of the large room, towards the dais which held three thrones decorated with gold and silver leaf, jewels sparkling everywhere it was possible to place jewels. The three thrones were for the King and Queen, together with a smaller throne for their sixteen year old son Charles, (the heir apparent, since the death of his brother Henry) who was to have his debut this evening. Above, a chandelier with hundreds of candles flickered in the solid gold of the many candle holders.

To the right of the thrones were the seats for Pocahontas, Tomocomo and Matachanna. These seats were tastefully decorated to show respect, whilst ensuring a distinction between the visiting Princess and the Monarch.

Tomocomo looked spectacular with his red paint, feathers and hair plaited on one side. He had brought with him a beautiful carved spear, and looked every inch a Powhatan warrior. Matachanna wore her simple suede shift and moccasin slippers, her long dark hair hanging down her back.

By contrast, Pocahontas's dress had been chosen with the greatest of care by Lady De La Warr. She looked stunning, although somewhat incongruous in a dress that was fit for royalty. The bodice was of the finest Italian silk, hand embroidered with flowers and ending in a point just under her tiny waist. From the delicate bodice fell the richest deep dark red velvet which dropped to the floor in cascades just allowing sight of her tiny cream silk slippers. The stiff white lace ruffle at her neck, accentuated her flawless brown skin, and her large bulbous sleeves contrasted with her small and slender hands encased in perfumed kidskin gloves. Her pearls adorned her neck at her insistence.

Indeed, Pocahontas knew they were a spectacle to behold, and held her head high. She was proud, and felt at ease being treated as royalty, as it was something that she had been used to - albeit in a very different setting. If only her father could see her now, she thought.

Many people were already gathered. All stared at the foreign visitors in disbelief. They had never seen people like this before. The noise escalated like an angry swarm of wasps as the crowd witnessed the Heathens walking up to the Dais and taking their seats next to where the King and Queen and Prince Charles were to sit. Pocahontas smiled regally and nodded.

Suddenly the trumpeters, dressed in bright red with gold braid, lined up along each side of the room raising their brass instruments with a flurry to announce the King, Queen and Prince. Everyone stood to attention as the trumpets blared and the Monarch's entourage proceeded towards the Dais. As they walked they nodded and waved to the crowds who were crammed into the seats on either side of the room. When they reached their thrones they turned, bowed their heads and sat down. The King then signalled for everyone in the room to be seated.

The "Vision of Delight" began.

Silence. Just the breathing of anticipation. A painted curtain fell to reveal a street, painted on shutters, and wings arranged in projecting series on each side of the stage, constantly changing, creating illusions of movement and depth. Moon and Night with their charioteers rose high above the heads of the audience. A tower, a house, a church. People moving in the richly created fantasy. Song, dance, lavish costumes, colours. Characters of Delight, Grace, Love, Harmony, Revel, Sport and Laughter... spoke to one another in song. "See, see, Delight sings, her sceptre and her crown are all of flame." Fantasy emerges and the music gets louder. Twelve French musicians signal the finale. A bower of flowers bursts open to reveal honeysuckle, Bryony and Jasmine. The main dancer, The Earl of Buckingham, the King's newest favourite and lover prances onto the stage, darting here and there in a fantastic display of human dexterity and talent.

The crowd gasps with delight. Laughing and clapping. The whole company of players descends onto the dance floor in a final tribute to the King and Queen.

The Duke of Buckingham's voice rose to a crescendo:
"Behold a king
Whose presence maketh
this perpetual spring...

King of the less and greater isles,
And all those happy when he smiles,
Advance, his favour calls you to advance,
And do your night's homage in a dance"

The music grew louder, the playfulness of it charging the audience with energy. The players beckoned the crowd to join them dancing and they spilled out from the seats bouncing onto the green carpet of the dance floor, unable to contain their glee.

The Duke of Buckingham walked sedately up to the Dais, bowed to the King with an intimate smile and turning, proffered his hand to the Queen who giggled childishly with delight infected by the atmosphere, as she followed him to the dance floor. The King grunted as he watched Prince Charles follow his mother to the dance floor where his sixteen-year-old spirit took flight amongst his people.

Pocahontas was taken aback as she watched the Lords and Ladies of every rank, all in their finery, let go of the stiff inhibitions they had previously portrayed. Laughing and twirling, flirting and bowing, they were infected with the gaiety and surreality of the masque they had just witnessed. They were in another world, a world where everything was allowed and fantasy was the norm. Serendipity. Music played and suns and moons floated overhead. Silver and gold glistened, laughter and ale mixed with the free abandon of lads and lasses without a care in the world.

As she watched, suddenly her face froze. A cloud descended around her, excluding her from merriment. He was prancing towards her, smiling the insincere smile of the devious. He bowed and held his sweaty hand out towards her.

"My Princess, how befitting that I should be the first Englishman that you should dance with."

She shuddered with disgust and looked around her to see who was watching. Could she refuse? Could she reject the hand of Sir Thomas Dale? His smile faded when she hesitated. He came closer to her and whispered in her ear so no one else could hear. "You and I are almost like husband and wife… you will always be mine." His face was menacing as he grabbed her arm and squeezed it until she gasped. She knew she could do nothing, so she rose from her seat, bowed to the King, and walked down the steps to the dance floor with Thomas Dale.

Pocahontas had been well versed in the dances of the court by Lady de la Warr, so she knew exactly what to do. She looked straight ahead, as he came closer to her, grabbing her around the waist. She concentrated on the dance steps, stiff with anger that he should invade her in such a way.

Everyone around her was free and whimsical, whereas she was bound with darkness, once again the prisoner of her abuser. The ale that had been flowing opened the gates for wild abandon and so no one saw her misery. Everyone was in their own bubble of whimsy as they were carried away with their own raucous revelry oblivious to her pain.

When Thomas Dale put his knee between her legs, and his hand traveled downward from her waist hidden by the folds of red velvet, she closed her eyes in disgust and tried in vain to pull away from his vice like grip. He smiled at his power as she scoured the room for people to see and help her - but there was no one.

"There, there Princess. This is what you have been waiting for, is it not?" he whispered with triumph in his voice.

"You will be mine until the day you die" he said as he pulled her from the hall into one of the side rooms and locked the door…

The silver and gold turn into dust and the sound of the music fades.

A hand reaches for me. His eyes are hazel, his hair is fair. But where is Kocoum? Ah - he is there, he is smiling that same beautiful smile, but stands apart. "Go, my love. Be happy, my love." he says. 'I am telling him 'No. No. I will always love only you Kocoum.' He puts his hand on his heart. He says "our love will survive - no matter what happens. I know I have not lost you; your love is not shared, it has expanded"

I try and touch his cheek, but he fades from out of my reach.

John is still there waiting. He looks at me, a tear runs down his cheek.

My love expands, I go to him.

Manito Aki is all around - he has given me permission. A message of truth has unfolded... I have been shown what I always knew but could not see...

Badger smiles, he always knew what I should do.

MOVE TO BRENTFORD

～⚶⚶⚶～

Pocahontas had had to restrain John, as he had exploded with rage when she told him how Dale had dared to approach her at the masque, even although she had not told him the extent of Dale's abuse. After hours of deliberation about Dale's continued bullying of Pocahontas, and the increasing threat of John's possible arrest by the king, their escape had been hastily arranged.

It had been an upheaval, but now they were finally there. Pocahontas looked out of the window of their new residence. It was difficult to believe that this was the same country that had filled her lungs with smog and made her gag with the stink of the streets. Here, the streams ran clear, and the air was crisp and fresh. There were open spaces and room to breathe. This was Brentford about ten miles from London, a world apart. It was cold, but it was bright, and Pocahontas's spirits had lifted as soon as she climbed out of the carriage.

The Percy family had lent them a villa in the grounds of the very grand Syon house.

George Percy and John were old friends. In 1609 they had both set sail on the 'Sea Venture' heading for Virginia and were blown off course in a hurricane. But for the good fortune of being wrecked on the Island of Bermuda they would both have suffered a watery death. They were marooned on Bermuda for ten months. So old friends re-united, eight years later, George had offered them accommodation for the rest of their stay in England.

She looked over to where John was holding BaBa as he played on a magnificent hobbyhorse that was in the nursery of the villa. BaBa was giggling with delight, his eyes twinkling as John moved him up and down and forwards and backwards on the bright red saddle of the grey dappled hobby horse, clicking his tongue mimicking the sound of hooves galloping. A flash of Kocoum playing with Ko-kee came into her mind. Kocoum and Ko-kee, John and Thomas. Her heart severed in two. How could she welcome the flower of joy into her heart when it grew in the soil of such pain and loss?

She became aware of Badger in the background watching her. She looked closer, and in his eyes she could see a little Powhatan boy laughing and happy.

Badger nodded. His message was clear.

She turned to look at Thomas.

Thomas looked at her and held out his arms "mama" he cried.

Pocahontas went to him, picking him up and drawing him into the warmth of her body. "Mama is here for you my Baba" she said, walking towards the window, glancing back to see that Badger had disappeared, leaving only his blessing for her to love again. Love extending, not cut in half. She did not have to choose, she could love both - both children and both men.

She buried her head in Thomas's neck, and then glanced out of the window.

"Oh look John, it is starting to snow again" she said. "Shall we take BaBa out and have a walk and a play?" Maybe the cold air would clear her thoughts..

They bundled themselves and little BaBa in warm clothing and headed out into the vast grounds of Syon house. The parkland seemed to go on forever, and no other houses could be seen from the white expanse that lay in front of them. Pocahontas carried BaBa on her back, sticking with the Powhatan tradition. She could feel his little warm body against her own, and she sighed with the pleasure of being in such a beautiful place with one of her babies and John. She looked over at John. Today for a change, she allowed her eyes to wander without turning away, taking in his strong physique and his smiling laughing face as he strode through the snow, kicking lumps of it into the air to make BaBa laugh. Suddenly he stopped and stooped down, grabbing a ball of snow in his hands he threw it at Pocahontas and BaBa.

The two of them shrieked as the cold snow thrown with such force found itself inside their outer garments. Pocahontas stamped her feet in protest.

"That is not fair - you caught us unawares, didn't he BaBa?"

"All's fair in love and war" replied John laughing at her and picking up more snow to throw in her direction. She ran towards him pushing him backwards into the snow. As he fell he threw his arms and legs out moving them backwards and forwards making angel wings in the soft white powder.

Pocahontas was hysterical with laughter, and BaBa squealed to see his father sprawled out on the ground. She had not laughed for so long - there was always duties to be done and sadness and cruelty in the air. Today it seemed to her as if a weight had been lifted from her shoulders. There was no one around except the three of them (and Badger). She could not remember the last time this had happened.

And Manito Aki had released her. She felt like the young woman that she was. Gone for now were thoughts of Thomas Dale, the peace process, or her failure to unite her people with the English. Just this one afternoon she was being real. She looked at John. For a fleeting moment, Kocoum flashed into her mind again, but just as quickly, he disappeared again. Kocoum was right, her love had expanded. She did not love Kocoum any less because she had fallen in love with John... and for the first time she allowed herself to admit to herself that she had fallen in love with John with a savage intensity that had been repressed for so long by guilt. She felt the freedom of surrendering to the truth.

It almost overwhelmed her as she allowed herself to look at him and really see him with her soul. She caught his hand which was warm and strong, and she strained to try and pull him up from the snow that was twinkling around him in the Winter sunlight. He looked startled at her contact with him, but smiled at her uncertainly, his hazel eyes full of hope with the change that he saw come over her so suddenly. He could feel the bond, despite the intangibility of it.

BaBa started to cry - he was cold, and he was bored with the cold white stuff that had made his clothes wet. His parents' attention had gone from him to each other, and he needed the attention back - so he kicked and wailed in protest. They looked at him and laughed.

"We had better get this little man back inside for some food and warmth" Pocahontas said. She was unwilling to break the spell and to let go of John's hand, unwilling to break the connection that pulsed through them both. This magic had been held back for so long and was like a dam about to burst. They walked back to the house, hand in hand holding on to each other like it was the first time that they had met, eyes meeting shyly and looking away. Secret smiles and beating hearts.

There was a roaring fire waiting for them when they arrived back at the villa. They took off their wet outer clothing, and dried the sodden and miserable little BaBa. The complaining toddler was given some hot milk and cake, and he happily started to play with the wooden blocks that John had given him, warm, replete, and content.

John and Pocahontas sat side by side, thighs touching, holding hands, watching BaBa play.

She blossomed. Her heart soared with the normality of being John's wife. He was tender and caring, and every night when at last they lay together in

310

one another's arms, his touch, like that of the gentlest feather brought her untold pleasure that took her to places she had never been before.

They went on long walks together with BaBa, and John introduced her to the joys of riding. Together they explored the countryside on horseback, seeing more of the beauty of his homeland without the politics and grubby commercialism of London.

For several weeks, they left behind the trials and tribulations of the Virginia Company - no glamorous receptions, no talk of tobacco, no tedious conversations, and debates about religious conversions. Just a small family living in peace and quiet, where they could explore one another and get to know each other as not only friends, but lovers.

As they crouched on the floor in the nursery together playing with BaBa, they heard a commotion outside. The housekeeper came crashing into the room, her face red with panic.

"My Lord - you have visitors. I was not expecting anyone, so I am not prepared." She was out of breath, with eyes wide, looking for instructions.

"It is fine Mary. Do not worry. I am sure that we can entertain whoever it is - even if it is not as we would have liked. If someone visits without any notice, they must be prepared for a very basic reception."

"Yes, My Lord." Mary curtsied.

"Who do we have the pleasure of receiving Mary?" he asked, trying to contain his irritation.

"Well M'Lord. Lord and Lady De La Warr are here, and so is Sir Thomas Dale, Capt. Samuel Argall and Mr. John Smith."

"Thank you, Mary, can you show them into the parlour and we will receive them as soon as we can. Please offer them some refreshments." Mary curtsied, turned and left the nursery.

Pocahontas's face had turned pale and she stared at the floor, stiff with emotion.

"What can they possibly want John?" she whispered. "Why is John Smith here? I never wanted to see him again, and now he has invaded our home. As for Thomas Dale - his coming can only bring us sorrow. He thinks he can do what he likes with me - but he is wrong. I despise him. How dare

311

he come here!" her voice became louder and stronger as she thought about the waiting guests. "And as if that is not enough - Samuel Argall - what possible reason can there be for him coming here? Can we just refuse to see them John?"

John picked up Thomas. "It may be that it is time for us to go back to Virginia Pocahontas. That is the only reason that I can think of for them coming here. The Virginia Company are in financial difficulties, and I know they resent paying your stipend."

"But why John Smith?"

"I don't know. We will have to meet with them to find out."

_____

As they walked into the room, John Smith walked towards Pocahontas, his face beaming. "Pocahontas, how lovely to see you again." He held out his hand to her. She ignored him, as if she had not see him and continued towards Lady De La Warr. She curtsied to her friend "Please sit down Lady De La Warr. I am afraid you have caught us somewhat unprepared for your visit." She smiled.

Lady De La Warr sat down, spreading her skirts around her. "We have some news from the Virginia Company, which Sir Thomas and Capt. Argall wanted to share with you, and Capt. Smith was very keen to join us as he has not seen you since before you were married."

John Smith ventured over to where the two ladies were sitting. "Yes, Pocahontas, it has been remiss of me not to visit you before now. My business engagements prevented me. But now that I am here, I cannot tell you how wonderful it is to see you again."

"So how have you been Lady De La Warr?" Pocahontas said, pointedly ignoring him again, a stern look on her face.

Thomas Dale strode over towards John, impatience written all over his face. "Forget all these "niceties". John, we must decide the future of this trip of yours. It can't go on forever as we are paying out good money for your "Princess" to stay here and basically do nothing. Capt. Argall is sailing back to Virginia in March, and we think that you should sail with him."

Pocahontas looked at the assembled group. How could things change in the space of ten minutes? Thomas Dale made her blood boil, and she could see John was trying to avoid looking at him. She knew he would have liked to take him outside and give him a hiding, but that was not going to get either of them anywhere. Dale was talking about sending them back to Virginia - the sooner the better now she and John had a chance of making a life together. But her heart could not settle on positive thoughts when John Smith was looking at her and smiling as though nothing had happened. What was *he* doing here? She could not look at him or speak to him. What was there to say to someone that had totally betrayed you? Her mind was whirling. She had arrows in her head all aimed at John Smith. She knew what she wanted to say to him, but she also knew that her anger would distort it and it would come out in a jumble of nonsense. So she decided to communicate her displeasure with silence.

She sat, with her hands in her lap, looking at the floor. She was vaguely aware that John had ordered Mary to bring refreshments and that there was a buzz of conversation as they discussed the logistics of the journey home. It seemed to go on for hours and hours, and the longer it lasted, the more she retreated into herself. She sensed people looking at her, and heard her name from time to time, but could not move. Would not move. How dare he! How dare he! Her father had bestowed John Smith, the greatest honour - the honour of becoming a Weroance, and he had betrayed him... The energy of the anger in her body was making her feel sick.

Finally, she heard everyone getting up and leaving the room. She sat alone with her thoughts - or so she believed.

He whispered gently. "Pocahontas, what is the matter?"

As she heard his voice, she jumped up, unsure who it was - she thought everyone had gone. She had not realised that the target of her displeasure remained. She blinked, forcing herself to look him in the eye. "What is the *matter*? What is the *matter*? I thought you were dead!" she shouted, tears of anger silently falling down her face."

"Yes, I know. I had to return to England very quickly as I was not well."

"You could have sent word. You just vanished leaving us to believe you had died in an explosion. All the while you have been in Virginia.... It is almost unbelievable."

"I was ashamed to leave you like that. I know I betrayed you and your father and I am sorry. I just could not face you."

"I do not understand. Remember how you came to Werowocomoco and talked with my father? Remember when he anointed you as his son making you as welcome as family? Remember that you promised my father that what was yours was his? You called him Father. You were like a father to me. You helped me to know your people, and we could have worked together for peace... you were part of our tribe, we wanted you... but you just threw me and my people aside... and now you come crawling back as though we are friends - friends do not betray one another as you have betrayed me." She turned her head away from him. Her heart was beating, and she was hot with the energy of her fury.

"Pocahontas, please listen to me. I know that I have done wrong in the past, but now I am here to make amends. I have always been on the side of you and your people. At the time I left, I could see that our people were starting to take over your land, to take over your way of life, and I could do nothing to stop it. I was ashamed, so I had to leave so I was not a part of it."

She turned and looked him full in the face, shaking with rage.

"So you ran rather than stay and work with us. You ran leaving us to the fate of your people, knowing all the while that we were hoping for a peace built on lies. You are telling me now that peace was never to be?"

He shook his head and looked at the ground. "I am sorry Pocahontas, your hopes for peace between our people are an illusion. I am here today to tell you that you cannot rely on the English to care about your wellbeing. You must know the truth. The English need land - your land is cleared and cultivated, so we will take it. If your people object to our taking your land and more - they will be killed."

"... and what of this charade of parading me around London? What is that all about?" she shouted at him.

"The investors want to know that not only are the English taking your land, they are taking your religion and your way of life. You have been proof that it is possible to convert the natives to Christianity. There are even plans afoot to create schools for your young men to educate them in the Christian way....And don't think it will be voluntary...children will be abducted and made to accept Christianity. There are already plans for a college at Henrico[1] - believe me, it is true. Edwin Sandys is organising everything, and the King is so keen on educating your young men that he has started fund raising to pay for it."

Pocahontas's eyes were wide with shock. "So, I have been an example of what can be done to bring my people into line? Our young men..." She stopped talking, deep in thought, her mind going round and round. Kokee... in time they might take *him*. Her visit, far from working towards peace and integration, was promoting the exploitation of her people. She was, in effect, validating the plan to overcome her people and force them to comply with English culture and religion.

"They are going to wipe us out..." she whispered, as the truth became clear.

"Sadly, that is the case. They have been delighted to see you around London looking so civilized and charismatic. Investors can see the possibilities of saving your people from their Heathen ways, and this makes them feel good about themselves. They can take your land from you and give you Christianity in return, whether you want it or not, and feel good about it at the same time."

Pocahontas was quiet. She was stunned. She felt that she was going to throw up, and struggled to hold herself together. Everything that she had worked for was a sham. These people were ruthless and cruel. She had never imagined such guile and deception possible from fellow human beings. Looking back there had been signs, of course there had been. The behaviour of Dale, the behaviour of Argall - she had chosen to see it as personal to them, not as a trait of their people. She suddenly realised that she had been so enthusiastic to welcome the strangers, that she had missed the reality of their intentions. How could she have known?

Her friendship with John Smith had been something special wasn't it?

Looking back now with new eyes she could see that maybe it had been a childhood infatuation that had clouded her judgment and made her idealize him and what he stood for.

She looked at him sitting here in front of her and saw him for what he really was. A diminished and pathetic old man who had taken her friendship and the friendship of her people and come running back to England when he saw that things were getting out of his control.

Maybe he was not to blame? Maybe he was just weak. The forces of evil were very strong in Virginia, maybe it was too much for one man to fight.

"So why are you telling me these things now when there is little that I can do?"

"I know it might not seem like it, but I have always cared for you Pocahontas. I regret not standing by you and being honest from the start - I regret encouraging you to think that there was ever any possibility that we could merge and be as one people. The English were never going to be just another tribe living under the rule of Powhatan. I regret feeding the flames of your hope for peace. I cannot protect you, the forces against your people are far too great. What I can do, is to finally tell you the truth, so that you can let your father know what he is really up against. He was always so kind, always willing to try. He fed us when we were starving, and he helped us when we were ill. He disagreed with Uttamatamakin who could see what our people were doing. Opechancanough was right Pocahontas. When you go back, you must tell them to fight. It may already be too late, but the Colony is still small and still struggling, and your people may yet have a chance to defeat them as the English are so incompetent. Fight, do not befriend." He shook his head with shame.

Pocahontas looked at her old friend. He was diminished in stature, overcome with genuine emotion. Despite her rage, part of her started to feel sorry for him. Perhaps they were both victims of the Virginia Company's greed.

She held out her hand to him. He took it as he looked into her eyes.

"You can stop this Pocahontas" he said quietly.

316

[1] Details in Appendix D

FLIGHT TO HEACHAM

We must go now!" shouted John. "We can't take the risk of Dale coming back here."

"John, I know you are trying to protect me, but if Dale wants to silence me, he will do it, one way or the other."

"No - if we can hide ourselves away until it is time to sail, he will have lost the opportunity."

She looked at him, sorrow in her eyes. "We can try" she said quietly and with little enthusiasm.

He grabbed her by the shoulders. He looked frantic. "We will take BaBa, and the three of us will just disappear. Heacham, my childhood home is at least a day's journey from here, and no one will know where we have gone. Matachanna and Tomocomo can stay here, and we won't even tell *them* where we are going. I will send word to my mother to prepare for our arrival." His speech was fast, and he was breathless trying to convince her.

"It *will* buy us some time John, but I fear for when we go back to London to board the ship to Virginia."

"We will have you well guarded, and there will be so many people around,

Dale would not dare to do anything to you. After all you are a guest of the King. It would not do him well to be seen to harm you."

"He will not be seen" she said in a monotone whisper, remembering how Kocoum had gone through this same process with her.

John would not give up. He was fired up, determined that he would protect her. John was determined that they would get to Virginia and start a new and exciting life together with her family. There was nothing he wanted more.

She watched him with sad eyes - she had to go along with the escape plan for his sake. She had to pretend that she believed everything was going to be alright, a bit like she had done with Kocoum all those years ago. Maybe they could just have these last couple of weeks together and enjoy BaBa and each other and not think further than that. She held her head up high. Yes, that was the only way forward. She *had* to make the most of these two weeks. Beyond that - if they all got to Virginia, their future would be the best that she had ever dreamed of. If not, at least she would have had this time with John and BaBa. She sighed and wrapped her arms around John's waist resting her head on his chest. He stroked her shiny black hair.

The daylight was very short in March, and they reached Heacham Manor on a cold dark night having travelled most of the day. Thomas was tired and cried when he was pulled out of the warm carriage to enter the house of his Grandparents and clung to John as he looked around the house that was so strange to him.

Pocahontas looked around her. It was a comfortable house, not as grand as some in London, but it had a certain charm and warmth that she immediately appreciated. Her mother in law and father in law were standing in the hallway to greet them as the butler opened the door. Dorothea, John's mother, stood erect, a middle-aged woman of breeding conveying the appearance of one with impeccable manners, keen not to let her son down at this first meeting with his new wife. Robert Redmayne, John's stepfather stood next to his wife - a rather rotund man with twinkling eyes, a large belly and a broad smile.

Pocahontas immediately warmed to Robert, but when she looked at his wife, she noticed the finely veiled shock in her mother in law's eyes as she extended her hand. She could see Dorothea struggling to know how to react and what to say to her when John rushed in. Dorothea had never met someone like Pocahontas before.

"Mother - I would like you to meet Pocahontas - she is a Powhatan Princess" he added. He smiled at his mother eagerly, hoping for a positive response. She nodded at her son, and seemed to relax having had a few moments to absorb the situation. Her eyes softened as she looked at BaBa, who was slumped in his fathers arms having fallen asleep again in the warmth of the house.

"... and who is this young man?" she smiled.

"This is our son Thomas. We call him BaBa" said John. "Your Grandson"

John's mother walked towards the sleeping child. "Poor little mite, he looks exhausted" she said.

"Well John," said Robert Redmayne, "It is so nice to welcome you home after such a long time. I hope that your journey has not been too arduous." He looked around for the parlour maid.

"Maisie, would you please show these good people the room that you have prepared for them. I am sure that they will want to refresh themselves before dinner.

Dorothea stepped forward. "Would you like Maisie to bring up some warm milk and bread and butter for the little one? He must be so hungry and confused." She smiled at Pocahontas.

Pocahontas bowed her head. "Thank you so much. I am sure that BaBa would be very grateful for that."

They went up the creaking wooden stairway that smelt of polish, the handrail smooth with the use of generations. Maisie showed them to their large bedroom. It was comfortable, the quality of the furniture still apparent showing through the dilapidation of years of use.

BaBa was still asleep, and rather than wake him up to have his milk, John laid him carefully in his cot which had thoughtfully been placed at the foot of their bed. John and Pocahontas washed and cleaned up after the journey, ready to go down for a meal with John's parents.

"They are very kind John" she said.

"I think my poor mother was a little shocked when you walked in and she saw you were not a blonde English girl. A Norfolk lady has never seen a Powhatan before, so I am sure we can forgive her." He walked over, put his arms around her waist and stooped to kiss her neck. "Once she got over her surprise, she did warm to you though, I could tell. She is obviously smitten with BaBa already."

Pocahontas smiled. "Yes, I did feel a little sorry for her. You should have told her what to expect... imagine being confronted with an Indian squaw as a daughter in law when you had never seen such a creature before."

"Mothers always worry about their sons, don't they?" John smiled and did not notice her face changing. Yes, she would always worry about her *two* sons, but tonight she would have to leave those thoughts in the back of her mind.

John looked over at the sleeping Thomas. "Oh, look at him, bless him, he has really passed out. I will call Maisie and she can sit with him while we have dinner. I don't want him to wake up in a strange room all alone."

They settled BaBa with Maisie and wandered downstairs. They were ushered into the large dining room. It was another lovely warm and inviting room with a large roaring fire in the grate and candles flickering on the table and around the walls. It was solid and safe. Plate after plate of basic steaming hot comforting food were brought to them and Pocahontas watched John's face softening as he looked around his old home.

"So how long will you be staying with us John" his mother asked, bringing John back to the present.

"We sail in a couple of weeks" said John. "We thought that we would come and see you and introduce Thomas to you, and have a little peace and quiet before we go back to Virginia. Life has been very hectic in London with all the Masques and dinners and parties, and I wanted to show Pocahontas where I grew up and at the same time let her rest. She has been looking a bit tired recently." He looked over at her, and she looked surprised that he had noticed how weary she had felt. "I would be grateful if you could keep our presence a secret. We don't really want any more attention from the Virginia Company." He laughed. Pocahontas knew it was a fake laugh. It was serious. By "Virginia Company", he had meant Dale.

"We would love to show you all off to the people in the village - but we completely understand John that discretion is required, and we will keep your visit quiet" said his step father. "Please use our house as your house and do whatever you like. I am sure you would like to show your new wife around your old home. BaBa would love the beach - but sadly it is a bit cold at this time of year. If the two of you want to go out and about, just feel free to use Maisie as a nanny.

John's mother butted in. "... and me of course. It has been quite a while since I have had a little one to fuss over and as you are not going to be here that long, I would like to spend as much time as I can with him ... and John is right - you *do* look a little tired Pocahontas. You must take this opportunity to rest." She held her hand over her mouth as she yawned. "Well, it is getting late, and I am sure the two of you are tired, as am I, so maybe we should all retire for the evening. If there is anything that you need please let us know." She smiled.

Pocahontas and John climbed the stairs again to retire for the night. Maisie was half asleep in the chair next to the cot, and she jumped up when they entered.

"Is everything alright Maisie?" said John.

"There hasn't been a peep out of him." Maisie smiled and curtsied.

"Thank you, Maisie, you may go now." The girl stooped to look at the sleeping child for one last time, then she left.

"He has had such a tiring day, poor little one" said John, brushing the hair back from his face and rearranging the blankets to make sure that he was warm.

"You are such a good father, John" said Pocahontas, pulling him towards her.

"I am such a good father, that I want lots and lots of babies."

She felt his soft mouth on hers and melted into him. His hands explored her body gently, as if she was a china doll, as he removed her clothes. He looked deeply into her eyes - nothing else existed except the two of them. He unfurled her shiny black hair and it fell like silk down to her waist. He ran his hand through her locks and then his finger traced her face, her cheeks, her mouth. He watched as his finger touched every part of her, stopping every now and then and stooping to lick and kiss the part that he was touching. He kept going down her silky brown body, teasing her with his light and sensual touch. She shuddered with ecstasy, amazed at how such a strong and masculine man could move with such delicacy, how he could make tears of anticipation come to her eyes. She loved him so much, there was nothing she could see or feel but him. She was his.

For both of them, life had always been about trying to stay in control in a chaotic world - at this moment there was no need for control, there was freedom just to love each other with wild abandon.

They laughed, they loved, they cried, and they held each other, in the springtime of blossoming love. They could not get enough of each other and Heacham Manor became their nest, shielded from the outside world. They talked for hours about how it was going to be when they got back to Virginia creating visions of certainty unmarred by any influence of darkness.

One day after eating breakfast Pocahontas rising from the table, looked suddenly excited. "I know what we should do today" she said. "I have the stone of a Mulberry tree that I kept as a souvenir from the King's masque. Why don't we plant it here at Heacham? It will be a lovely tree that will give your mother blossom in the spring, and lovely fruit in the summer."

John looked up at her and smiled. "That is a novel idea, do you really think it will grow?"

323

"Of course it will grow! … and when it does, there will be something here at Heacham that is part of us. We will have made a difference." Her face was serious. "To my people, planting is giving back something to the universe. We will plant a tree that will grow for many generations. When we are both dead, and gone, the tree will still be here - no one will remember *us*, but this tree is a symbol of how life and love go on, and when it dies its seeds will bear more trees."

John went over to her and embraced her. "We will plant the seed." His eyes were sad. "Your people take from Nature what they need to survive, but always give back. Sadly, my people do not understand that this is the only way. You teach me so many things."

They went into the garden with BaBa, and John dug a hole for the seed. "We must mark it, so that people know it is here. I will make sure that Maisie looks after it until it is big enough to look after itself" he said. He marked the spot with a wooden stake, and they stood hand in hand, thinking and praying that their offering would be accepted by the universe. A thanks for the two weeks that they had spent at Heachem. The two most important weeks of their lives so far.

John was trying to learn Algonquin. English had always been the language that he and Pocahontas spoke together. But, if he was planning to live with her people, he had to know how to communicate with them. They were sitting in the living room in front of a roaring fire, Pocahontas was reeling off vocabulary at John, leaning against him as she watched Thomas play with a pile of wooden bricks.

"So how do you say 'I love you' in Algonquin? She asked him.

"Oh no - I am sure you have not told me that one - you are cheating…"

"Well, it is 'Kuwumaras'. Ku..wu..ma..ras. Got it?" John nodded like an obedient child.

"Say it then" she said. He tried, and she laughed at him.

"So alright, here is an easy one - tell me John, what is the word for child in

Algonquin?" she asked him, raising her eyebrows, and looking very serious.

He looked up at the ceiling as if he could find the answer there. Then he shook his head.

"I don't remember that one" he said shaking his head and wriggling with discomfort at his stupidity. "I am not very good at this am I?"

She rolled her eyes in pretend chastisement, when actually she was rather charmed by his embarrassment. "Well, it is "mukkie."

She suddenly turned around to look at him, smiling. She grabbed his hand fiercely and placed it on her belly. "Mukkie" she whispered.

He looked confused.

"That is why I have been so tired."

THE FINAL JOURNEY

oing back to London was like the end of a perfect dream. Pocahontas looked out at the beautiful English countryside and re-lived memories of the past two weeks, smiling to herself as each picture of their time at Heacham came into her mind. She held John's hand and BaBa sat on John's lap.

As the time passed, and they gradually approached London, the sights and smells started to change. There were more houses, more horses, more people, more filth. The rubbish in the streets began to appear with the stink and the smog, and Pocahontas remembered how horrible it had been. She sighed, longing for the refreshing cold crisp breezes of the countryside. Here, very few trees had been planted, and nature had been lost to the "progress" of the developing City. People were frenzied with trying to survive, competing for scarce resources, most having never known the beautiful countryside.

Nothing was said as they rumbled onto the quay, the cobblestones jiggling and crashing below the wheels of the carriage. BaBa started to cry, being jolted backwards and forwards, sensing the tension in the air. John held him close, murmuring to him. Pocahontas's newly pregnant body suddenly made her want to vomit - and her tiredness overcame her as she took in the sights and sounds of the quay with a sense of disgust. People were shouting, smoke was rising from fires at the side of the quay selling hot food, and prostitutes paraded up and down, their makeup hiding poxed and malnourished faces, grim with the cold. This was not a happy place and she did not want to be here. She felt hemmed in by the claustrophobic atmosphere, struggling to breathe in the damp and smoky air. She wanted to be back at Heacham beside a roaring fire sipping a mug of hot ale. She thought she might faint, but concentrated on holding onto John and breathing deeply to maintain her consciousness.

As the carriage drew up to the ship, they saw the rest of their party had already arrived. Matachanna, Tomocomo and the other Powhatans were assembled with their belongings waiting to board the ship. Admiral Argall was shouting orders and pointing here there and everywhere impatient to organise what seemed like chaos. He caught sight of the pale and fragile figure of Pocahontas as she walked towards the ship holding onto John's elbow.

"Good morning Princess" he said. "Are you alright? You look a little unwell."

Pocahontas just nodded at him. John answered for her. "It has been a long journey as we have come all the way from Norfolk. Pocahontas is just a little tired and hungry. Perhaps we could go aboard and get settled in. I am sure she will feel better then."

Argall nodded. "Of course, John. Take her on board and find where you are to sleep. I am sure you can find something to eat and refresh yourselves. I am afraid that we will not be setting sail any time soon as the wind and the tide are not with us."

Pocahontas's heart sank. The longer they stayed, the longer she would be in danger. She felt nauseous and still a little faint. Perhaps it was a little girl this time? Often baby girls caused more sickness than boys. How lovely it would be for John and her to have a little girl. She sighed as she walked up the gangplank, knowing that this was going to be a difficult journey. The journey across the ocean was hard at the best of times, but with a pregnancy as well, it was going to be very difficult. But she could do it - the thought of landing in Virginia and seeing her people again pulled her forwards until she got to the simple cot that was going to be her bed for the next six weeks. She flopped down and closed her eyes sighing.

"Are you alright Pocahontas?" John's eyebrows were drawn, and his body was tense. Thomas was clinging to him like a frightened little monkey.

Pocahontas smiled at him. "Don't worry John. I am feeling very tired and a little sick, but that is the price you pay when your body is welcoming a little baby." John took her hand and squeezed it.

"Here, have a nibble of these biscuits and a sip of ale - you need to feed that little one… "

She did as she was told and then lay back staring at the ceiling. "Why don't you take Thomas up onto the deck and he can watch the sailors getting the ship ready to sail? I will just have a little rest. I will be fine when I have had a sleep." She smiled at him, and pulled BaBa towards her. "You go upstairs with Daddy, BaBa, and see the men doing all their jobs. There is lots to see, and you can come back down and tell me all about it." She hugged him.

John carried BaBa up to the deck and left Pocahontas to rest. She took another nibble of the biscuit and sipped the ale, resting her head down on the cot, feeling the movement of the ship bobbing gently up and down. The nausea was starting to lift, and she closed her eyes, drifting off into a deep sleep.

An hour later, she awoke to see John and BaBa, flushed with the fun that they had had on the deck coming towards her."Argall says we won't be sailing for at least another two days. We just have to bide our time until then. At least we can venture off the ship from time to time, and we will not have to rely on that horrible dried meat for food! Here are some sugarplums that Argall gave me for you. He sends his compliments and hopes that you are feeling better."

"I am feeling better. I just needed a rest, that is all. It is very common in early pregnancy" she said. She looked at the confectionery. "How uncharacteristically kind of him." She picked one up and nibbled the corner.

"Actually, it is very nice. Here BaBa - try this, it is nice and sweet" she said handing it over to the toddler. BaBa took it and nibbled it, spitting it out immediately. "No" he shouted. Pocahontas laughed. "I will have to eat it all then" she said popping it into her mouth. "I am eating for two after all" she said.

The next day, Pocahontas woke up her tummy rumbling, and she started to vomit. She thought back to her last two pregnancies, neither of which had made her physically sick. It must be a little girl she thought smiling, despite the griping of her stomach, imagining her little girl in John's arms, she smiled. Who would she look like? BaBa would be so thrilled to have a sibling... she wretched again. There was nothing left in her body to bring up though.

Over the next couple of days, John became increasingly shocked by the downturn in Pocahontas's condition. He spent all day by her side. He had asked Matachanna to look after Thomas as he could not bear to leave Pocahontas. His nights were spent pacing up and down, his mind cycling through ups and downs - imagining the worst, imagining the best, trying to think what he could do to help, and feeling totally powerless.

At last the wind was in their favour, and they were ready to set sail.

"Pocahontas are you sure that you are well enough to do this journey?"

She could just about raise her head from the cot. "Oh, darling John, do not worry. It will be fine. It is just this baby fighting to let me know her power." She held out her hand to him. "Just hold me for a while."

John went over and lay down on the cot next to her, cradling her head on his chest, feeling her shallow breathing.

They both felt the shudder of the ship as she pulled away from the quay. They lay together feeling the rocking. Every now and then Pocahontas had to vomit into the bowl that had been provided for her.

Her pains were getting worse and she clutched her stomach in agony. "John, this doesn't seem right. The pain is getting worse very quickly. I hope I am not going to lose the baby." Tears started to run down her face. She suddenly pulled away and vomited again - noticing streaks of blood. She froze with fear. What was happening to her? She looked at John.

He held her close. "We cannot continue with this journey, Pocahontas. I will go and tell Argall that we need to stop."

She was very weak, but she raised her head. "John, we must go - I must tell my father..."

"Do not worry about that now Pocahontas - we just need to get you well"

John climbed up to the top deck and saw Admiral Argall in full flow making sure that the ship navigated the Thames efficiently.

"Argall...! Argall...! " he shouted. Argall looked in his direction and signalled for John to go to him. John ran.

Breathless he came face to face with Argall. "We have to make land. Pocahontas is very ill. She needs medical attention."

"What? No, I cannot stop the journey now. We are already well behind schedule, and we must take the chance when the weather is with us John. I am sorry, I cannot dock the ship now."

"You must Sir. She may die if you do not."

Argall sighed. What a shame this had happened before they reached the open sea. To refuse the request to land would seem callous and open to questioning. He would just play for time.

"It is difficult to find somewhere to land out here. We are now 25 miles from London. Our only chance is maybe Greenwich" he replied.

"If you do not land, her death will be on your conscience" said John.

The river was getting wider as they navigated Long Reach and Erith, where the tower of the church could be seen at Swanscombe. Eventually the church and inn at Gravesend appeared. Admiral Argall dropped the anchor, and watched as John, Matachanna and several other native Powhatans carried the barely conscious Pocahontas off the ship to the Inn.

Pocahontas could only look up at the grey sky and call on Ahone to save her and her baby. She had known that she was in danger but had never considered pregnancy to be her enemy. How ironic, she thought to herself.

She lay in a bed in the Christopher Inn, thankful to be on dry land where the nausea subsided slightly without the movement of the ship.

The doctor came in. He was an older grey-haired man with kindly eyes. He looked at her and smiled, and as he did so, she vomited once again and fell back on the bed exhausted, beads of sweat appearing on her forehead.

The doctor examined the vomit and felt her pulse. He stopped and shook his head, pausing. "Your illness is not from your pregnancy madame - I fear you have been poisoned."

There was silence in the room as everyone absorbed what had been said.

Then it became clear. "Can anything be done" John asked, tears welling up in his eyes.

"No there is nothing that I can do. I am sorry." The doctor bowed his head and stroked Pocahontas's brow. "I am so sorry, my dear - but your symptoms lead me to believe that arsenic was used and I have no antidote."

"Wait, wait... I always carry the Powhatan powders for snake bites with me. Would that do anything?" It was Matachanna, eyes wide and frantic.

The doctor looked at her. "I have no knowledge of Native medicine Madame. But, you will not do her any harm by trying. I have nothing that I can offer her."

John sprang up. "We must try it. It saved her with a snake bite - maybe it can save her again. We must try it."

Pocahontas lay, sweat continuing to bead onto her forehead. She was flushed, and crying out with the pain of the cramps in her stomach.Every now and then she shouted for a bowl and John had to help her to sit up momentarily as she vomited and then collapsed back down onto the bed.

Matachanna made up a solution of the Powhatan powders, and helped her to sit up again. She sipped the liquid, every now and then choking and spluttering. Her breathing was rapid and she could hardly open her eyes for the pain and exhaustion as she took in the Powhatan remedy.

"It may take a little while to take effect" said Matachanna.

"Thank you Matachanna" whispered John. "I will stay with her and take care of her. Maybe she can get a little rest." His face was full of fear.

Pocahontas sank into the bed, all energy gone. She sighed and closed her eyes. John sat on the bed next to her holding her hand. As she slept the vomiting ceased. John was frantic thinking about it. It had to have been Dale. Dale was going to win. He wanted Pocahontas silenced forever. He sat for hours thinking, remembering, praying. He started to get tired and lay down on the bed next to her. He felt her warmth, and the movement of her shallow breathing. He held her hand and felt her pulse, weak and irregular. They slept together for three hours in the darkened room.

John woke up when he felt Pocahontas move next to him. He looked at her and saw that she had sat up and was smiling at him. "John, I think the powders have worked - I feel a lot better. I am still very weak, but the stomach cramps have gone, and I no longer feel the need to vomit."

John could hardly believe it. "Pocahontas - you beat him. You are going to live. We are going to Virginia!" He was bursting with happiness, and pulled her towards him, feeling her body so fragile and small. "I must call Matachanna and the others and let them know that you are getting better."

"No John. Wait a few minutes. I just want to be with you alone."

He nodded and pulled her head into his shoulder. "I was so worried about you. I don't know what I would do if anything ever happened to you." Pocahontas could not see his tears, but she felt his body trembling with emotion.

"Well, those powders seem to have made me better, so you do not have to think about losing me just yet. We have so much more to do together John. We must go back and tell my father about the plans the English have for Virginia… and BaBa - we will see him grow up together. Our lovely BaBa… Ko-kee and BaBa can grow up as brothers. We have a beautiful future ahead." She stopped for a moment and looked into his eyes.

"I was wondering - as this baby is definitely a little girl. I was thinking about names. What do you think about the name Nuttah? In English it means 'My Heart'. Our two hearts joined in her."

John paused. He was overcome with joy. He had her back, and they were naming the baby. "Nu-tt-ah" he sighed out the name. "It is beautiful" he said. "It is the most beautiful name I have ever heard apart from Pocahontas."

Pocahontas suddenly clutched her stomach, her eyes momentarily filled with fear. Then she realized, and peace overcame her. She reached up and kissed John's cheek. John felt her small body convulse, and he knew.

"All men must die… it is enough that BaBa and Ko-Kee will live… I love you" she whispered, as she felt the room getting hazy and she started to

drift. Then she remembered her father's words as she sat upon his knee…
"if you love someone deeply, you never lose them, they live on in your heart
even after death." She touched the pearls around her neck that her father
had given her on her wedding day. A smile touched her lips as she took her
last breath, closing her eyes.

Badger took her hand and led her into the next world.

*The pain is taken away. I see John collapsed on the floor weeping -I stoop
down and kiss my beloved and he looks up to see that I have gone. I give
my heart to him. Nuttah. But I must go, even though my heart is heavy, as
my tears fall.*

*I look to the sky and see Hurit's leaf floating down towards me. It is a
perfect whole, no longer torn as a symbol of my separation from Kocoum.
I hold it to my heart. "I am here Pocahontas, I am here… I will always be
here" he whispers. I feel his hand like on the night of my Huskanasquua.. I
find joy, my eternal love at last, but my heart is broken too. I am leaving
my fair love, only our tree goes on to bear fruit. My tears will always fall
for him, but I cannot walk in two worlds. I hold two worlds always in my
heart.*

*Now I see the Universe. There are no boundaries. I am free to roam. I
am Beloved Woman, like Nikomis the woman that fell from the sky. Am
I a mirror of her? Her two sons, Okee and Ahone, one standing for peace
and one for destruction. My two sons Ko-kee and BaBa, from two different
worlds. Will one stand for good and one stand for destruction as in the
prophesy of the woman that fell from the sky? No. Manito Aki knows
that peace is in both of their hearts as their mother stood for Peace. I am
different from the Woman That Fell From The Sky. A new cycle has begun.*

*The Gods are taking me, it is true, they have not forsaken me, even
although my time on earth has ended - I see the sun, the moon. I see a small
boy playing with a greyhound, he looks up and sees the white bird – he
smiles and waves, a tear in his eye.. Djoodjoo… he whispers. He knows I
will forever watch over him.*

I see a little English toddler – Badger is in the corner. BaBa… I blow a kiss...he knows I am always here... Badger will watch over him...

And Nuttah... who died with me will always be by my side.

I roam and roam and I see the large grey sharp buildings standing tall and ugly. They are cutting the forest down with shiny tools and big machines, the earth is dry and dusty, it cannot bear fruit. They starve the beautiful world of nourishment. The beasts are quivering and starving. The oceans with dolphins tangled and bound so they cannot move, and turtles drowning. It is raining, it is hot, the black air is choking Bear and Fox and the people that cut the trees. Where are my people now that the world has grown older? Where are the Powhatan that lived with Nature, the ones that took but always gave back? Manito Aki promised to save them.

Ah, I see them. Small. Tiny. But alive amongst the concrete and tarmac - a minute oasis in the midst of death. The voice of Manito Aki floats on the wind... those who nurture the world survive, those who take from her perish through their own greed...

Manito Aki has saved them - They have the souls of Nature, they are kind, they understand, they are strong, they see what others do not see and because of that, they live in harmony with the Universe. I am the messenger of Manito Aki. I am the Beloved Woman, and the name of Pocahontas and that of my people will not be forgotten. When greed blackens the sun, my people's harmony with the Universe will regenerate the world. Manito Aki always knew. It is not war or peace; it is harmony with Nature and kindness that ensures survival.

The End

FOLLOW UP

Pocahontas

Pocahontas died on 21st March 1617- the Spring Equinox, the anniversary of her Dream vision. She was buried at St. George's church. Her death was entered into the register of burial of the parish of Gravesend. The entry reads:

"March 21 - Rebecca Wrolfe wyffe of Thomas Wrolfe gent. A Virginia Lady borne was buried in the Chauncel."

In 1727 the church was destroyed by fire. In 1897 some charred bones were found possibly belonging to Pocahontas and they were re-interred, but the exact location is unknown.

Powhatan

On hearing the news of the death of his beautiful daughter, Pocahontas, Powhatan was heartbroken and he died within the year.

John Rolfe

John continued to cultivate tobacco in Virginia, and he married Jane Pierce, the daughter of his friend George Pierce who had been marooned with him in Bermuda. They had a daughter called Elizabeth. John died in 1622 - this is the year of the great Powhatan Uprising. Some say that he died at the hands of the Powhatan.

Thomas Rolfe

When his mother died in Gravesend, his father wanted to take him back to Virginia, but at the start of the journey he became too ill. The ship docked at Plymouth and Thomas was given into the care of Sir Lewis Stukey until his Uncle, John Rolfe's brother Henry, could collect him. He spent his childhood in England with his father's family and never saw his father again.

When Thomas grew up, he travelled to Virginia (around 1635). His passage was paid for by John Rolfe's father in law (father of John's third wife Jane Pierce). After a time in Virginia Thomas sought permission to visit his uncle Opechankeno - and also to meet his mother's sister "Cleopatra" believed to be one of the squaws that went with Pocahontas to London.

Thomas married Jane Pythress and took up the substantial lands in Virginia that his father had left him, becoming a Leutenant in the English militia.

Little Kocoum

Pocahontas's first son survived. It is believed that Wayne Newton, the American singer, is thought to be one of his descendants.

Thomas Savage

Thomas Savage continued as an interpreter, and by 1624 he had married Hannah, and they had a son called John. As Hannah had paid her own way when she emigrated in 1621, she was given fifty acres in her own name.

Thomas continued working in Jamestown. He is said to have died in the early 1630's.

Sir Thomas Dale

As he was in Virginia longer than expected, his Company command in London was seized by a Capt. Willoughby and he had to petition to have his wages paid. King James came to his aid, and he received £1,000 in back pay. In September 1617 he was nominated for command of the English Naval Expedition to the East Indies to promote English commerce. He took the role of Admiral of the Fleet and was paid £480 per year.

He eventually died on 19th August 1619 of an illness, probably Typhoid or Dysentery.

Admiral Samuel Argall

Returned as Governor of Virginia but requested that someone else take over. Lord De La Warr was due to take over command and set sail in April 1618, however he died en route.

Many complaints were made about Argall's running of the Colony, and he left Virginia in March 1618 under a cloud. He was accused of arrogant and aggressive conduct and taking profits for himself as well as doing private deals with the Indians.

He defended himself against charges and was cleared. He then commanded a ship in the 1620 attack on Algiers. He was appointed Admiral of New England and was knighted by James 1 in June 1622.

In 1624, Argall was appointed to the Mandeville Commission, and he oversaw the reorganization of Virginia after the dissolution of the Virginia Company. He voted to surrender the company's charter but was defeated in his bid for election as the Royal Colony's Governor.

After commanding a large English fleet in an abortive attack on Cádiz he died at sea aboard the 'Swiftsure' on January 24 1626. He is buried at St. Gluvias Parish Church in Falmouth.

John Smith

John Smith never returned to Jamestown. He explored and mapped an area North of Virginia which he called 'New England'. His efforts to establish a Colony in 'New England' were stalled when he was captured by French pirates. After his release, he returned to England and concentrated on his writing. He died on 21st June 1631.

Development of Tobacco

John Rolfe relentlessly persevered with various methods of curing tobacco. The seeds he is thought to have brought from Bermuda grew strong and tall in Virginia. Even the natives were surprised at the height of the plants at four to six feet as opposed to their native specimens of half that size. By 1617 he exported 20,000 tons and by 1618, 40,000 tons. There was a contest between the two main producers, Spain and Virginia.

It is interesting to note King James's extreme abhorrence of tobacco. He believed that it damaged health. In his book, "A counter-Blaste to Tobacco" (1604) he said of tobacco:

"An unctuous and oily kin of soote as has been found in some great Tobacco takers. Smoke will infect the air, is dangerous to the lungs and hurtful to health of the whole body… A man [may] smoke himselfe to death with it (and many have done.

Despite the King's overt disgust with smoking, and his imposition of large duty on its importion, its popularity increased.

1600's Pope bans smoking in holy places.

1614 there were 7000 Tobacco shops in and around London.

In 1700 African slaves worked on Tobacco plantations long before they worked in cotton fields.

From John Rolfe's humble beginnings, Tobacco consumption continued to grow. In 20th century, almost the entire generation returning from the 1st World War was addicted.

In 1924 over 70 billion cigarettes were sold in the USA.

1930s Britain had the highest lung cancer death rate in the world.

In 2017 15% of global deaths was the result of tobacco.

20% of adults in the world smoke tobacco - in some countries it is over 40%.

Tobacco smoking is now on the decline with UK rates falling from a high of 38% to 22%.

Native Americans

It would take a whole book to discuss the fate of Native peoples following the invasion of foreign powers, and there are many out there that you can explore. I can only give a very brief outline here.

Every tribe of Indigenous people not only have their own names, they have their own languages and culture, so it is impossible to wholly generalize. Each area of, what is now, the USA was invaded by different foreign powers. Each tribe dealt with this differently. What *can* be generalized is the abuse and lack of respect indigenous people endured.

The story is a harrowing one of forced schooling, forced removal to reservations, forced sterilization (as late as 1970s) and discrimination accompanied by horrific death from disease. By 1900 Native Americans controlled a mere 3% of the 2.4 billion acres that had originally been theirs.

It is difficult to be precise about the number of Natives that died in the course of the invasion. Researchers have estimated there to have been approximately 60.5 million people living in the Americas prior to European contact. Between 1492 – 1600 90% of the population died, and of course, this trend continued.

Academics at University College, London have put forward the theory that so many Native Americans were killed through war and disease (smallpox, measles and influenza brought in by the colonizers) following invasion of their lands, that the rapid population decline and subsequent reduction in the cultivation of land, forced an increase in Carbon-dioxide-absorbing trees and vegetation, that triggered a mini ice age.

The death and destruction went on for hundreds of years. Native Americans were not even considered to be American citizens until 1924, and they were not allowed to vote until much later. The last state to guarantee voting rights for Native people was Utah in 1962, although it is still difficult for some Native Americans to vote because of language barriers, lack of transportation, lack of residential addresses etc.

Today Native Americans have the highest poverty rate of any major group, with a quarter living below the poverty line.

However, the story may not be all doom and gloom.

The Standing Rock Sioux Tribe and other Native American environmental groups have shown that their strength endures.They have fought for years against The Dakota Access Pipeline, an oil route from North Dakota to Illinois. The pipeline is less than a mile from the Sioux reservation and they argue that a spill could pollute the water they rely on for fishing, drinking and religious ceremonies. Under President Obama it looked like they were going to win, but four days into his Presidency, Donald Trump approved the pipeline. However, now the legal battle has almost been won as the Company has been directed to close it down as of August 2020 - subject to appeal.

And from being unrecognised as tribes, as of 29th January 2018, Virginia has seven federally recognized tribes, the Pamunkey and Mattaponi amongst them. This was a fight hard won over many years and allows the tribes to ensure the continuity of their identity. In all there are 574 Federally recognised tribes, 229 of which are in Alaska.

Helen Roundtree, who has written many wonderful and informative books about the Powhatan states:

"The Powhatan Indian identity has already survived nearly four centuries of culture change, spin off to and from the English population, and times of repressive laws alternating with times of lenience. If the Powhatans did not completely disappear in the century and more between 1725 and 1830, when a quiet exit would have been easy, they are not likely to disappear in the next generation or two because of a further increase in associations with whites....

The Powhatans are ample proof that the "Vanishing Indian" is indeed a myth" (Roundtree, H.C., The Powhatan Indians of Virginia Through Four Centuries, p.277)

FOLLOW UP

APPENDIX A

Letter from John Rolfe to Sir Thomas Dale

Honorable Sir, and most worthy Governor:

When your leisure shall best serve you to peruse these lines, I trust in God, the beginning will not strike you into a greater admiration, then the end will give you good content. It is a matter of no small moment, concerning my own particular, which here I impart unto you, and which toucheth me so nearly, as the tenderness of my salvation. Howbeit I freely subject myself to your grave and mature judgement, deliberation, approbation, and determination; assuring myself of your zealous admonitions, and godly comforts, either persuading me to desist, or encouraging me to persist therein, with a religious and godly care, for which (from the very instant, that this began to root itself within the secret bosom of my breast) my daily and earnest prayers have been, still are, and ever shall be produced forth with as sincere a godly zeal as I possibly may to be directed, aided and governed in all my thoughts, words, and deeds, to the glory of God, and for my eternal consolation. To persevere wherein I never had more need, nor (till now) could ever imagine to have been moved with the like occasion.

But (my case standing as it doth) what better worldly refuge can I here seek, then to shelter myself under the safety of your favorable protection? And did not my ease proceed from an unspotted conscience, I should not dare to offer to your view and approved judgement, these passions of my troubled soul, so full of fear and trembling in hypocrisy and dissimulation. But knowing my own innocency and godly fervor, in the whole prosecution hereof, I doubt not of your benign acceptance, and clement construction. As for malicious depravers, and turbulent spirits, to whom nothing is tasteful but what pleaseth their unsavory palate, I pass not for them, being well assured in my persuasion (by the often trial and proving of myself, in my holiest meditations and prayers) that I am called hereunto by the spirit of God; and it shall be sufficient for me to be protected by yourself in all virtuous and pious endeavors. And for my more happy proceeding herein, my daily oblations shall ever be addressed to bring to pass so good effects, that yourself, and all the world may truly say: This is the work of God, and it is marvelous in our eyes.

But to avoid tedious preambles, and to come nearer the matter: first suffer me with your patience, to sweep and make clean the way wherein I walk, from all suspicions and doubts, which may be covered therein, and faithfully to reveal unto you, what should move me hereunto.

Let therefore this my well advised protestation, which here I make between God and my own conscience, be a sufficient witness, at the dreadful day of judgement (when the secret of all men's hearts shall be opened) to condemn me herein, if my chiefest intent and purpose be not, to strive with all my power of body and mind, in the undertaking of so mighty a matter, no way led (so far forth as man's weakness may permit) with the unbridled desire of carnal affection: but for the good of this plantation, for the honor of our country, for the glory of God, for my own salvation, and for the converting to the true knowledge of God and Jesus Christ, an unbelieving creature, namely Pocahontas. To whom my hearty and best thoughts are, and have a long time been so entangled, and enthralled in so intricate a labyrinth, that I was even awearied to unwind myself thereout. But almighty God, who never faileth His [people who] truly invoke his holy name, hath opened the gate, and led me by the hand that I might plainly see and discern the safe paths wherein to tread.

To you therefore (most noble Sir) the patron and Father of us in this country do I utter the effects of this settled and long continued affection (which hath made a mighty war in my meditations) and here I do truly relate, to what issue this dangerous combat is come unto, wherein I have not only examined, but throughly tried and pared my thoughts even to the quick, before I could find any fit wholesome and apt applications to cure so dangerous an ulcer. I never failed to offer my daily and faithful prayers to God, for his sacred and holy assistance. I forgot not to set before mine eyes the frailty of mankind, his proneness to evil, his indulgency of wicked thoughts, with many other imperfections wherein man is daily ensnared, and oftentimes overthrown, and them compared to my present estate. Nor was I ignorant of the heavy displeasure which almighty God conceived against the sons of Levi and Israel for marrying strange wives, nor of the inconveniences which may thereby arise, with other the like good motions which made me look about warily and with good circumspection, into the grounds and principal agitations, which thus should provoke me to be in love with one whose education hath been rude, her manners barbarous, her generation accursed, and so discrepant in all nurture from myself, that oftentimes with fear and trembling, I have ended my private controversy with this: surely these are wicked instigations, hatched by him who seeketh and delighteth in man's destruction; and so with fervent prayers to be ever preserved from such diabolical assaults (as I took those to be) I have taken some rest.

Thus, when I had thought I had obtained my peace and quietness, behold another, but more gracious temptation hath made breaches into my holiest and strongest meditations; with which I have been put to a new trail, in a straighter manner then the former. For besides the many passions and sufferings which I have daily, hourly, yea and in my sleep endured, even awaking me to astonishment, taxing me with remissness, and carelessness, refusing and neglecting to perform the duty of a good Christian, pulling me by the ear, and crying: why dost not thou endeavor to make her a Christian? And these have happened to my greater wonder, even when she hath been farthest separated from me, which in common reason (were it not an undoubted work of God) might breed forgetfulness of a far more worthy creature. Besides, I say the holy spirit of God often demanded of me, why I was created?

If not for transitory pleasures and worldly vanities, but to labor in the Lord's vineyard, there to sow and plant, to nourish and increase the fruits thereof, daily adding, with the good husband in the Gospel, somewhat to the talent, that in the end the fruits may be reaped, to the comfort of the laborer in this life, and his salvation in the world to come? And if this be, as undoubtedly this is, the service Jesus Christ requireth of his best servant, woe unto him that hath these instruments of piety put into his hands and wilfully despiseth to work with them. Likewise, adding hereunto her great appearance of love to me, her desire to be taught and instructed in the knowledge of God, her capableness of understanding, her aptness and willingness to receive any good impression, and also the spiritual, besides her own incitements stirring me up hereunto.

What should I do? Shall I be of so untoward a disposition, as to refuse to lead the blind into the right way? Shall I be so unnatural, as not to give bread to the hungry? or uncharitable, as not to cover the naked? Shall I despise to actuate these pious duties of a Christian? Shall the base fear of displeasing the world overpower and withhold me from revealing unto man these spiritual works of the Lord, which in my meditations and prayers, I have daily made known unto him? God forbid. I assuredly trust He hath thus dealt with me for my eternal felicity, and for his glory. And I hope so to be guided by his heavenly grace, that in the end by my faithful pains, and Christianlike labor, I shall attain to that blessed promise, Pronounced by that holy Prophet Daniel unto the righteous that bring many unto the knowledge of God. Namely, that they shall shine like the stars forever and ever. A sweeter comfort cannot be to a true Christian, nor a greater encouragement for him to labor all the days of his life, in the performance thereof, nor a greater gain of consolation, to be desired at the hour of death, and in the day of judgement.

Again by my reading, and conference with honest and religious persons, have I received no small encouragement, besides serena mea conscientia, the clearness of my conscience, clean from the filth of impurity, quae est instar muri ahenei, which is unto me, as a brazen wall. If I should set down at large, the perturbations and godly motions, which have striven within me, I should but make a tedious and unnecessary volume. But I doubt not these shall be sufficient both to certify you of my true intents, in discharging of my duty to God, and to yourself, to whose gracious providence I humbly submit myself, for his glory, your honor, our Countrys good, the benefit of this Plantation, and for the converting of one unregenerate, to regeneration; which I beseech God to grant, for his dear Son Christ Jesus his sake.

Now if the vulgar sort, who square all mens actions by the base rule of their own filthiness, shall tax or taunt me in this my godly labor: let them know, it is not any hungry appetite, to gorge myself with incontinency; sure (if I would, and were so sensually inclined) I might satisfy such desire, though not without a seared conscience, yet with Christians more pleasing to the eye, and less fearful in the offence unlawfully committed. Nor am I in so desperate an estate, that I regard not what becometh of me; nor am I out of hope but one day to see my Country, nor so void of friends, nor mean in birth, but there to obtain a match to my great content. Nor have I ignorantly passed over my hopes there, or regardlessly seek to loose the love of my friends, by taking this course. I know them all, and have not rashly overslipped any.

But shall it please God thus to dispose of me (which I earnestly desire to fulfill my ends before set down) I will heartily accept of it as a godly tax appointed me, and I will never cease (God assisting me) until I have accomplished, and brought to perfection so holy a work, in which I will daily pray God to bless me, to mine, and her eternal happiness. And thus desiring no longer to live, to enjoy the blessings of God, then this my resolution doth tend to such godly ends, as are by me before declared: not doubting of your favorable acceptance, I take my leave, beseeching Almighty God to rain down upon you, such plenitude of his heavenly graces, as your heart can wish and desire, and so I rest,

At your command most willing to be disposed of,

346

John Rolfe

APPENDIX B

NOVA BRITANNIA

God that hath said by Solomon: Cast thy bread upon the waters, and after many daies thou shalt find it: he will give the blessing: And as for supplanting the savages, we have no such intent: Our intrusion into their possessions shall tend to their great good, and no way to their hurt, unlesse as unbridled beastes, they procure it to themselves: Wee purpose to proclaime and make it knowne to them all, by some publike interpretation that our comming thither is to plant our selves in their countrie: yet not to supplant and roote them out, but to bring them from their base condition to a farre better: First, in regard of God the Creator, and of Jesus Christ their Redeemer, if they will beleeve in him. And secondly, in respect of earthly blessings, whereof they have now no comfortable use, but in beastly brutish manner, with promise to defend them against all publike and private enemies. Wee can remember since Don Jon Daquila with his forces invading Ireland, a noble civill kingdome, where all (except a few runagates) were setled in the truth of Religion, and lived by wholsome laws, under the milde government of Christian Kings and Princes, long before his grandsiers cradle: yet hée thought it no robberie to proclaime and publish to the world, that his comming thither, was to none other end, but to free their Nation from their bondage, and tyrannous subjection, and to bring the blind soules to Catholike religion: a plausible pretence, the least end of his thought.

But if this were coyned in those dayes by the Printers themselves, to passe for currant thorow the world, howsoever base it was indéede, wée hope they will be as favourable to our case, and give as frée passage and allowance to our invasion, much more currant, and so farre different, as not to bring a people (according to our proverbe) out of the frying panne into the fire, but to make their condition truely more happy, by a mutuall enterchange and commerce in this sort: That as to our great expence and charge, wée make adventures, to impart our divine riches, to their inestimable gaine, and to cover their naked miserie with civill use of foode, and clothing, and to traine them by gentle meanes to those manuall artes and skill, which they so much affect, and doe admire to sée in us: so in lewe of this, wée require nothing at their hands, but a quiet residence to us and ours, that by our owne labour and toyle, we may worke this goode unto them and recompence our owne adventures, costs and travells in the ende: wherein, they shall be most friendly welcome to conjoyne their labours with ours, and shall enjoy equall priviledges with us, in whatsoever good successe, time or meanes may bring to passe. To which purpose, wee may verily beleeve, that God hath reserved in this last age of the world, an infinite number of those lost and scattered sheepe, to be won and recovered by our meanes, of whom so many as obstinately refuse to unite themselves unto us, or shall maligne or disturbe our plantation, our chattle, or whatsoever belonging to us: they shall be held and reputed recusant, withstanding their owne good: and shall be dealt with as enemies of the Common-wealth of their countrie: whereby how much good we shall performe to those that be good, and how little injury to any, will easily appeare, by comparing our present happinesse with our former ancient miseries, wherein wee had continued brutish, poore and naked Britanes to this day, if Julius Cæsar with his Romane Legions (or some other) had not laid the ground to make us tame and civill.

APPENDIX C

Abstract from Generall Historie by John Smith.Letter from John Smith to Queen Ann, June 1616

THE MOST ADMIRED QUEEN:

The love I bear my God, my King, and Country hath so oft emboldened me in the worst of extreme dangers, that now honesty doth contrain me [to] presume thus far beyond myself, to present Your Majesty this short discourse. If gratitude be a deadly poison to all honest virtues, I must be guilty of that crime if I should omit any means to be thankful.

So it is that some ten years ago, being in Virginia and taken prisoner by the power of Powhatan their chief King, I received from this great Savage exceeding great courtesy, especially from his son Nantaquaus the manliest, comliest, boldest spirit I ever saw in a savage, and his sister Pocahontas, the King's most dear and well-beloved daughter, being but a child of twelve or thirteen years of age, whose compassionate pitiful heart, of my desperate estate, gave me much cause to respect her: I being the first Christian this proud King and his grim attendants ever saw: and thus enthralled in their barbarous power, I cannot say I felt the least occasion of want that was in the power of those my mortal foes to prevent, not-withstanding all their threats.

After some six weeks fatting amongst those savage courtiers, at the minute of my execution, she hazarded the beating out of her own brains to save mine; and not only that, but so prevailed with her father, that I was safely conducted to Jamestown: where I found about eight and thirtie miserable poor and sick creatures, to keep possession of all those large territories of Virginia; such was the weakness of this poor Commonwealth, as had the savages not fed us, we directly had starved. And this relief, most gracious Queen, was commonly brought us by this Lady Pocahontas.

Notwithstanding all these passages, when inconstant Fortune turned our peace to war, this tender Virgin would still not spare to dare to visit us, and by our jars [brawls, with the Indians?] have been oft appeased, and our wants still supplied; were it the policy of her father thus to emply her, or the ordinance of God thus to make her His instrument, or her extraordinary affection to our Nation, I know not: but of this I am sure; when her father with the utmost of his plicy and power sought to surprise me, having but eighteen with me, the dark night could not affright her from coming through the irksome woods, and with watered eyes gave me intelligence, with her best advice to escap his fury; which had he known, he had surely slain her.

Jamestown with her wild train she as freely frequented as her father's habitation; and during the time of two or three years, she next under God, was still the instrument to preserve this Colony from death, famine and utter confusion; which if in those times [it] had once been dissolved, Virginia might have line [lain] as it was at our first arrival to this day.

Since then, this business having een turned and varied by many accidents from that I left it at; it is most certain, after a long and troublesome war after my departure, betwixt her father and our Colony; all which time she was not heard of.

About two years after, she herself was taken prisoner, being so detained near two years longer, the Colony by that means was relieved, peace concluded; and at last rejecting her barbarous condition, was married to an English gentleman, with whom at this present she is in England; the first Christian ever of that Nation, the first Virginian ever spake English, or had a child in marriage by an Englishman; a matter surely, if my meaning be truly considered and well understood, worthy a Prince's understanding.

Thus, most gracious Lady, I have related to Your Majesty, what at your best leisure our approved histories will account you at large, and done in the time of Your Majesty's life; and however this might be presented you from a more worthy pen, it cannot from a more honest heart. As yet I never begged anything from the state, or any [person]; and it is my want of ability and her exceeding desert, your birth, means and authority, her birth, virtue, want and simplcity, doth make me thus bold humbly to beseech Your Majesty to take this knowledge of her, though it be rom one so unworthy to be the reporter as myself, her husband's estate not being able to make her fit to attend Your Majesty.

The most and least I can do is to tell you this, because none so oft hath tried it as myself, and the rather being of so great a spirit, how ever her stture, she should dnot be well receied, seeing this Kingdom may rightly have a dingdom by her means; her present love to us and Christianity might turn to such scorn and fury, as to divert all this good to the worst of evil. Where finding so great a Queen should do her some honor mor than she can imagine, for being so kind to your servants and subjects, would so ravish her with content, as endear her dearest blood to effect that [which] Your Majesty and all the King's honest subjects most earnestly desire.

And so I humbly Kiss your gracious hands.

APPENDIX D

CHARTER OF THE COLLEGE AT HENRICUS

Whereas by special grant and licence from His Majesty, a general contribution over the Realm hath been made for the building and planting of a college for the training up of the children of those Infidels in true Religion, moral virtue, and civility, and for other godlyness. We do therefore, according o a former Grant and order, hereby ratifie, confirm and ordain that a convenient place be chosen and set out for the planting of a Univrsity at the said Henrico in time to come, and that in the mean time preparation be there made for the building of the said College for the Children of the Infidels, according to such instructions as we shall deliver. And we will and ordain that ten thousand acres, partly of the lands they impaled [settled; or impaled, as in setting up palisades], and partly of the land within the territory of the said Henrico, be allotted and set out for the endowing of the said University and College with convenient possessions.

Notes taken from "Jamestown Colony: A Political Social, and Cultural History by Frank E. Gizzard, Jr.; D. Boyd Smith

Nicholas Ferrar, the elder - left £300 to establish a college in Jamestown colony for the purpose of educating at least "ten of teh Infidels children placed in it. His endowment was to support "three discreete and godly men in the Colonie, which shall honestly bring up three of the Infidels children in Christian Religion, and some good course to live by."

East India School

Shortly after the College at Henricus was chartered in 1618, members of the East India Company sailing back to England from the New World aboard the ship "Royal James" began collecting money to establish a "collegiate or free school" at Charles City (present day City Point), to be associated with the new college. The purpose of the school was twofold: to prepare English students for eventual attendance at the College at Henricus and to introduce young Indian boys - kidnapped and enslaved - to English culture and to Christianity. Appropriately named the East India School in honor of its early benefactors, the school was assigned 1,000 acres for the support of its master and usher. The school actually opened, but most of its occupants were killed in the Indian Massacre of 1622. Renewed efforts to establish the school failed.

REFERENCES

Allen, P. G., Pocahontas, Medicine Woman, Spy, Entrepreneur, Diplomat (2004)

Barbour, P.L., "Pocahontas and her World, (1970)

Bernhard, V., A Tale of Two Colonies, What really happened in Virginia and Bermuda

Charles River Editors "The Lives, Legends and Legacies of Pocahontas & John Smith"

Custalow, Dr., L., & Daniel, A. L.,
"The True Story of Pocahontas, The Other side of History, (2007)

Glover, L. & Smith, D.B, "The Shipwreck that Saved Jamestown" (2008)

Kupperman, K. O., "Pocahontas and the English Boys" (2019)

Mortimer, I., "The Time Traveller's guide to Elizabethan England" (2012)

Mossiker, F., "Pocahontas, The Life and The Legend" (1976)

Orlin, L. C., "Material London ca.1600" (2000)

Roundtree, H. C., "The Powhatan Indians of Virginia, Their Traditional Culture" (1989)

Roundtree, H. C., "Pocahontas's People, The Powhatan Indians of Virginia through Four
Centuries," (1990)

Rolfe, J.E., "Pocahontas and her two Husbands (2017)

Roundtree, H.C. "Pocahontas, Powhatan, Opechancanough, Three Indian Lives changed
by Jamestown
Roundtree, H.C. "Pocahontas's People, The Powhatan Indians of Virginia Through Four
Centuries, (1990)

Scarboro, D.D., "The Establisher, The Story of Sir Thomas Dale, Marshal and Deputy
Governor Of the Virginia Colony", Jamestown, 1611-166 (2005)

Spelman, H. "Relation of Virginia - a Boys Memoir of Life with the Powhatans and Patwomecks "(original reprinted 2019)

Tormey, J., "John Rolfe of Virginia" (2006)

Townsend, C., "Pocahontas and the Powhatan Dilemma" (2004)
Warner, C.D., "The Story of Pocahontas" (A public Domain book)

««»»

Thank You for Reading

I hope that you enjoyed this, my second novel. My first novel, which followed John Rolfe's early life was called:

'Tempest - Bermuda 1609'

You can find it at:
   https://www.amazon.co.uk/dp/B07L39JG3T and www.amazon.com/d-p/B07L39JG3T
   or paperback editions can be ordered from bookstores.

If you bought this book through Amazon, I would be *very* grateful if you could leave a review with your honest opinion of the book. Or you can contact me at suewrightauthor@gmail.com with any comments. I am a newbie in the book market, and it is so nice to get feedback and helpful comments. I read all of my reviews and always take into account what is said to improve my writing . I love writing, and I love sharing my work - I would be so very grateful for feedback to know what I am doing right and what might need a little more work. Writing is a lonely place - but communication with readers and knowing what they want gives me motivation to keep on writing and improving my skills.

   Reviews and feedback do matter to me, and I know it takes time - but I will be forever grateful!

Thanks for your help.
Sue

Made in the USA
Middletown, DE
21 March 2022